INDY
RACE AND RITUAL

Terry Reed

PRESIDIO PRESS

Library of Congress Cataloging in Publication Data
Reed, Kenneth T
   Indy, race & ritual.

   Includes index.
   1. Indianapolis Speedway Race — History. I. Title.
GV1033.5.I55R43   796.7'2'06877252   79-25342
ISBN 0-89141-075-9

Book and Cover Design by Joe Roter

Published by Presidio Press,
San Rafael, California 94902
Printed in the United States of America

For Susan
You were there.

We love the things we love for what they are.

ROBERT FROST

CONTENTS

PREFACE

*T*he beloved World War II war correspondent Ernie Pyle was once quoted as saying, "I would rather win that race than anything in the world. I would rather be Ralph DePalma than President." The race to which he referred is the Indianapolis 500-mile classic which has been run on or near Memorial Day some sixty-three times. Ralph dePalma, as every bona fide Indianapolis enthusiast well knows, won the race of 1915 and competed in nine other 500 milers on the fabulous two-and-a-half-mile brick course west of the Indiana capital. Anyone truly smitten with the aura and mystique of the race and all of the many curious customs and rituals that it entails will also understand the spirit in which Pyle made his remarks. He was not speaking in jest.

This book, although it is concerned ostensibly with several different aspects of the most celebrated automobile race in the world, is personal in that it represents more than thirty years of reflection on and experience with what might be called the Indianapolis scene. That scene, although it is an annually recurring juncture in my life, is one that I have never, to this day, played any direct role in. I have never driven a racing car. I have never constructed a racing car. I have never driven the track at Indianapolis. I have never known very intimately anybody who did any of these things. It is ironic, in other words, that something so crucial in my life should be so removed from it. The remarks that follow are therefore those of an outsider, and the particular point of view expressed here reflects a line of accumulated views and opinions not necessarily embraced by a consensus of confirmed Indianapolis-watchers. Quite the contrary. Some of these perspectives may strike knowledgeable readers as variously subversive, hyperbolic, hostile, forgiving. My answer is that I have made every possible effort to be accurate with respect to both fact and conclusion.

In recent years there has been increasing attention given to the subject of sports in America. Minimally, we have come to understand that the meaning of sporting activities extends deeper and more pervasively in our culture than we once might have suspected. To assert that professional sports are merely a diversion for the spectator and a livelihood for the participant is to underestimate the significance of such methodically ritualized game playing. At Indianapolis, the particular form and function of the 500-mile race, for instance, is a microcosm of the American Way, and an invaluable index to predominantly middle-class values and aspirations. As an American institution, the race is a product of the minds that constructed the track, perfected the cars, established the rules, and selected the driving personnel. If attentive enough, one will recognize that virtually all aspects of the Indianapolis 500, regardless of how ludicrous and how frivolous, hardly represent insignificant aspects of the national mentality.

A good proportion of this inquiry is historical, and much of that history centers on the four turns at Indianapolis where the driving is the most demanding. Most of the legend of the Indianapolis Motor Speedway has evolved from the dangerous curves that have claimed lives while at the same time dispatched others to triumph and international acclaim. The turns at Indianapolis have a story of their own to tell, and much of that story is narrated here in order to illuminate best the curious lore that has elevated the Speedway into the most enigmatic rectangle anywhere in America.

This inquiry began in 1974 at a lodge hidden among the mollifying Pocono Mountains of eastern Pennsylvania, where

Leon Mandel, then senior editor of *Car and Driver* magazine, spent three days of unremitting persuasiveness urging that this book should be written. After it was begun, the unenviable task of lighting the way to its conclusion passed to Adele Horwitz, editor in chief at Presidio Press in San Rafael, California. To these persons, and to the dozens of individuals from inside the world of Indianapolis racing who gave so freely of their time and their candid opinions on a thousand aspects of the 500-mile race, I shall always remain grateful.

Prerace festivities on the main straightaway, 1946.

INTRODUCTION

Speedway, Indiana

6 A.M.

Memorial Day, 1950

*I*t is one of those sultry Indiana mornings as the sun rises over what 175,000 spectators presume will be the thirty-fourth running of the Indianapolis 500-mile motor race. My father and I are visiting the track for the first time. This is a pilgrimage (both festive and solemn) that will become a ritual with us for thirty more years. The uneasiness I experience is partly a consequence of having ridden all night from Grand Rapids, Michigan, in the back seat of a chartreuse '49 Ford, and partly a consequence of anxiety. As the yellow Ford passes over the ominous north chute of the Indianapolis Motor Speedway, I steal a first glance at two of those famous (some would say infamous) turns, the outsides of which are circumscribed by a continuous ribbon of white retaining wall that curves in the distance and rolls gracefully out of range. Among the things the wall retains is an enormous profusion — a mongol horde — of infield dwellers, a substantial part of whom have stationed themselves for the day beneath a grove

*of sycamores toward the north end of the main straightaway.
Even at this early hour, the infield is well on its way to becoming a frenetic disarray of beer bottles, partially eaten
breakfasts, abandoned pages from the morning* Indianapolis
Star, *and other forms of offal.*

This is race day.

*The stellar performance will come at the stroke of eleven: it
is the legendary and spectacular 500 miles of Indianapolis.
Although the start of the race itself is still five hours away, I
have the distinct sensation of déjà vu, of having witnessed
this whole remarkable madcap panorama before. In 1948 and
1949 I had listened, with an attentiveness uncharacteristic of
me, to Sid Collins, the self-proclaimed Voice of the 500, and to
his histrionic, syndicated WIBC Mutual Network worldwide
bang-em-up race broadcast. I had also been foraging through
copies of a weekly motor racing tabloid, a gossipy digest
printed in New York called* Illustrated Speedway News, *and
through the monthly issues of a magazine with the visionary
title of* Speed Age.

Speed Age! Today, the same yellowed copies of it and the
tabloid are arranged in tidy, chronological piles along my attic
bookshelves, and they are as accessible there as they are
through the back staircase of my consciousness. But where is
Sid Collins? He has receded into that very curious fabric of
automobile racing folklore that belongs primarily in central-
most Indiana. On May 2, 1977, the esteemed bachelor sports-
caster, who had been afflicted with a terminal illness known
as amyotrophic lateral sclerosis (Lou Gehrig's disease), was
discovered hanged in his Indianapolis apartment. He was fifty-
four.

I was twelve years old on Memorial Day in 1950, and this
was my first really significant motor race. I say "really
significant" because I had spectated prior to 1950 at quite a
number of relatively insignificant midget car races staged by a
coterie of drivers who towed north to Michigan (mostly from
Illinois, Indiana, and Ohio), to run a card of weekly racing
heats on a certifiable deathtrap of a racecourse known as
Bigelow Field. To call Bigelow field a racecourse is an exag-
geration that should not go unchallenged. It was, to be more
precise about it, a ramshackle baseball park with an irregu-

larly shaped, rutty dirt track carved on its perimeter. Whereas rival semi-professional baseball teams did their level best to strike each other out on Saturday nights at Bigelow Field, there was an entirely different kind of striking out that took place there on Wednesdays, when a not-too-scrupulous entrepreneur named Jim Williams promoted his weekly midget car races, even in light snowfalls, before ever-dwindling numbers of paying enthusiasts. The races themselves kept an irate neighborhood awake most of the night with deafening twenty-five-lap encounters that, at their financial nadir, paid a total driver purse of two hundred dollars. Williams liberally allowed fifteen minutes at the conclusion of the program for the men to load their equipment before he turned the ballpark lights out.

The men who competed at Bigelow Field did so at extraordinary peril, for the hazards of that amorphous, potholed smokepath were as extreme as they were numerous. The green wooden guardrailing that extended from home plate to first base had a fearful tendency to splinter when brushed (much less hit head-on) by a racer pointed the wrong way. Then there were wooden utility poles that were positioned on the track itself. One such pole (will I ever forget?) was responsible for the demise of a local favorite named Cecil Clees, whose racer struck it, flew perhaps fifteen feet in space, and then fell back on him. It was not exactly good clean fun to see that kind of thing, or to observe another ludicrously hazardous aspect of Bigelow Field, the so-called home plate curve, where broadsliding, mudhurling cars attempted to negotiate over and around a deeply imbedded cement home plate marker without actually hitting it. When struck at precisely the right tilt (which it not infrequently was), the marker would cause the car to dig in and flip over. But even this was not the worst aspect of Bigelow Field; the worst aspect was a baseball dugout situated between third and home. On a July night in 1949 a diminutive and likable Indiana driver named Ralph Reel decapitated himself there when his errant Offenhauser-powered midget racer plunged into the dugout that faced the ball diamond. Following a brief intermission during which a grounds attendant hosed the dugout clean of telltale signs, track activity resumed.

Bigelow Field's carnival of carnage was almost the only side of automobile racing that I knew about prior to my Indianapolis sojourn in 1950. Violent and pointless as it was, the prospect of these small, scaled-down versions of larger Indianapolis prototypes had, by this time, seduced me to the immensely powerful mystique of open wheel automobile racing. It occurred to me then that barnstorming the country racing small-bodied, well-crafted, hand-constructed, open-topped cars powered by Ford V-8 60s was a splendidly romantic way of life, a life not so different from signing on with the Ringling Brothers. I was not mistaken about that romantic aura; it was really there. But what I did not quite understand at the time was that these men (little-known individuals of minor league heroic dimension like Bernie Jacobson, Ray Elliott, Lou Scally, Neil Carter, and Corkey Singer) raced more for the thrills than for the money. I had been under the impression that they amassed great fortunes and lived regally, but I was mistaken about that; they were fortunate if winnings exceeded expenses.

Having little else to interest me at that stage of my youth, I came to admire the low-budget mechanical creativity and craftmanship that many (if not all) of the well-polished, tiny machines represented to me at the time. Most of them had been constructed from scratch by ingenious, predominantly ersatz engineers more at peace with cutting torches than slide rules, who modified engines of various and not especially exotic origins (such as Fords, Willys, Drake cycles, and Alto outboards), hammered bodies out of cold steel, and fitted the driver's cockpit upholstery. The result of all this labor was a thing of great, sometimes enduring beauty that would occasionally go to its final resting place in an automotive museum some thirty years later. So intrigued was I with this shade-tree, filling-station resourcefulness and ingenuity that at the conclusion of a night's dusty competition I exercised extraordinary self-control to keep from fondling the sweaty steering wheels and brake handles. Later, having ingratiated myself with an itinerant, noseless, track-mauled dirt-track jockey with the improbable name of Willie Wik, his face and hands badly disfigured from burn scars, I was accorded the honor of steering his number 8 cream-colored racer on the track and into position for the night's eighteen-car featured race. And when Willie was at speed (seldom over sixty-five miles an hour on a short track like Bigelow Field), it was the greatest spectacle in all of western Michigan. Willie and his roughneck racing pals, who flirted regularly with catastrophe by wearing flimsy helmets (many of which had seen gridiron action), protruded precariously out of the tops of their lilliputian racers. Evidently unconcerned about the possibility (let's call it the eventuality) of burns, breaks, and abrasions, the drivers generally wore tee shirts on muggy nights, and gave little or no thought to the use of substantial seatbelts, shoulder harnesses, and rollover bars. Their brazen disregard for a few commonsensical safety precautions cost them dearly.

As a spectator, I progressed from the minors to the majors when I renounced Bigelow Field and headed toward Indianapolis in 1950. Anyone who is not conversant with motor racing in America needs to be informed, right off, that Indianapolis is auto racing's premier event. It is, however, neither the longest automobile race in the world, nor the fastest. Indy is the preeminent motorsporting contest because it is the richest, and by all odds the most prestigious. That it is the richest is easily documented. The total prize money paid in 1911 for the initial 500-mile race came to $27,550. It had reached $97,600 by 1930, $201,135 by 1950 and $400,000 by 1961, and has exceeded a million dollars each year since 1970. Prize money paid out to contestants in other racing events is dwarfed by contrast. That Indy is the most prestigious contest is a little more difficult to substantiate. The late Peter Revson, himself a superbly able and stylish Indianapolis performer, put it succinctly: "An American driver of any stature doesn't have much of a choice about Indianapolis; he has to be there. Usually he has an American sponsor, and so far as the sponsor is concerned, Indianapolis is the most important race in the world in terms of the promotion of his product." Revson's remarks are to the point: Anyone wishing to establish his full motor-racing legitimacy in America is obliged, as soon as possible, to pay his Indianapolis dues. I learned that from no less a personage that Mickey Rooney, whose 1949 B-grade racing picture, *The Big Wheel*, had as one of its enduring social messages the unassailable supremacy of Indianapolis. In about the third reel Rooney moves with tight-jawed determination through the ranks of midget and big car (now called sprint car) pilots until he presents himself one fine day before the golden gates of the home of the brave itself, the Indianapolis Motor Speedway. Here the puckish driver not only loses the race, but also sustains debilitating burns in pursuit of Indy's elusive checkered flag. A year or two after *The Big Wheel* there appeared a somewhat more plausible racing picture entitled *To Please a Lady*, with Clark Gable ensconced behind the wheel this time, but both the point and the romantic plot were essentially the same.

The romanticism of *To Please a Lady* was not entirely the felicitous invention of Hollywood moviemakers. The picture was shot partly on location at Indianapolis in 1950, where the general run of drivers led, and continued to lead, lives every bit as colorful as the one Gable portrayed on the screen opposite his celluloid bitch-goddess Barbara Stanwyck. When the 1950 race was flagged off, its participants were as hell-for-leather as the fictional Mike Brannon whom Gable had, with a certain verisimilitude, impersonated on the screen. I refer, of course, to men with the magnetic crowd appeal of Walt Faulkner, Troy Ruttman, Duane Carter, Tony Bettenhausen, Bill Holland, and Johnnie Parsons. At a moment in history when, unlike today, drivers had to get their living done in a hurry because of a decidedly telescoped life expectancy, it is ironic that only Faulkner and Bettenhausen were fated (if that is the word) to perish in racing-related accidents. Could careers as ephemeral and mercurial as theirs fail to possess a romantic coloration?

I think not. And when other boys my age were keeping abreast of American League batting averages, I secluded myself behind the family's three-trunked chokecherry tree and thumbed issues of *Speed Age* for belated word on the exploits of three dozen "dirt-track gladiators" (as they were once referred to by an over-zealous press agent) while they tested their courage and luck on other tracks of varying lengths, contours, and surfaces. Among the better recognized half-mile ovals were the treacherous, steeply banked saucers of the Middle West (Dayton, Ohio; Fort Wayne, Winchester; and Salem, Indiana); the half-mile dirt tracks (Reading,

Williams Grove, and Allentown, Pennsylvania; New Bremen, Ohio; and Terre Haute, Indiana); and the dazzling one-mile dirt courses (Langhorne, Pennsylvania; Trenton, New Jersey; Syracuse, New York; Detroit, Michigan; Indianapolis State Fairgrounds; Milwaukee, Wisconsin; Springfield and Du-Quoin, Illinois; Denver, Colorado; and Bay Meadows, Del Mar, and Sacramento, California).

In short, I had never seen a group of really accomplished, professional drivers on a track at the same time, until they blew past me at Indianapolis on Memorial Day in 1950 like three simultaneously hell-bent freight trains. What a sight! Like all Indianapolis contestants, each man hoped that even if he could not win, he could at least hold tight for the full 500 miles. It wasn't to be, however. That sultry Indiana day became a little too sultry at precisely 1:41 P.M. With the race leader at 345 miles, the race was red flagged (halted) when the sky suddenly blackened and sent down a brief but determined rainstorm so strong in its intensity that visibility was severely impaired. The winner of the race was Johnnie Parsons, a skitterish, soaking wet, thirty-one-year-old Californian from Van Nuys driving a huge, canary yellow Wynn's Friction Proofing Special powered by a 270-cubic-inch Meyer and Drake Offenhauser engine equipped with a cracked block. Parsons, whose free-floating anxieties had kept him wakeful most of the previous night, expressed confidence that he would have triumphed anyway, had the race gone the full distance. His remark, of course, was the purest of speculation. We all understood that.

Memorial Day, as it turned out, was the high water mark in Parson's eventful career, although he persisted in driving competitively for several more years, and much later in life successfully undertook to drive an automobile around the world. For me, however, it was only the beginning of an intense attachment to the Indianapolis scene, an attachment perhaps best described as addictive. The reasons for that addiction are not easy for me to account for, although I have observed that my gut-level response to Indianapolis is comparable to other people's gut-level response to Churchill Downs and the Kentucky Derby. An Indy addiction, however, may often prove incurable. An annual stroll through the

Speedway's garage area, a place sacred to many, known as Gasoline Alley, will reveal that the same faces are back again and again: former drivers, mechanics, and stooges (mechanics' helpers), among the prodigious numbers of ubiquitous hangers-on. Part of what draws them from near and far is the realization that the 500-mile race, like the Kentucky Derby, is a uniquely American rite of springtime. By April, the track's wintery drabness is transformed into a modern pastoral. Freshly mown acres of lawn, around which the sights, smells, and sounds of newly constructed or refurbished racing cars of varied shapes and colors appear, contrast with the two-and-a-half-mile asphalt rectangle that constitutes the track itself.

When the cars make their long-awaited appearance on the track early in May, they are as apt a symbol as any of the Machine's insolent intrusion into the great Edenic garden of America. Henry Thoreau, startled at hearing the whistle from the Fitchburg Railroad disturb the sylvan serenity of Walden Pond, would experience much the same sensation at Indianapolis. Racing cars at Indy, like the cars he observed on the Fitchburg Railroad, are nothing if not appropriate emblems of defiant American ingenuity: ruggedly individual (despite their ostensible similarity), uncompromisingly competitive, blatantly representative of the free enterprise system that is responsible for their construction and for the products and services they advertise. Forthrightly commercial, American racing cars have become low-flying billboards that huckster such diverse things as bluejeans, sauerkraut, and money management.

In the main, America's big time racing establishment embraces a profoundly American mentality. That was as true in 1950, when a number of the drivers that afternoon were not long discharged from service in World War II, as it is today. A good proportion of Indianapolis drivers, particularly during the Nixon years, were eager to show their colors. They attended a 1971 presidential reception and rolled their racing cars on the White House lawn for the occasion. They proudly displayed decals of resplendent American flags on their cars and lacquered helmets. But even these are only outward signs of a staunch devotion to the American Way. A cursory glance at the 1976 entry list at Indianapolis will show that two racing machines were entered as "Spirit of America Racers," while another was christened the "Spirit of Public Enterprise." Parallels between the mainstream of American life and the month-long solemnization of speed in Hoosierland are imposing enough to render the entire Indianapolis undertaking a very microcosm of America in more ways than one. Both car and driver are, as the cliché has it, here today and gone tomorrow; machine and man become a part of a no deposit, no return, throwaway consumer mentality. Indy cars, as a rule, grow obsolete very rapidly, their chassis and engine components being modified substantially with each passing year. Indeed, the drivers themselves are also the victims of creeping obsolescence, and have a partially valid reputation for changing domestic circumstances almost as often as they change rides. As a continuing occupation, driving racing cars is a career with a tenure as brief as most other professional sporting activities. And although Indianapolis drivers are not a particularly youthful assemblage (the average age comes to around thirty-five), they find their salad days in racing pretty well numbered after the vulnerable age of forty. Only a dozen or so regulars — the likes of the brothers Unser, the redoubtable A. J. Foyt, and Johnny Rutherford — have managed through the years to make a steady, well-paying occupation out of an inherently unsteady undertaking: driving at Indianapolis. But even for them, the coming of May means that they must prove once again that they are equal to the challenge of Indianapolis. They must also defend their sporting reputations all over again. Many drivers, regardless of how well esteemed they once may have been, find themselves suddenly persona non grata for having failed to qualify for the previous year's race or for having failed to move up front once the race was under way.

Once the race is under way, American style breakneck, devil-take-the-hindmost competition prevails among those who have a realistic chance of copping the 200-lap race. Usually not more than ten of the thirty-three race day starters have anything but a remote chance of surviving the 500 miles a winner. While rules pertaining to every facet of the race exist, part of the game, from the standpoint of the crew chiefs, is to take every conceivable advantage possible. Some surreptitiously overstep the rules entirely, particularly in the preparation of racing cars, and the attitude has prevailed for some time that one is never actually cheating unless one gets caught at it, an attitude not so different from the corporate morality that puts up the money for the cars in the first place. This is not to convey to the casual observer that cheating is a significant part of the formula for winning. To bend the rules may be as American as apple pie, but it seldom has a major effect on the order or finish of a single race and is probably insignificant in the long run.

Drivers often share the attitude toward driving the race that their crew chiefs have as they are preparing for it, although drivers cheat to a lesser extent; for whereas mechanics labor mostly in the inner sanctums of their air-conditioned Gasoline Alley garages, drivers do their stuff in public. Most racing drivers are both clannish and benevolent to one another off-track. On track, it's a different attitude. Indy's heavier hitters will attest, quite openly, that winning is the whole objective. Beneath the superficial glitter of big league auto racing is the very real presence of big business, which insists upon a coordinated effort at winning. That coordination involves, among other things, (1) a visionary, ahead-of-the-game car builder, (2) an engine man who can not only make the engine run fast, but run fast all day, (3) a smart, heavy-footed driver who can wring the most out of his machine without making a tactical mistake, (4) a crew chief who speaks the driver's language and who can see to the car's total preparation, (5) a charitable sponsor (or sponsors) accustomed to spending large sums of money, and very importantly, (6) truckloads of good luck. The entire enterprise is as tentative, commercial, and competitive as the twentieth-century America in which it has flourished.

I would suspect that as long as the Speedway (in racing parlance "the Speedway" can refer only to Indianapolis) is literally as well as symbolically attuned to certain basic, highly cherished American values, it will not lose its immense vitality. Nor will those fiercely loyal camp followers (among whom I count myself a member) cease to make a minimum of one annual visit to the Speedway, even on those days when the eighty-nine garages that line Gasoline Alley are not occupied.

They return for mysterious reasons not easily comprehended outside of racing's subculture. There can be no gainsaying that for huge numbers of people the track embodies some kind of mystic meaning that verges at times on the spiritual. To some, the notion of spirituality arising out of alcohol fumes and burned rubber may seem vaguely preposterous, if not altogether ludicrous. Ludicrous or not, the 500 miles of Indianapolis provide a meaningful exercise which, besides being a celebration of fertility, spring, and a new racing season, has its established litany and sacrificial victims. It is as close to the spiritual, in any event, as hordes of its litter-spewing customers ever get. Aerial bombs, nostalgic anthems, invocations, and threnodies become the order of the day. Convertibles bearing video heroes, tinhorn politicians, and vestal virgins circle the track slowly. They wave to the crowds. The crowds cheer their approval. Once the race is on, it is expressly emblematic of such primal forces as luck, chance, and accident, which are pitted against such admirable human qualities as skill, determination, and daring. With the fickle turning of Fortune's wheel, this Maytime scenario with its main actors and chorus is set into motion. Part of that drama is orchestrated to the last word and gesture; part of it is left to the caprice of the gods. The world of sports is, after all, the world of symbolic action.

About those sacrificial victims: Auto racing's fallen have been placed before the twin altars of Speed and Competition. If bleeding corpses and screaming ambulances come to mind at the mention of Indianapolis, it is small wonder; the Speedway has had its share of both since its initial construction in 1909. In 1933, when the country was suffering through one of its more miserable years, the Speedway followed suit. The final May tally reached a new record: five men dead and one seriously injured. It is more than a little paradoxical that although current speeds at Indianapolis are roughly 70 miles per hour faster than they were in 1933, fatalities and lesser injuries are dramatically fewer today. The reason for the decline is that the racing fraternity has taken a serious, if belated, interest in safety. After 1973, for example, when drivers flirted with, and finally attained, lap speeds during practice and qualification that reached over 200 miles per hour, gestures were made by the United States Auto Club sanctioning body to temper speeds which almost everyone seemed to agree had escalated out of control. The speed tempering was accomplished in three primary ways: (1) by limiting the area of body wings, (2) by limiting the cubic inch displacement of racing engines, and (3) by limiting intake manifold pressure. In spite of these measures, enterprising car builders and mechanics have, in time, discovered means of driving speeds upward once more to keep pace with the competition. From an aesthetic point of view, it makes little difference whether the speeds on race day are at 165 miles per hour or 195 miles per hour. It is a seasoned spectator who can tell the difference without a stopwatch. It is partly the prospect of seeing lap and race records broken that lures the railbirds out, however, and increased speeds translate into increased gate receipts, which translate into higher purses.

Higher speeds also improve chances for mishaps. Particularly in recent years, drivers have been involved in accidents that are terrifying beyond belief, and still managed to walk away essentially or completely unharmed. Among the critical factors that save lives on race tracks are (1) improved screening of drivers to ascertain their temperamental and experiential fitness to compete, (2) flame retardant clothing, (3) full-face helmets, (4) fuel tank bladders, (5) fuel systems that shut off automatically upon impact, (6) onboard fire extinguishers, (7) effective driver rescue systems, (8) improved tires, and (9) Magnafluxing, a means of identifying internal weaknesses in metal through the use of X ray. When automobiles crash, energy is dissipated through a process of bending and breaking. As wheels and other pieces are shed, the racing car is slowed in the process. Earlier racers with stiff axles and truck spindles were more apt to hook something (such as a wall) and flip over. Today, as this initial energy dissipation process occurs, the driver usually remains in a relatively safe structural cocoon. It is interesting that this byproduct of a faster design, which was fought tooth-and-nail by the Indy establishment as unsafe, turned out to be quite the opposite.

Come what may, however, the spectre of death hovers over motor racing. Few other forms of sporting activity are obliged to deal with the prospect of fatal injury, and none handle it in quite the way that the racing fraternity does. While drivers have anything but a cavalier attitude toward mortality, they probably fear it less than the average Presbyterian bank teller. The medical newsmagazine *MD* reported in March 1978 that California State University psychologist Keith Johnsgard "conducted studies of more than 500 racing drivers and reached conclusions that confound the image of persons with a death-wish bent on self-destruction." He found that the typical driver was happy-go-lucky in general attitude, markedly superior in abstract intelligence, about average in self-control, below average in anxiety... Drivers," the report continued, "commonly exhibited a need to lead and a need to be noticed, particularly by women."

The prevailing attitude toward death on the part of most drivers can best be described as fatalistic, as for example driver Sam Posey's reaction to the 1973 death at Indianapolis of fellow driver David "Swede" Savage: "Swede was killed because his number was up, just like anybody else." Savage's number happened to be up on his fifty-seventh circuit of the Speedway. Driver Jimmy Caruthers, who eventually succumbed to cancer in 1975, lost his spectacular midget-racing brother Danny "Kid" Caruthers in a California midget racing accident some years back, and was teammate to Art Pollard, a late-blooming, avuncular, but hard-charging Indy favorite who was killed while exiting the southwest turn on the first morning of time trials in 1973. Clint Brawner, then chief mechanic on the Cobre Tire cars driven by Caruthers and Pollard, later wrote in his autobiographic *Indy 500 Mechanic* about the death of the latter: "Caruthers visited the accident scene. He talked with various eyewitnesses (although so-called eyewitnesses invariably have conflicting stories) to try to find out why it happened. And then Jimmy walked stolidly back to the pits, belted himself into his Eagle, and when it was his turn to qualify hit a blazing 195 mph for ten miles — faster than he'd ever gone before. Race drivers, like mechanics, are a breed apart."

Drivers of the sort who compete at Indianapolis may be a breed apart, but they also leave less to chance than the casual observer (believing that racing car drivers are little more than

(a) Rick Mears, '79 winner, before qualifying.
(b) That's the car. (c) Roger Penske, owner, strides
towards finish line.

a band of wild kids with a magnificently developed death-wish)
might suspect. Not surprisingly, most front-line drivers race
as little as possible for as much as they can get in financial
return. The Speedway's all-time record first place payout
went to Al Unser, who in 1970 was awarded $271,697.12, more
than a thousand dollars higher than Californian Rick Mears
collected for his 1979 winning effort. And while it is occasionally possible for a driver to enter as many as four race meets of
various kinds in the course of a week, very few professional
drivers are willing to assume so much risk over so little time.
The better paid chauffeurs who follow the championship trail
(the rich Indy car circuit) compete relatively little, selecting

races with the maximum payoff potential: Trenton and Milwaukee (which are no longer dirt tracks); Phoenix, Arizona; Pocono, Pennsylvania; College Station, Texas; Ontario, California; or Brooklyn, Michigan. Then there are those drivers who restrict themselves to what the United States Auto Club refers to as auto racing's "triple crown": the 500-mile races at Ontario, Indianapolis, and Pocono. A driver may restrict himself so severely because of safety and the question of potential risk versus potential earning. Still another reason is that for a driver whose annual income exceeds, say, $75,000, the prospect of clobbering himself for 40 percent of a $1,000 sprint car payoff seems hardly sensible, especially in view of the tax penalties. Few well-heeled drivers (and there are a number) are willing to accept the high risk and the low pay that result from racing midgets and sprint cars. The occasionally successful driver who will "stand on the gas" (another favorite racing phrase) with verve and determination in comparatively low-paying races is respectfully referred to in the business as "a real racer." Traditionally, the driver's share of his winnings comes to the standard 40 percent, although it goes without saying that some can command more, others less. The now legendary A. J. Foyt, Indy's only four-time winner, is easily the most talented and accomplished driver in the annals of the sport, and is also the classic, prototypical "real racer" because of his willingness to compete, at whim, in almost any kind of four-wheel motor mayhem. Not far behind Foyt is Duane Carter *fils* (known in the sport as "Pancho"), who has not permitted the generous championship trail prize money to sate his appetite for going flat out on the United States Auto Club's preposterously dangerous sprint car circuit. Showing more spunk and race savvy than his very successful driver-father, who was an Indy regular between 1948 and 1963, Carter won the United States Auto Club's national midget title in 1972, and the sprint car title in 1974 and again in 1976. In 1978, Carter added still another laurel to his career by clinching the championship dirt-racing title.

Part of the measure of a real racer is his ability to bounce back after adversity, and this the 1973 California State College business administration graduate did over the long winter of 1977-1978. It was on the second day of December in

1977 that Carter, testing a Lightning-Cosworth Indy car at the Phoenix International Raceway, spun into the inner guard rail at a speed well in excess of 150 miles an hour, sheared off six supporting posts, and caught fire. His injuries (a ruptured bladder, multiple fractures of his hands, arms, and wrists, in addition to a pelvis fractured in two places) were hardly severe enough to keep him long out of the racing wars. After buckling himself into a sprint car at Indianapolis Raceway Park on the following April 8, Carter time trialed second fastest ("second quick" in racing patois) in a field of thirty-four, and then won the forty-lap "feature." On the following afternoon, at Winchester, Indiana (evidencing a limp and complaining about a "sore tailbone" from the previous night's escapades), Carter won again.

Racing's camp followers derive considerable satisfaction from such feats of courage and resilience. It is part of what keeps them lining up at the ticket booth. Ticket lines are the longest at the Indianapolis Motor Speedway, and the crowd that assembles there on race day is alleged to be the world's largest single day sporting swarm. The reasons for the attraction of an estimated 325,000 persons have been hotly debated through the years. The popular notion is that crowds congregate in the delightful anticipation that they may see someone mutilated. Except in the instance of a pathological few, this could not be so. Spectators at race tracks are far more intrigued with the idea that a calamity *might* occur than that it *will* occur. Crowd reaction to catastrophe is unfailingly predictable. Spectators become mute and terrified. A few pick up and leave. It is these same people, however, who "get off" (as a friend of mine puts it) at the prospect of thirty-three race day contestants wheeling past the start-finish line at 220 miles an hour.

There are, of course, other reasons why people find the Speedway a fertile place to congregate. Some go there to pick pockets. Beer guzzlers have traditionally found it an ideal site for a bacchanal. Still others, like the braless teenagers who entrench themselves in that muddy mire known euphemistically as the Snake Pit (inside turn one) discover social and sexual fulfillment. Probably a majority of the aggressively middle-class male customers find a vicarious thrill in the purifying prospect of speed and sound and color. But there are many who derive some satisfaction from seeing and hearing the Indianapolis script reread every year. For them, the May ritual begins with daily practice sessions which culminate in two weekends of time trials, the object of which is to identify the thirty-three fastest cars from out of an entry list that usually numbers somewhere between sixty and ninety cars. A time trial run consists of a driver's being out alone and at speed for four electronically timed laps. After all entrants have had an opportunity to make a qualification attempt in the four days designated for that purpose, the eleven-row three-abreast lineup is established.

Once the race is underway, the practiced Indianapolis observer takes positively nothing for granted. He expects the unexpected. Consider, for instance, the start of the race. That otherwise orderly high-speed procession of thirty-three cars three abreast has resulted in some of the most extraordinary debacles ever perpetrated on the public. Unquestionably the most breathtaking prospect in all of sportsdom, Indianapolis starts have not infrequently gone completely awry, as for example in 1957 when a car driven by an irascible Oklahoman named Elmer George (the now deceased son-in-law of the now deceased owner-president of the Indianapolis Motor Speedway, Tony Hulman) drilled the tail of a car driven by Eddie Russo on the relatively slow pace lap prior to the actual start; in 1958, when a totally bungled start indirectly resulted in an eight-car pileup and the death of popular Pat O'Connor; in 1964, when an explosive, seven-car wreck claimed the lives, by fire, of sports car racer Dave McDonald and Eddie Sachs, racing's "clown prince"; in 1966, when the unfurling of Pat Vidan's green bunting initiated an eleven-car shunt on the main straightaway; in 1971, when the pace car, driven by a less-than-able Indianapolis Dodge dealer named Eldon Palmer, drove headlong into a portable grandstand full of news photographers; and in 1973, when wealthy David "Salt" Walther's fiery end-for-end starting-line flips in his father's McLaren Offenhauser left him gravely injured and put several of his competitors out of action for the day.

Much of the psychological effect that captivates visitors is the aura of the Speedway's 539 acres, which are now listed on

Out of control Dodge pace car about to crash, 1971.   David Knox

the National Register of Historic Places. The track grounds, while not particularly impressive when viewed from an aircraft landing at nearby Indianapolis International Airport, are large enough to contain two golf courses (an eighteen-hole championship course liberally peppered with pine trees which is adjacent to the backstretch on the outside of the track, and a short course in the infield known as the "Track Nine"), a field hospital, a ninety-six-unit motel, a row of trackside apartments designated as VIP suites, and a huge infield automotive museum-office building complex. Until his retirement in the summer of 1977, owlish Clarence Cagle was responsible for overall supervision of the Speedway grounds and kept them

Westward view of south chute the day after the 1977 race.

A sign painter methodically letters the name of each
car and driver on the pit wall.

Indianapolis Star

admirably well manicured until May, when they were defiled with tons of refuse deposited there by spectators. Renowned as an enthusiastic and tireless worker, Cagle (who occupied a home on the grounds facing West Sixteenth Street) became famous for his sixteen-hour workdays, weekends included.

Anyone troubled with an active Oedipal complex will stay well clear of the Speedway's main gate, ominously situated where three roads (West Sixteenth, Georgetown, and Crawfordsville) converge in the municipality of Speedway, Indiana. The city limits of Indianapolis begin at the track's easternmost edge. As a community, Speedway's denizens range from the lower middle class, who occupy the medium-seedy dwellings on the east side, to the upper middle class, who occupy some medium-elegant dwellings on the west side. Speedway is unquestionably the dead center of automobile racing in America, and because of the track's all but unsullied reputation in the racing world, a number of drivers who compete there (or would like to compete there) live in reasonably close proximity, especially in the summer. If your name is Billy Puterbaugh and you have made it fairly big in United States Auto Club competition circles, you reside in the same home that 1955 Indianapolis winner Bob Sweikert once occupied a few hundred yards away from the Speedway grounds on a partially paved street known as North Luett. The Speedway holds a spell over you. Puterbaugh: "I'm over at the Speedway every day, and I've thought about it, and walked around it, and everything else. I just made my mind up that my life wasn't complete until I made that race."

But it is not only for the sake of convenience that the racing community lives in such places as Speedway City, Indianapolis, Brownsburg, and Lebanon, and tends not to stray too far from the sow's teat. For them, the Speedway repesents the perpetual hope for some future bonanza. Activity hums in the shops of such better known car fabricator-mechanics as A. J. Watson, George Bignotti, and Grant King. And while scores of drivers have for years listed exotic-sounding California addresses, their actual presence has been close to the watering holes, drugstores, and racing shops in and around Speedway, Indiana.

Both town and track have changed since Johnnie Parsons

won the 500-mile race in 1950. The quarter-mile Sixteenth Street Speedway directly across from the big tracks, where some drivers who drove at the Speedway competed in midget races on the evening before they drove at the Speedway, no longer exists, having been removed to make way for that ratty American institution, the shopping center. Rosner's Rexall, where Peter DePaolo dined after he won the 1925 race, still stands at the corner of West Sixteenth and Main near the Speedway's main gate. Three-quarters of a mile to the east stands Mates White Front Cafe, once a popular hangout and the scene of some memorable barroom brawls. Mates has exchanged its gallery of framed driver portraits behind the oaken bar for a gallery of strippers highlighted by the occasional appearance of Miss Nude Universe. On Sunday mornings, the pyramid of empty beer cans at Mates' rear door becomes the closest thing in central Indiana to Mt. Everest.

While the quality of life outside the boundaries of the Indianapolis Motor Speedway has not necessarily improved in the years since 1950, the Speedway itself has gradually meliorated since Anton "Tony" Hulman Jr. negotiated the purchase of the track in 1945 from World War I flying ace Eddie Rickenbacker. If the Indianapolis Motor Speedway is in some sense the lengthened shadow of a man, then the man is Tony Hulman. By the time of Hulman's fatal heart attack in 1978, the Speedway had undergone a nearly complete metamorphosis without the loss of its essential character. The Yale-educated Hulman, a Terre Haute, Indiana sportsman and entrepreneur, so loved the Speedway that, until the day of his passing, he is said to have invested more in it than he derived from it. The refurbishment of the Speedway, which had lain fallow during World War II except for some government-authorized tire testing, was slow, painstaking, and costly. Nearly having fallen to the wrecker's ball and become an urban housing development following the war, the track's resuscitation was gradual. Even in 1950, as old photographs will attest, there were weeds still growing through cracks in the racing surface on Memorial Day. But Hulman's rescue of the Indianapolis Motor Speedway had other implications as well, because it also underwrote the future of traditional, conservative, midwestern heartland, roundy-round oval track auto racing by giving it a permanent home.

Today, the Speedway has been redeemed and improved to the point that the acclaimed rectangle once known as the Brickyard now consists of a smooth asphalt span that exposes one yard of original brick at the start-finish line. To racing crackpots, even a single brick embodies some great microcosmic significance. When the south chute was excavated in 1973 to make way for an expanded underpass for automobile traffic, I was myself one of those who rummaged through the rubble in search of an authentic Speedway brick. But whereas the original bricks have been paved over repeatedly with layers of asphalt, the old prewar grandstands have been superceded by huge metal and concrete structures that reach skyward. The "new" Chinese pagoda constructed next to the starting line in 1926 after the "old" (1913) pagoda burned to the ground in 1925 is gone. In its place is an imposing aluminum and glass structure known as the Master Control Tower where, because of inadequate ventilation, legions of press, radio, and television reporters compete for what little oxygen there is on race day. New tunnels have been created, like the one in the south chute, while existing ones have been expanded. By 1974 the northwest turn had been widened considerably to create a safer entryway to the pit area. At the same time, retaining walls were raised to a minimum height of thirty-two inches.

A chronicle of systematic improvements to the track and grounds is itself the record of the Speedway's growth as a national institution. But even this elaborate program of maintenance and melioration is but part of the story, and it says relatively little about the mystique that eveywhere surrounds the most significant of all motor-racing courses in the world. To begin to feel that mystique, one has little recourse but to walk, unattended, over the two-and-one-half miles of what the front office stationery calls "The Greatest Race Course in the World." We're headed there presently.

Chapter 1

THE LAYOUT!
A STROLL AROUND
THE SPEEDWAY

Speedway gates open for qualification crowds at six o'clock in the morning, and the swarms of people continue until midafternoon, when they tend to evacuate gradually. At the six o'clock close of activity, the noontime throngs have been reduced substantially. Most of the qualification attendees, their arms and faces sunburnt and their bellies awash with beer, have by this time elected to go elsewhere.

It is on this initial day of qualification that the "hot dogs" (fast runners) on the Speedway's April 15 entry list are most apt to make a flat-out qualification attempt; for although the thirty-three fastest qualifiers run in the race, second day qualifiers line up in order behind first day qualifiers, third day qualifiers start behind second day qualifiers, and fourth day runners start the race at the end of the field on race day. A number of first day runners make a qualification attempt in the hope that they will earn the money, the prestige, and the clear advantage that goes with starting the 500-mile race on the pole (the pole being the inside position of the trio of cars that comprise the first of eleven rows of racing cars on race day). On the evening prior to the first Saturday of qualification runs, the day that the pole car will be determined, a representative from each car draws a number that determines the order in which that car will make a qualification run. To draw a low number is not necessarily a tactical advantage; the track may well be too hot for the racing tire compound to work properly, and the driver may be secretly quaking from something akin to stagefright brought on by hundreds of thousands of pairs of eyes fixed on him. Some racing teams prefer to wait, if possible, until late in the afternoon, when long grandstand shadows begin to appear on the track and the mobs begin to disappear, before they make a qualification fling. The surface of the track may have cooled by this time, the tires may grab just a little more effectively than they did earlier in the day, and the fuel-injected engines may be turning healthier rpm's. Cooler and therefore denser air will produce more power. The result, although the track surface may be a little greasier than it was earlier in the day, can be a fortuitous gain of perhaps one to three precious miles per hour, and therefore a better (and safer) race day starting position.

Once this initial day of qualifying is completed, the objective for most of the remaining would-be contestants is to divine the car-driver combination that will generate sufficient speed to clear the thirty-three car cut. To this end, Indy's chief mechanics apply every toolbox trick there is to coax even one more mile an hour. They jack the weight of the chassis to favor one wheel or another, they experiment with varied tire combinations, they adjust airfoils, and they threaten or humor the driver — whichever seems to bring results. A driver who does not strike a good working relationship with his car may, like some disenchanted lover, go looking for another machine to drive. In the middle of such frantic activity, beleaguered Gasoline Alley assumes a different personality. No longer a pleasant place to loll away a lazy day, the Alley becomes all business as it loses its penchant for convivial horseplay.

Outside of its wire fenced boundaries, a seemingly endless succession of strolling curiosity seekers fouls the grounds with a variety of ordure: sandwich wrappers, discarded drinking cups, and white hunks of trampled Styrofoam. Everywhere, as far as the eye can see, it is a city in which deputations of the Marion County Sheriff's Department patrol the acreage on horseback in a futile attempt to create order out of disorder. Less conspicuous are the detectives in mufti who monitor the infield in search of rowdies, underage drinkers, potheads, gamblers, and occasional hookers.

On the track, along congested pit row, and in the tension-filled enclaves of Gasoline Alley, the race qualifying procedure is played out. For a number of racing teams who have been assured, because of quick qualification speeds, of a place in the select race day lineup, the month's main objective has been fulfilled. They may have an eighty-to-one chance of winning the race, but with clenched teeth, good luck, and considerable help from their friends, they have also managed to hold car and driver together for four laps under the electric eye timer. The driver, although he assuredly will not win the race, has kept his reputation alive, satisfied his car owner, saved face for his sponsors, and assured himself of the butter-and-egg money (about $20,000) that will come to a bottom-end Indianapolis finish. Although the race looms a week away, he has quelled the greater number of his anxieties.

It can be safely said that, with good counsel, the novice spectator at Indianapolis can discover in the 500-mile chase a very invigorating, pleasurable, and exciting outing, if he will but attend to certain details well in advance; for just as there is an art to competing at Indianapolis, so too is there an art to spectating it. Accommodations (should accommodations be necessary) in and around Indianapolis should be settled as much as a year in advance, although they not infrequently entail a three-day minimum tenancy at race-inflated prices. Tickets, obtainable from the Speedway front office, can be ordered on the day following one 500-mile race for the following year's extravaganza. Most serious spectators (in addition to quite a few thousand not-so-serious spectators) prefer to situate themselves somewhere along the main straightaway and at a judicious distance from the grid itself. The higher up a spectator positions himself, the better he can find the perspective on the day's activity that suits him best. The farther he is from the track itself, the less likely he is to be inadvertently on the receiving end of some unforeseen mishap. The next thing he does is order a May subscription to one of the Indianapolis dailies.

To get the full beauty of it, the diligent spectator arrives at the Indianapolis Motor Speedway at the earliest possible moment after five o'clock in the morning on race day, for if it is cornball, down-home Americana he is in search of, he is certain to close the day with a full cup. When, amid aerial bombs and thousands of parti-colored helium-filled balloons, the race gets underway at eleven o'clock, it is the spectator within half a mile of the starting line who will be kept better aware of the day's progress. From that general vantage point, he can see the Speedway's chief starter Pat Vidan orchestrate the field into motion, but he can also view a reasonably accurate electronic scoring tower that illuminates with computerized imprecision the order in which cars are running. Most importantly, perhaps, he is also in a position to witness pit activity, which, in the opinion of many knowledgeable onlookers, is half the race day fun. Most important of all, it is the denizens of the main straightaway who experience the greatest orgasm in sports, the flagging-off of the Indianapolis 500. The prospect alone is easily worth the crowd crush and the price of admission. Once the Big Race is on, the only near-necessity for the complete spectator (besides such life-sustaining things as food and drink) is a set of radio headphones which will both muffle the hyena howl of engines and receive messages from the Speedway's own radio network. Once the race has been run, many of the spectators dash to the nearest television set to confirm that what they saw was in fact what actually happened.

To the uninitiated, preparations as elaborate and methodical as these may appear to carry fansmanship beyond the pale, but not so. The true, hard-bitten Indy devotee, well aware that every little bump and wobble on the racecourse will in time be painstakingly chronicled, debated, discussed, and evaluated from varying perspectives in the days to come, possesses an all but insatiable desire for total knowledge of the colorful Indianapolis scene. People like him flock to Indianapolis every year, partly out of pure habit and partly out of the gnawing prospect that not to appear means they would miss something that they consider somehow significant. Not wishing to interrupt their long-standing records of habitual race attendance, they wend their way back to Indianapolis every May, just as I do, regardless of impedimenta.

Sometimes the impedimenta seem inordinately great. At the age of eighty, Larry Maine Bisceglia has driven his camper truck from Yuma, Arizona to be the first spectator (theoretically, anyway) in line at Indianapolis every year since 1949, and he has seen all of the post-World War II 500-mile races. Shirley Murphy, on the other hand, who had a financial interest in A. J. Foyt's winning cars in 1964 and 1967, has never missed a race at Indianapolis, and that includes the premier event in 1911. Murphy was present again in 1978, though very nearly sightless, as the financial backer of the only woman driver to run at Indianapolis, formidable and feminine Janet Guthrie. Somewhere out there on the main straight on race day is Freeman Downing of Boston. Downing is totally blind.

The infield scene on race day differs markedly from the scene that prevails from the grandstands. Infielders are perhaps more inclined to abandon themselves in holiday revelry, which is the primary reason for their being on hand in the first place. But before there are any spectators on the grounds on race day itself, thousands of other persons, each with a role to play, have reported for duty. Among them are about twenty-four hundred safety patrolmen, eleven hundred concessions workers, and two hundred fifty physicians and nurses. These numbers do not include drivers, car owners, sponsors, mechanics, newspeople, firemen, roving bands of cops, and who knows whom. Many of them enter the Speedway while there is still a cover of darkness. Once inside, a good number of them breakfast at the dragnasty cafeteria expressly reserved for the racing clan, while others wend their way to Mass said by a priest standing on the back of a pickup truck within the fumy confines of Gasoline Alley. Others have been known to climb atop the garage roofs to witness the coming of five o'clock, the violet hour when the public gates are thrown open. Like the detonation of some eighty-megaton turd bomb, the Speedway's twelve means of ingress are flung open to accommodate what turns out to be the seamier side of the race day rabble, the ones who opted to wait all night (maybe even

(a) Janet Guthrie waiting for signal to start the time trial, 1979. (b) On her way.

David Knox

all week) somewhere outside the gates so that at this precise moment they might sprint toward one of the coveted spaces along the infield fencing and view the proceedings from the discomfort of their automobiles. It at last becomes clear what the actual meaning of race day is. First, it is the motorcycle contingent. They worm their way noisily to the front of the traffic, which by this time is backed up for blocks, and charge triumphantly toward the infield ahead of anyone else. After the motorcycles come carloads of glassy-eyed mummers, their mouths tasting like the inside of a shellac can, who can lay siege in a sixty-mile-an-hour run across the infield in a sprint that would make the most hardened of Indianapolis drivers cower in terror.

By nine o'clock a good portion of the 264,000 reserved seat holders have arrived. If there is one thing that concerns them more than the prospect of viewing the race itself, it is the weather. Anxiously, they scan the heavens for any hint of inclement signs, while band after high-kicking high school band (each one seeming a little more off key than the last) parades smartly around the track. Unhappily, what the weather-scanners sometimes see resembles more of a hurricane than a hint. In recent years (1973, 1975, and 1976), driving rains washed out part, if not all, of the race day festivities. At Indianapolis, there can be no racing on a wet track, one good reason being that the fifteen-inch-wide treadless Goodyear tires, even at relatively modest rates of speed, will hydroplane over accumulated water on the track surface, turning the race into a thoroughgoing fiasco of spinning cars piloted by an incorrigible gang of sex-crazed orangutans over a frozen lake.

The overwhelming question on race morning, therefore, is the state of the weather in Terre Haute (seventy miles to the southwest), because the rain that falls in Terre Haute falls a short time later over the Speedway. So while rain-racing at Indianapolis is out of the question, the Speedway's aging battalion of officialdom has been understandably hesitant to halt such a momentous thing as the 500-mile race, especially when everyone present appears to be having such a good time. The traditional policy at Indy has been to call it a day if rains should fall after 51 percent of the race (101 laps) has been registered by the leading car. By that time it's usually a *fait accompli* unless there is some reasonable chance that the track may dry soon enough before night. Once the track has had a thorough soaking, however, chary railbirds know from experience that there will be a two-hour minimum until it is race-ready again. In 1976, as luck would have it, the race ended in a typhoon at just about the moment leader John Rutherford logged his 101-lap minimum.

Race day throng as seen from Gasoline Alley.

David Knox

*   *   *

It is an exceptionally hot mid-July day in Indiana. There are no howling turbocharged Cosworth engines to deafen me, only a chirping that originates with infield crickets and with a caravan of pullcarts that trail behind a party of lady golfers. Virtually all of the racing crowd has vanished temporarily, and the golfers, like ants after a picnic, have fallen heir to the Speedway. At this time of the year the infield seems to lie fallow, gathering strength for the next onslaught that awaits it some ten months and two weeks from today. I leave the ladies to their hooks and handicaps, and I move to more familiar ground by passing the white field hospital (reconstructed in 1948) where Clark Gable was taken after a simulated crash in *To Please a Lady.* From here I walk toward a dormant Gasoline Alley and through its gates, unchallenged.

Gasoline Alley consists of little more than two long sad-looking weathered white and green buildings situated parallel to each other. To racing afficionados, this is indeed the center of motor racing in America, and the spirits and legends that dwell there are anything but passive; they're somewhere in the woodwork, behind a door, under a sunbleached roof, in the oil-stained asphalt pavement. Precisely where one goes to find the quintessential Indianapolis Motor Speedway is a question. But in Gasoline Alley there is a certain apotheosis that only persons with leaden sensibilities can ignore totally. When summer winds waft through the eighty-eight garages situated there, it is very like a scene from *The Last Picture Show:* forlorn and abandoned. Although there are eighty-eight garage stalls, the garages are numbered to eighty-nine because garage 13 does not exist (not too surprisingly). Time was in Gasoline Alley when women, peanuts, and green racing cars did not exist either, although they had been discredited long before New York's Janet Guthrie appeared at the track in 1977 driving a green Bryant Heating and Cooling Special. Today, however, the prohibition of the number 13 appears to be as sacrosanct as anything in holy writ. The appearance of these Gasoline Alley garages is easily enough to underwhelm even the most enthusiastic of first-time Speedway visitors,

Gasoline Alley.

but to old-line racing cuckoos they are revered as though they were a piece of the Cross or a brick from the track.

The Gasoline Alley garage compound is a place abounding in signs and messages. In our time, the scarred and layered paint that covers the two rows of garages puts one in mind of an abused picnic table, and the bruised exteriors of the buildings bespeak the arduousness of a life in racing. Thirty new garages were erected in 1915 when Woodrow Wilson occupied the Oval Office, and before America had become involved in the first World War. Most of the 1915 structures still exist, although a number of them were destroyed in a fire that swept through Gasoline Alley at seven o'clock on race morning in 1941. It was at that hour that three-time Indianapolis winner Wilbur Shaw, a leading contestant on that day, heard the scream of fire engines over the sound of the shower he was enjoying in his landlady Mrs. Furguson's Speedway bathroom. Hurriedly dried and dressed, Shaw arrived in Gasoline Alley soon enough to see the south row of garages ablaze, allegedly the fault of someone's careless handling of a heater. While the Indianapolis fire department declared time out while they searched for a usable hydrant, half of the garage area was consumed. Said one on-the-scene reporter: It was "unquestionably the biggest thrill that the people at the track have ever experienced." The 1941 race went on more than two hours late and short one car (George Barringer's rear-engine, four-wheel drive, blue and white number 34 Miller Special). For Shaw, the day that had begun miserably ended that way. On lap 152 the right rear wheel on his Maserati weakened enough to send him into the wall on the southwest turn, leaving him temporarily paralyzed from the waist down. Shaw claimed that the accident was caused by a wheel which he either knew or suspected to be faulty. It was marked so that it would not be used, but the mark was washed off during the fire.

Although the Indianapolis Motor Speedway had ceased activities during the 1917-1918 war years, 500-mile races went into another hiatus between 1942 and 1945. It was on November 14, 1945 that Tony Hulman purchased the track, reportedly for about $750,000. With his characteristic prudence, he added eight more garages in 1948, plus eight more in 1952, two in 1953, four in 1962, and fourteen in 1967. But there is more to Gasoline Alley than meets the eye, because all the eye perceives is a succession of cramped and often mangy garage stalls. In reality, the history of American motor racing is etched deeply in the grain of those wooden structures, and its brilliant yesterdays are emblematic of the emerging American character. America's fabled love affair with the automobile has found its most colorful expression through the years on racecourses at county fairs and makeshift race tracks, none of them so justly celebrated as the one at Indianapolis.

My personal Stations of the Cross include certain points in Gasoline Alley and around the track itself. Even on this July afternoon, with almost nobody in sight, I sense that because of my peripheral connections with the racing scene in general, I am really not wanted here. But among the nearly deserted row of garages facing me is number 14. This was the space that Bob Sweikert and his builder-mechanic A. J. Watson occupied back in 1955 when they won the race. I was a tender eighteen in 1955, and without anybody on the inside who would shepherd me through the gates to Gasoline Alley. As a consequence, I stood on the outside just after the race had concluded and observed Sweikert, then a twenty-nine-year-old former University of California student who had just earned 40 percent of his $76,138.63 for coming home first in the thirty-ninth running of the Indianapolis 500. That was the race in which Billy Vukovich (known to the press as "The Mad Russian," but who was neither mad nor Russian) had not survived a backstretch pile-up that also involved Johnny Boyd, Al Keller, and Rodger Ward. For a competitive man like Sweikert, Vukovich's demise meant that Sweikert had "backed into" an Indianapolis win without Vukovich's having raced him all 500 miles to the drop of the checkered flag.

At the conclusion of the race Sweikert had received the usual accolades, including being kissed by his wife Dolores and by Dinah Shore. Back in Gasoline Alley, Sweikert retired to the dimmed privacy of garage 14. I pressed closer to the wire fence for a better glimpse of him and his pink and white racer. Behind the car, Sweikert, his crew chief and mechanic A. J. Watson (whose Indy cars even today are a reflection of himself: tidy and well-scrubbed), and car owner Jack Zink smiled as they waved to newspaper cameramen and reporters. Sweikert then disappeared into Zink's garage. A crowd collected and eventually eclipsed my view of garage 14. After that, somebody pushed its door partially closed. I crossed the litter-strewn infield and lost myself in the mobs that were burgeoning across West Sixteenth Street.

But there is more to the story. A year later, Bob Sweikert returned to Indy one final time, switched racing teams, brushed the wall during the race, and finally limped his bright yellow D-A Lubricants Special to the finish line in sixth place.

Bill Vukovich greeted by Speedway president Tony Hulman, 1955. (Vukovich did not survive the race.)

Shortly after that, on June 17, 1956, Sweikert lay dead in the emergency room of southern Indiana's Washington Memorial Hospital, the victim of devastating head injuries sustained in a sprint car race when his car vaulted the wall on the first turn of the treacherous, steeply-banked, paved half-mile track that is still in operation about a mile west of Salem, Indiana. Six years later, a rusty wheel from Sweikert's car dropped from a tree where it had been lodged all the while.

Even in the heat of summer there is still activity in Gasoline Alley. Popular Dick Simon, once a ski-jumping standout, a national parachuting champion, an official in the Mormon

Church, and an insurance holding company board chairman, is today at work mending the brakes on his racing car. Across the way is Larry Dickson, winner of more than one hundred thirty automobile races. The two men have driven in seventeen Indy 500-mile races between them. Dickson shrugs and says that as time goes on, races are becoming harder to win.

Gasoline Alley exudes the earthy and intermingled organic scents of tar and oil; for one whose every moment is consumed by motor racing, this is a delicious aroma. Futhermore, the redolence that is always present here is supplemented by other distinguishing signs, such as the automotive logotypes that are affixed in great numbers against garage windows and on the doors of beer-burdened garage refrigerators. For Gasoline Alley is, among many other wonderful things, the heavenly city of stickers and decals that say things like "Goodyear" or "Champion" or "Valvoline" or "Perfect Circle" or "Premier" or "Die Hard" or "Bear" or "Sunnen" or "Monroe" or "Wagner" on them. Indeed, this is the place where a man is known by the products he finds a way to use. There are other messages, as well, and these are designed — make no mistake about it — to protect the apartheid culture of the racing clans from any unwanted intrusion from the outside world: No Admittance. Keep Out. Crew Only.

A pickup truck parked between garage rows has the legend COON HUNTERS DO IT AT NIGHT stuck to its rear bumper, while on its front bumper the inscription reads CHRIST IS THE ANSWER. Around the corner in front of garage 3, there is a wooden bench holding an engine cowling that has been freshly sprayed in rich blue. The sun's reflection on the moist azure paint blinds me momentarily.

I leave Gasoline Alley and walk out to trackside, passing beneath a banner that reads, from behind, YELLA ENILOSAG. Like some Dantean bandroll warning all who pass beneath to be wary of what's before them, the drapeau that flies between Gasoline Alley and the way to the track seems to imply a warning. And why shouldn't it? The racetrack that lies in wait out there has, over the decades, proven itself to be a man killer in more ways than one. If it has yielded more broken dreams than broken bodies, then it is all the more formidable. This is racing's ultimate arena. The pit wall is lettered with the names of every car and every driver from the previous year's race, and the lettering remains there throughout the winter, until the coming of another Indiana May. Coats of white paint have been spread many times on the pit wall, and famous racing names have superceded still other famous racing names. The roadway, parallel to the track, is called the "pit": itself an anachronistic misnomer, suggesting the existence of trenches from which to examine the underside of an automobile. Here there are no pits in the original sense of the word, but a lane that extends for perhaps half a mile. On race day, each car has its assigned place for hurried service stops, and each car has its own fuel storage tank pitside. It is forbidden to add oil during the race, or to accept fuel from any storage tank except one's own. To add oil is prohibited because it suggests that a car is blowing (or leaking) its original supply on the track, making the course even more hazardous. To add fuel from another car's storage tank means that one is exceeding the mandated fuel allotment for the 500 miles. The old bromide that races are won and lost in the pits has more than a grain of truth to it, because seconds squandered during sloppy or otherwise inefficient pit stops will result in a car's being set back in the race standings. Pit crews (limit: five crew members over the pit wall on race day) not wanting to blemish what they expect will be their driver's peerless performance in the race, act with as much precision and dispatch as they are capable of. Fifteen or twenty seconds, depending entirely on what must be accomplished, is a respectable amount of time to keep the driver waiting for fuel and tires.

If there are debacles connected with the start of the race itself, there have been a great many remarkable (if understandable) pit blunders, as well. Two examples come to mind. Charismatic but somewhat articulate Lloyd Ruby from Wichita Falls, Texas has an immense sentimental claque at the Speedway and has had a win on the bricks within his grasp on several occasions, only to have some terrible thing happen. In 1969, for instance, Ruby had his Wynn's Spitfire running to near perfection. Having begun the day in twentieth starting position, Ruby had pressed his car into first place by the 105th lap when he slithered very rapidly down pit lane for a fillup.

With more than $805,000 in prize money at stake, he was eager to rejoin the fray. So eager was he, in fact, that his car moved out of the pits before the fuel nozzle had been removed from the side of his car. The result was that the tension of the fuel rig ruptured his tank.

Then there was 1972, one of the fat years when total prize money exceeded a million dollars. Huge (six feet two inches and 200 pounds) Jerry Grant of Irvine, California was ahead with 187 of his 200 laps behind him. His tank as parched as his throat, Grant wheeled his purple number 48 "Mystery Eagle" into the pit area of teammate Bobby Unser, took on fuel, and headed back on the course. Meanwhile, a rival crew chief filed a protest with the chief steward alleging that Grant had accepted fuel from the wrong storage tank (a villainous act, inasmuch as each contestant has a fuel limitation during the race), and the protest was upheld. The result this time was that none of Grant's laps were scored after his 187th and the car that would have finished second was set back to twelfth, meaning an estimated loss for Grant and his associates of $72,000 in prize money.

Just as Gasoline Alley is filled with messages of varying sorts, so too is pit row. Whereas the flashing of pit signs to cars in competition was once virtually the only way of communication between crew and driver, two-way radios have more recently come into vogue. Other messages are those painted on the cement of pit lane itself. The pavement in front of each driver's stop-off is not infrequently decorated with a combination of curlicues, stripes, and other cryptic reminders for both crew and driver on race day. Certain rectangles and circles, for example, mark the spot where the driver is expected to set his front wheels during the pit stop. To bring a racer to a complete stop after having had it at 225 miles per hour only a few moments before requires some doing. Drivers are immersed in a strange, heady, high-velocity world on the track, and to leave that world is, like many other of life's interruptions, a necessary, if unwelcome distraction. But from the vantage point of the pits themselves (always the worst place to spectate on the whole racetrack) there are pavement hieroglyphics that a pit man needs to take seriously, such as the huge pair of footprints illuminated in Day-Glo red in A. J. Foyt's pit to assist in the preferred stance for a refuel man during a stop: left foot aggressively forward, right foot back and open. There is also the curious reminder painted in the cement in front of David "Salt" Walther's pit space which reads: JIM! SALT'S WATER.

To walk the racing surface at Indianapolis can be a quietly enlightening experience, particularly if one has been accustomed to seeing race cars turn the two-and-one-half-mile track in under a minute. On foot, a leisurely and contemplative circuit of the raceway will take about forty-five minutes, and the perspectives one gets are quite different from those available from any grandstand. Whereas most auto racing tracks are oval in contour, Indianapolis is much less so. Resembling a rectangle more than an oval, both the front and back straights run precisely north-south and measure 3,300 feet in length, about five-eighths of a mile. At each end of the course is a short straightaway called a *chute*, measuring 660 feet or about one-eighth of a mile. The two chutes and two straightaways are linked by four turns, each one covering a distance of 1,320 feet, which is a quarter of a mile. If it were possible to lift those four turns and position them together, the result would be a one-mile circle. The width of the track ranges from 60 feet on the turns to a very confined 50 feet on the straight sections. At its maximum, the banking on each turn reaches nine degrees and twelve minutes.

The faster one moves around the track, the more the turns seem to become right angles, and the more the banking seems to disappear. Most conventional race tracks in America, regardless of length, have what is spoken of as four "corners." On the Indy car circuit, the so-called Championship Trail, there are three noteworthy exceptions. One of them is the Pocono Raceway, a two-and-a-half-mile, three-cornered track located amid the serene Pocono Mountains of northeast Pennsylvania. Another is Greater Gotham's difficult Trenton Speedway, a mile-and-a-half course with a troublesome right hand dogleg in the middle of the backstretch. The Phoenix International Runway is a one-mile course of similar contour. Traditionally, however, the prevailing American racing mentality seems to demand a four-turn race track with the competition moving in a counter clockwise direction. The Indianapolis lay out looks something like this:

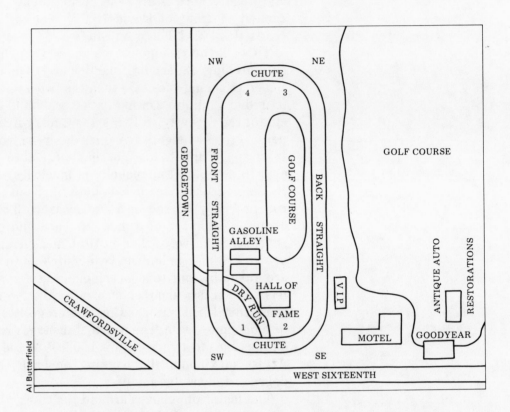

Today, all but one yard of the original 1909 brick surface is covered with asphalt, and that one yard is situated at the start-finish line, which is as good a place as any to begin a walking tour of the track itself. If you had X-ray vision and could read the inscription on the underside of some bricks, you would discover the following legend: W. C. Co., Culver Block, Pat. May 21, 1901. If you own a brick with that inscription, you have the genuine Indianapolis Motor Speedway brickyard brick article. It will serve well as a doorstop or as a relic of Americana that will, on three out of ten occasions, amaze your guests.

If from this brick cross-section you cast your eyes toward

the first (southwest) turn, you should bear in mind that on race day there may be (conservatively) a congregation amounting to 150,000 surprisingly knowledgeable and interested persons like Freeman Downing out there occupying the reserved seats that are visible from here. But on a day like today, I seem to be the only person in immediate view. The temperature exceeds 90° F and an oily vapor seems to be emanating from the asphalt. As I begin to stroll down the main straight, towering grandstands mark the way. To approach the first turn at Indy is to realize that it cuts to the left very suddenly. At the beginning of the first corner the track is intersected by Dry Run Creek, known to Speedway regulars as Ditch Creek. It flows beneath the track, curves with the contour of the southwest turn, and then passes beneath the track once again in the middle of the south chute, where the track's banking levels out to the point that it has only enough pitch left to allow the water to roll off. From the south chute there is a clear view of the Hall of Fame, situated in the infield, which serves as an office building, a repository of antique street and competition vehicles, and a tourist shop. From the outside, it puts one in mind of a mausoleum fitted out with a billowing American flag and a decorative fountain in the form of a miniature geyser. Near the flag stands a huge memorial in homage, for some reason, to Louis Chevrolet, who exercised his limited racing luck at Indianapolis between 1915 and 1920. Here is a place for weary wayfarers to pause and refresh themselves beneath the stern bust of Chevrolet, which faces east. Beneath the bust is inscribed the rigorous admonition: "Never Give Up."

About sixty automobiles of yesterday repose inside the Hall of Fame, racing's Temple of Karnak. They are under the constant surveillance of affable, plainclothes security men. Among the automotive collection is Ray Harroun's Marmon Wasp, the same wasp that, in six hours, forty-two minutes, and eight seconds, captured the first Indianapolis 500 in 1911 at an average speed of just under seventy-five miles per hour. A short distance from the yellow Marmon stands a more recent relic, the silent pink and white Zink Special, a roadster, that Sweikert won with on Memorial Day in 1955.

In the south chute the whiteness of the retaining walls masks impact marks, some of them made long ago. The present thirty-two-inch wall stands in front of an earlier one which is still in evidence and which was part of the original 1909 construction. In the immense heat of this July afternoon a workman is applying still another coat of white paint to it. He too perspires freely and invites me to join him in his day labor.

At the exit of turn two is what the Speedway management calls "500 Hospitality Suites" or the "VIP Suites," which symbolize racing's close connections with the world of private enterprise. The particular mentality that prevails at Indianapolis has long been taken (and at times taken in) by the sort of individual who fancies himself a Very Important Person. In May at Indianapolis they are as thick as fleas, but the core of the racing establishment (the people who have actual hands-on relationships with racing cars) remains predictably indifferent to anything other than the arduous task of preparing for and running the race itself. Persons outside the establishment are far more inclined to stand in awe at the prospect of visiting actors, politicians, and corporate magnates. Racing people, on the other hand, are quick to warm up to anyone who can offer financial support in the form of sponsorship dollars. When actor Paul Newman (appearing somewhat incognito) passed much of May 1977 in Gasoline Alley with a racing team in which he had a financial interest, he seemed to be regarded more as a serious participant than as a celebrity-actor.

The "500 Hospitality Suites" situated adjacent to the southeast turn are, perhaps more than any other location, home base for visiting celebrities. As track locations go, however, those same terraced suites overlooking the track from the outside are not particularly good vantage points. They have redeeming features such as bars, bathrooms (at least one such bathroom has gold plumbing fixtures), closed circuit television, sofas, and tilt-back chairs. When the race is on, VIP tipplers miss seeing the action from the front straightaway, except on their closed circuit television receivers, but they seem not to mind. What price luxury? It cannot be said of the occupants of the VIP Suites that they necessarily fail to get their race day licks in, however. On the twenty-fifth lap of the 1976 race, they received an uncommon thrill when affable Tom Sneva of Spokane, Washington (once a junor high school principal and later a national driving champion) brushed wheels with Canadian ace Eldon Rasmussen. Neither accused the other of triggering the violent accident that followed: Sneva's bright blue and yellow Norton Spirit spirited end-for-end directly alongside the VIP Suites, letting fly with certain choice and costly pieces of shrapnel (an engine here, a little sheet metal there). Sneva, who miraculously evaded serious injury in one of the Speedway's all-time meaner-looking didos, indirectly caused quite a number of spilled gin and tonics up there in the Indiana National Bank suite as its terrified guests dove for cover.

Beyond the VIP Suites is that great expanse of Speedway backstretch which, on a day as intensely hot as this one, literally shimmers in the distance. Halfway up the backstretch the sound of traffic emanating from West Sixteenth Street has died down considerably and has been replaced by the sounds of birds and insects from the infield golf course. Very old trees with amputated limbs line the backstretch on the outside. Here too are somewhat anomalous polo barns now designated as a maintenance depot. Nearby stand a collection of race car refueling rigs from races long past. On one of the rigs is a faded Mobil flying red horse that, prior to Ashland Oil's near-monopoly on racing lubricants and fuel, was a commonplace logotype at the Speedway in the 1950s.

The unpainted retaining wall extending along the backstretch is scarred with still more impact marks. As I run my hand along one of those gouges in the cement, up comes one of the Speedway's white minibusses driven by an elderly guide entrusted with a gaggle of tourists. The man stops his bus in front of me, swivels around in his seat, and addresses his passengers in a wearisome tone of voice: "And here," he says, "the boys hit 227 miles an hour!" The tourists look around them, silently and incredulously. The old man pauses for a few moments to allow the wonder of his disclosure to be comprehended fully. He then puts the bus back into gear and motors slowly up the backstretch into turn three, the northeast.

The banking in the northeast, like the banking in the other three turns, strikes a maximum pitch of nine degrees and twelve minutes. Like the southwest turn, it tends to flatten out as it leads into the chute. The north chute, like the south chute, has an outer edge that is a mere five inches more elevated than the inner edge. It was back on race morning in 1950 that my father and I passed over this part of the track as a means of entering the infield. Today, it is no longer possible to do that; traffic now enters and departs the Speedway through a four-lane underpass that runs beneath the chute.

Just ahead of me is the fourth and final turn at Indianapolis, the northwest, which is perhaps the most forgiving of the four in the sense that the drivers have more racing room through here than they do elsewhere. The extra margin of track down toward the apron allows them to dip low and inside as they prepare to enter the pits. Drivers here come upon a yellow line painted on the track, which they cut below as they decelerate down the main straight and into the pit row. At about the place where the yellow line begins, the unhurried traveler can enjoy a reasonably clear view of ladies toilet #16, a facility around which considerable consternation centered in the middle sixties. In 1966 the Speedway (as a kind of extra added attraction) sponsored a balloon race in memory of a 1909 publicity stunt at the track's grand opening. Carl Fisher, who had originally masterminded construction of the Speedway, had been an avid balloonist. But this time a balloon chanced to fall directly on Ladies #16 and an occupant in the midst of her ablutions. As the falling balloon up-ended the facility, another woman attempted single-handedly to hold the building in place, but to no avail. The occupant proceeded to bring suit against the Speedway for alleged damages, and the controversy was eventually settled out of court. Today, in a rare expression of official levity, the sides of Ladies #16 are decorated with the painted figures of red and yellow ascension balloons.

From the north end of the main straightaway it is especially evident that the homestretch is fully grandstanded on both sides of the track. The huge sycamore that grew for generations on the inside left at the exit of turn four grows there no longer. It was near the shade of this tree that Dave McDonald and Eddie Sachs were burned fatally at the beginning of the 1964 race. It is fearfully evident from this vantage point that the main straightaway narrows to the point of leaving little, if any, room for error. In the event of a calamity, a driver can take refuge almost nowhere on the main straight, with its retaining walls on both sides of the course. Today, as I have noted, this place is very nearly deserted, and as a consequence the Speedway shows a different side of its personality. The names of all the cars and drivers are still painted on the pit wall from the previous year's race, and a somewhat forlorn ABC Sports banner billows even now from the roof of the paddock grandstand.

All of these sights and sounds and impressions are part of my own private Indianapolis. I have brought friends here on numerous occasions to share my response to the surroundings and their powerful ambience, but they have not always heard my message; they have viewed the place as an elaborate two-and-a-half-mile asphalt strip surrouned by steel and aluminum grandstand and situated comfortably on 539 acres. They have often show a disinclination toward my point of view: that Indy epitomizes the essence of Americana perhaps more than anything in Washington or Philadelphia or Boston.

*   *   *

The genesis and development of the Indianapolis Motor Speedway has been told and retold as a part of racing's cultural legacy. It requires no special genius to recognize that the track has been, since its inception, another expression of America's intrigue with the automobile as a symbol of rugged independence. More specifically, the Speedway was originally an adjunct of Indianapolis as an automobile manufacturing center. At one time some 250 kinds of cars were produced there, and until 1905 there were more automobiles manufactured in Indianapolis (automobiles such as the Overland and the Marmon) than there were in Detroit. Indeed, four of the original five entrepreneurs who invested money in the construction of the IMS by acquiring the 320-acre Pressley farm were men with automotive connections. At the time of purchase there seemed to be two fundamental motives in mind. First, they wanted to clear a profit by staging automobile races on a relatively long, paved track. Second, they wanted to create a dynamic automotive showplace. Their more public raison d'etre, however, was to create a kind of theatrical automotive proving ground in various senses of term. Until the 1960s there was still considerable lip service given to Indianapolis as a place where passenger automobiles benefited from the automotive research and development on the Speedway. The brochures at the entrance to the track's Hall of Fame assure the casual visitor that the track has made "contributions each year to the development of spark plugs, piston rings, turbochargers, suspension systems and aerodynamic designs which have increased the safety, performance and comfort qualities of modern passenger cars." To assert this gives the Speedway a certain rational justification for being, although it is questionable that much of a strong case could be made for the Speedway's (or racing's, for that matter) demonstrated contribution toward the evolution of the modern street automobile. Today, although automotive-related corporations and businesses make themselves very visible at Indianapolis, they come to advertise rather than to develop their products.

The original five investors in the Indiana Motor Parkway Grounds are today objects of veneration among racing's historic retinue. Carl G. Fisher and his partner James Allison manufactured a somewhat hazardous automobile carbide gas headlamp called the Prest-O-Lite. Frank H. Wheeler, the third partner, was at the helm of the Wheeler-Schebler Carburetor Company. Wheeler's friend Arthur Newby headed the National Motor Vehicle Company. The fifth man, Stoughton Fletcher, was a banker. In Speedway today, Fisher, Allison, Wheeler, and Newby all have public elementary schools named after them.

The five entrepreneurs secured the options necessary to purchase the original 320-acre plot (consisting of four eighty-acre farming tracts) for $72,000 in 1908, just as Fletcher asked to be dropped from the alliance of partners altogether. Fletcher's departure, executed before the articles of incorporation had been filed, meant that the Speedway was now entirely in the hands of men with a stake in the future of the automobile in America. It was playboy Carl Fisher who, more than any of his remaining three partners, was conversant with automobile racing and who, besides being a balloonist, had himself driven in a number of rough-and-tumble dirt-track races. His dirt-

Speedway founders prepare for an inspection tour of the grounds, 1909.

track experience had taught him, if nothing else, that he disliked dirt tracks. He disliked their dust, their mud, and their inadequate guardrailings. The thing that interested Fisher was relatively long (three- to five-mile) dustless race course, and his original plan was to make the new speedway on the Pressley farm into a three-mile rectangular track. Upon closer scrutiny, it became evident that the three-mile length was not feasible: the engineers would have been obliged to construct the track too close to property lines, leaving inadequate space to erect grandstands. A two-and-one-half-mile course was plotted out instead; even so, the south chute was but a short distance from what little horse and buggy traffic existed at the time on West Sixteenth Street.

Under the supervision of a New York engineer named Park Taliaferro Andrews, the configuration of the track was carved out, and the paving began. After the course had been rolled out with considerable precision by a fifteen-ton, three-wheeled steamroller, Andrews called for a two-inch layer of creek gravel; this, in turn, was subjected to a fifteen-ton roller. He then called for two inches of limestone, which he subjected to an eight-ton roller. Two gallons of taroid were poured over each square yard, and over the taroid went half an inch of stone chips to fill any remaining holes in the track surface. Andrews ordered still another layer of taroid (of a lower melting point than the first), and on top of all this, he added one more layer of crushed stone, ranging from dust particles to half-inch pieces. He then gave it a final going-over with a three-ton roller.

The paving of the track was painstaking, but alas, it did not hold up. After the staging of the June 15, 1909 balloon race, and after some failed attempts at motorcycle racing, auto racing began at the Speedway on August 19. Three days (Thursday-Friday-Saturday) of racing were staged with ghastly results. Andrews' pampered track surface could not withstand the stresses placed upon it by motor racing, and the breakup of the track was a major factor in making the Speedway's christening a bloody one. On September 1, 1909, the *Automobile Trade Journal* reported quite matter-of-factly that the "inauguration of the great Indianapolis Motor Speedway witnessed the breaking of American track records, and the loss of several lives." Driving a Knox in the first day's 250-mile race, William Bourque had worked his way into second position when the race reached its halfway point. As Bourque moved down the main straightaway, his car dove into a chuckhole and swerved toward the inside of the track, where it passed through two fences and struck a tree. Both Bourque and his riding mehanic, Harry Holcolm, perished as the entire front end of the Knox was torn away in the melee. On Saturday, driver Charley Merz's National shredded a tire in turn one, soared over the wall (which was perpendicular to the ground, but not to the banked turn), and landed about a hundred feet outside the track in Dry Run Creek. Merz was treated for bruises, but his riding mechanic Claude Kellum was dead at the scene, along with two spectators, James West of Indianapolis and Homer Joliff from nearby Franklin, Indiana. Several others were reported injured. Harry Tapking was removed from the grounds with a compound fracture of the right arm, a broken nose, and some scalp lacserations. As

Tapking was being carried out, driver Bruce Keene, at the switchboard of a Marmon, struck a wooden post in the second turn and was cut very badly about the head and neck. Race officials, who had seen about enough of this nonsense for three days, called off the 300-mile race after 235 miles had been run. The track surface was a mess, and Fisher was more than discouraged.

But Fisher and his associates had invested too much money to consider backing down at this point. Their only option was to invest still more money in the Speedway, and to do it quickly. They felt, not without reason, that they were in hot water with the American Automobile Association (AAA), which was the race sanctioning body, and they knew that more races on the present surface would cost more lives. To improve the track surface, there were but two ways to go: concrete or brick. Brick had the advantage of lasting longer, but it had the disadvantage of costing half again as much as concrete. They elected the brick surface and followed the recommendations of the National Paving Brick Manufacturers' Association; an order was placed with the Wabash Clay Company for 3,200,000 paving bricks, each weighing a little under ten pounds. Also needed were more than fourteen miles of drainage tile and enough concrete to construct a nine- by thirty-three-inch retaining wall along the curves and in front of the main grandstand.

Andrews lost no time. Some five hundred carloads of brick and eight carloads of cement soon arrived on West Sixteenth Street. Bricks were fed to the bricklayers by means of a portable belt conveyer powered by an automobile engine. After a two-inch cushion of sand was spread over the old surface, the bricks were set in place and then flattened true with a three-ton steam roller. Following an inspection of the placed bricks for grade and plane, a thin, batterlike filler consisting of equal parts sand and Portland cement was applied between the bricks with a scoop shovel. An hour later came another coat, this one applied with a squeegee. Some work was done at night with the aid of Prest-O-Lite lamps, and during a single nine-hour workday some 140,000 bricks were set in place.

Miraculously, the Speedway was race-ready after only sixty-three days of paving. On Friday, December 17, only one

Looking north on the bricked backstretch from the
golfers' bridge, 1936.

brick was missing from the Speedway — a gold-plated coin-
silver block weighing over fifty pounds and valued at $500. On
the day that the gold brick was to be placed in position, two little factors contributed to the less-than-abundant crowd that
turned out for the occasion: First, it was Friday, a working
day; second, the temperature hovered around the zero mark.
Notwithstanding, there were (according to a reporter who
joined the ranks of bystanders who seemed to have been called to muster in a Siberian prison camp) "opening speeches,
congratulatory opportunities, the meeting of workers in the
vineyard, they who stood shoulder to shoulder in the good
fight." Among the many winter hostages assembled on that
miserable day was Indiana's governor, the Honorable Thomas
R. Marshall. Assisting him in the placement of the fifty-two-

pound "Gold Paver" was his beleaguered private secretary Mark Thistlewait, who (and not without difficulty) eased the gold brick into its hole. The discrete circle around the starting line clapped politely, no doubt to improve circulation.

*   *   *

This, then, is part of the story of how the Speedway came into being. It is important to understand, however, that the current condition of the place is necessarily different from the way it appeared in 1909, or for that matter, in 1949. Scarcely anything at the Speedway has escaped alteration or demolition since 1909. The track changed hands in August 1927 when Eddie Rickenbacker assumed control. After the 1935 race had been run, a retaining wall perpendicular to the banking of the turns replaced the wall that had been constructed under the direction of Andrews in 1909. It was in 1936 that the inside concrete walls on the turns were removed and replaced by safety aprons. A year later the brick turns were resurfaced with asphalt, and in the year after that the only exposed brick was to be found in the middle of the front and back straights. With the resumption of racing in 1946, the Hulman administration embarked on a systematic and aggressive program of improvements in a variety of areas: grandstands, garages, pits, fences, commercial shops, museums, motel and golf facilities, bars, and other less apparent amenities.

Chapter 2

STAGGER
AND BOOST

With the evolution of the Speedway has come the sometimes bizarre evolution of mechanical creations competing there. To chronicle the progress of the contemporary Indianapolis racing car, however, is every bit as arduous as tracing the ascent of man. In it's role as an automotive proving ground, the track has been visited by a veritable rogue's gallery of mechanical perversities, each of them, one might suppose, an expression of its creator's maverick instincts. Theoretcially, ventures into mechanical perversity are undertaken with the notion of improving the breed. The mechanical breed, needless to say, has not always improved with each innovative experiment. Even comparatively ordinary racing machines are quite extraordinary in design and function, and the quest to identify a really strange automobile in Gasoline Alley is something like searching for a snowflake in a blizzard.

Indy cars are perhaps no more peculiar than Indy people, and it is difficult to know where to begin and where to end in describing the rolling curiosities at the Speedway. A few examples, however, may suffice. In 1948, Tennessee truckline owner Pat Clancy (in the words of automotive writer William Jeanes) "rightly reasoned that more rubber on the road would

1947, Pop Dreyer's shop on West Washington Street
in Indianapolis. The man with the hat (with the
hatband) is Dreyer.

Indianapolis Motor Speedway

mean higher cornering speeds." The result was a six-wheel
racer (a concept revived in the 1970s for Grand Prix competition) that Clancy, his car builder A. J. Bowen, and driver Billy
DeVore brought to the Speedway. The machine had all of the
theatrical charisma of a carnival fat lady, and lumbered home
to a creditable twelfth place. "The performance was not such
to send development engineers back to their drawing boards
with dreams of multi-wheeled cars," according to on-the-spot
technical writer Russ Catlin, but when the same subversive
vehicle returned the following year to the Speedway, it broke

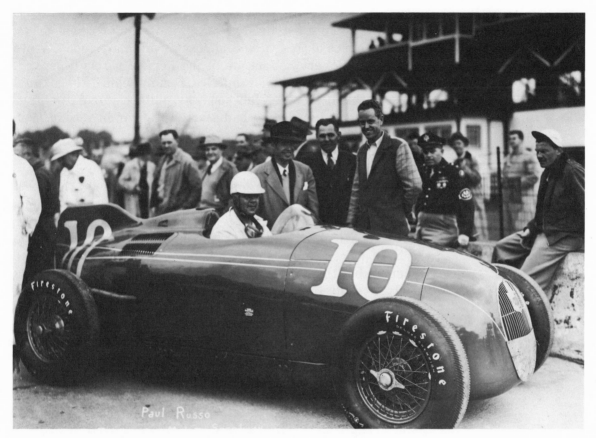

Paul Russo in the 1946 twin-engine Fageol Twin Coach Special. (In the center of the trio behind him is Louis Meyer, three-time Indianapolis winner.)

an overburdened driveshaft after sixty-five laps and finished twenty-second.

The Clancy six-wheeler was neither the first nor the last automotive outcast ever to attempt Indy. Lou Fageol, a bus builder from Kent, Ohio, had appeared at the Speedway in 1946 with his 2,510-pound Twin Coach Special, a seemingly belligerent, fubsy car that looked very like a pregnant blowfish with an atrophic tailfin. Beneath the hoods rested two 91-cubic-inch midget car Offenhauser engines, one at each end of the car. Minor adjustments made it theoretically possible to achieve front drive, rear drive, or four-wheel drive. "Performance of this car was almost surprisingly good," wrote optimistic Robert T. Jackson of the Perfect Circle Company. "It appears to ride and handle extremely well." For sixteen laps of the 1946 race, Jackson was quite right. After that, chunky Paul Russo, who had started the car in second position, banged the wall on the track's northeast turn, broke a leg, and finished dead last.

Although outré cars have come and gone at the Speedway, perhaps none were as memorably freakish as the 1964 "sidecar" carried to Indianapolis by Daytona Beach mechanic Smokey Yunick. Fitted out with a conventional four-cylinder 251.9-cubic-inch Offenhauser, the engine was mounted in the rear of what remotely resembled a drag-racing chassis. The remarkable thing was the driver's location outside the car's body in a tiny Harley Davidson-inspired capsule to the left of the car proper. Asked by a reporter whether hanging the driver insecurely out there in mid-air was not inordinately hazardous and vulnerable, Yunick replied confidently, "The only safe place is in the garage, and you can drop a hammer on your foot there." Exiting the first turn of its first qualifying lap with gamey Florida stock car racer Bobby Jones aboard, the car (listed in the program as the Hurst Floor Shift Special) spun, caught the retaining wall, and was destroyed. Its driver, fortunately, managed to escape unhurt.

To a degree, innovation has been an ingredient of the Indianapolis scene that has helped tease spectators through the gates. It is also occasionally true, as with all laudable research and development endeavors, that today's exception becomes tomorrow's rule. Whereas Jack Brabham's underpowered Cooper Climax was the lone rear-engine machine in the 1961 race (although by no means the first rear-ender seen at Indianapolis), only five years passed before all but one of the thirty-three race day starters were rear engine automobiles, the last of the old 1950s front-engine roadsters being driver Bobby Grim's supercharged Racing Associates car. Quipped a disenfranchised and disgruntled roadster-builder from Glendale, California named Frank Kurtis, "If a car with a horse turd on the hood wins at Indy, then everybody wants to design one with a horse turd on the hood."

A morose Bobby Jones is at the controls of the Hurst Floor Shift Special while defiant car builder Smokey Yunick stands behind, 1964.

Indianapolis Motor Speedway

The more one knows about Indy, nut by bolt, the more rewarding is the spectating. Unquestionably, one of the dark areas to the large majority of spectators at Indianapolis is the arcane world of esoteric bloat-budget racing machinery that one finds in such profusion there. If some rudimentary understanding of one's own street automobile were not preplexing enough, the insides of Indy cars are written off by most racing enthusiasts as being decidedly outside their sphere of comprehension. In a sense, they're correct, but in another sense, they're not; for the technical side of motor racing is as difficult or as simple as one cares to make it, and to discuss principles is not always to discuss specifics. Fielding a car at Indianapolis is anything but an exact science, as the characteristically contradictory technical opinions of mechanics in Gasoline Alley will attest.

It is with hesitancy that I raise the question of technical strategies at Indianapolis at all, for although I am among the more seasoned spectators there, I am neither an engineer nor a mechanic. Indeed, it was late in my spectating career that I began to take an interest in things mechanical at all. Before that I paid almost no attention to the things I now scrutinize quite closely. I refer, of course, to racing tires, body designs, and engines. A substantial number of opinions about such things exist, but one proposition that would not fail in a Gasoline Alley referendum vote is the notion that, after more than eighty years of bump-and-run motor racing in various places and under varied conditions, there is a great deal that remains a mystery. For those who spend their days and nights attempting to solve it, it is an intriguing source of both challenge and discouragement. The racing clan that gathers faithfully at the Indianapolis Motor Speedway is justly famous for its resistance to agreement on nearly anything it routinely does, and when the subject turns to things mechanical, the spectrum of view and opinion is broad enough to defy consensus altogether.

An intelligent outsider would assume that Indianapolis is a true engineering nirvana, inasmuch as the cars that compete there are allegedly the most sophisticated and *au courant* racing marvels assembled anywhere in the world of wheels. But here is where paradox enters the picture. Most of the engineering to be found at Indianapolis is hit and miss, for there is an historical antipathy that has existed between old-line Indianapolis car builder-mechanics and book-learned engineers. The mechanical mentality at the Brickyard is largely divided between the academics (engineers) and the pragmatists (mechanics). The latter faction, being the clear majority, prevails over the former. To them the proof is in the performance. No questions asked. To the best of my knowledge, there are no credentialed, certified, capped-and-gowned engineers among the many chief mechanics who haunt Gasoline Alley, although some of the better financed and more liberal-minded among them have ready and easy access to engineering counsel, should they ask for it. But like the proverbial deathbed nonbeliever, Indy's chief mechanics seem to solicit engineering advice only after all else has failed, and maybe not even then. Ironically, even the United States Auto Club's eighty-member Technical Committee consists primarily of nonengineers, like their chairman Jack Beckley; while they are entirely competent, their knowledge comes from years of hands-on experience with the vagaries of racing car innards.

Engineers find it vaguely amusing that instead of calculating the stresses brought to bear on, say, suspension components while those components are still on the drawing board, an out-in-the-barn Indy car constructor will divine strengths and weaknesses more or less by experience and by seat-of-the-pants intuition. If a part should break, he returns to his shop bent on constructing a beefed-up replacement part more likely to bear up.

Pragmatic Indy chief mechanics, on the other hand, are quick to point out that the concepts engineers extract from their SAE papers and their musty textbooks are misleading, if not entirely unworkable in practice. Says chief mechanic A: "If an engineer walked in here and told me that my car was put together wrong, I'd ask why. Then he'd have me in for a year seminar on the subject. I just don't have time for that. There's no engineer who understands race cars, anyway. But if Jack Beckley were to walk in here and say that the car was all wrong, you can bet that I'd have a careful look at it." Says chief mechanic B: "I'm no engineer and I can't think of many times when I asked for any help from one except once when a part kept breaking." Says chief mechanic C: "What is an engineer? He's a person with a piece of paper that says he's an engineer. After you see the paper, you don't have to fire him, after all. Everything's cool." But is it really?

To enrich the controversy, the views and opinions of one chief mechanic about racing car design and preparation will invite a hearty guffaw from another chief mechanic, although both are honor graduates of the same trial-and-error school of mechanical ingenuity. If it is difference of opinion that makes a horserace, so too does it make an auto race. Being the hide-bound American institution that it is, the Speedway mentality, with its latent resentment toward rationally "scientific" approaches to problem solving, is another expression of down home Yankee self-reliance and anti-intellectualism. "Against rationalism as a pretension and a method," wrote pragmatic spokesman William James in 1907, "pragmatism is fully armed and militant."

Set in 1972, the 500-mile record of 162.962 miles per hour at Indianapolis is still the property of the late Mark Donohue. Ironically, Donohue laid no credit for his many and lucrative successes in motor racing to his B.S. degree in mechanical engineering from Brown University in 1959. "The fact that I went to college," said Donohue, "makes me unusual in racing circles. There are drivers who never even finished high school. But a college degree doesn't mean a thing in this sport. People think that I have some sort of 'unfair advantage' because I know more about the technical side of racing than other drivers. That's nonsense." Yet it was Donohue, according to fellow engineer Paul Van Valkenburgh, who proved "mathematically and experimentally" that "to keep the tire and the car on the perimeter of the friction circle at all times is a measurably faster way around a race track."

If preparing a car for Indianapolis is as complex a task as one cares to make it, a pragmatic mechanic, like a pragmatic driver, is satisfied when the engine functions well and the car behaves itself at competition speeds on the raceway. A common complaint among chief mechanics is that the driver, besides being hopelessly lazy, knows little or nothing about the insides of a racing car. Said outstanding mechanic and car builder Clint Brawner about his once equally outstanding driver Eddie Sachs, "He knew nothing about race cars. Absolutely nothing. I could leave off half the car, and he'd never know the difference." Regardless of how much (as in the case of Mark Donohue) or how little (as in the case of Eddie Sachs) the driver seems to understand about the technical side of an Indianapolis racer, the game is not only to make the car run fast, but to make it run fast all day. Half the battle at Indy is endurance; the other half is speed. As winner Al Unser crossed the finish line in the 1978 race, only thirteen other wilted cars and drivers were still on the track. One of the drivers, exhausted George Snider, required oxygen.

Although very few spectators give it much thought, the technology involved in racing tires alone is incredibly complex. After Firestone's defeat by default in the great battle of the tires, the final round of which came in 1974, Goodyear has enjoyed a cozy corner on the rubber goods at the Speedway, cheerfully providing free tires and technical advice to competitors in return for substantial promotional and advertising perks. But although racing tires at Indy are somehow improved with the coming of each new season, Goodyear is willing to surrender almost no specifics. "The current state of the art in race tire development for the Speedway," writes Goodyear public relations man Dick Ralstin, "is classified as being available only for the use of Goodyear race tire engineers." The reason for Goodyear's refusal to comment on current tire activity at Indianapolis is explained by veteran Gasoline Alley car builder and mechanic who holds his thumb and index finger a quarter of an inch apart and remarks that if Goodyear engineers were to surrender only *that* much of their current tire technology, potential racing tire competitors "would be in their underwear overnight."

Even so, certain information about tires at Indy is in fairly common currency around Gasoline Alley. It is known, for example, that in 1979 Goodyear offered Indianapolis contestants one rear and two front constructions, each of them available in two different rubber compounds. One of the compounds was on the gummy side while the other was harder. The relative hardness of a tire can be detected by a device called a durometer, which resembles a stopwatch with a needle protruding from its bottom. The precise composition of Indianapolis tires, whether they be gummy, medium, or hard, is one of Indy's more compulsively guarded secrets. According to one garage area wag, they contain goat droppings and chicken fat. Whether the rubber (if indeed there be much rubber in the compound at all) is natural or synthetic, its properties are controlled by the introduction of such chemicals as carbon black, to the end that a compromise is struck between safety, traction, and durability. (Interesting aside: Goodyear's nutburger Pike's Peak tire, designed some time back to last the duration of one high-speed charge up the seven-mile road to the pinnacle of Pike's Peak itself, allegedly consisted partly of pulvarized walnut shells).

Certain principles involving racing tires are assumed to apply — such as Pat Clancy's notion that the more rubber on the track, the better the traction in the turns where it's needed most. Today Indy's tires are thin-walled (to minimize heat generation), leaky (Who cares? They're only in use for a few hours), and treadless (the more rubber on the road, the better). Designed to last about one race, they measure fifteen inches of tread on the rear and eleven inches on the front. Their extreme width, however, takes its toll in the resultant drag effect, which is, of course, aerodynamically undesirable.

Out on pit row, there is much consternation over tire temperatures under racing conditions, although the temperatures themselves (like almost every other factor in racing car preparation) are variously interpreted. Theoretically, a racing tire functions at its best in a certain temperature range, although there are small differences of opinion over what that range actually is. Drivers come in after turning high-speed laps on the track and show concern that a tire is either not hot enough or too hot. During such tire testing sessions there is an effort made, sometimes through camber correction, to strike a consistent temperature (detected through the use of a pyrometer) across the tire, from left to right, to find its theoretical maximum coefficient of friction. If tire temperatures are not as high as they ought to be, it may mean the tires are not being taxed to their maximum potential, and that the driver could be moving around the track a great deal faster than he is. If the right front tire is inordinately hot, it may mean that the car is "pushing" or understeering. Because an automobile has a tendency to list rightward as it moves through the turns, and because most of the car's weight is in the rear where the engine is situated, the tire that shoulders the most work and therefore tends to be the hottest is the right rear. The left front tire works the least and tends to run the coolest. Theoretically, it would be desirable to place equal weight and strike equal temperatures on all four tires, although in practice it is impossible to achieve such a balance because of the tremendous right sideforces brought to bear when the car executes its left turns.

Besides *toe-in* (a kind of cross-eyed tire setting) on both front and rear of a racing car at Indy, mechanics achieve what they refer to as *stagger* to the right rear tire by inflating it to a greater circumference than the left rear tire. In times past, the folksy method of enlarging the right rear tire was to spin it on an axle while teasing it with a torch to the temperature of a medium-rare steak. The result was a kind of misshapen doughnut taller and wider than its original configuration. One chief mechanic was overheard saying, "Now, we've got us a good right rear." The object of stagger, all the same, is to compensate for the absence of a differential (present on street automobiles) and to aid it in rounding the turns where the outer wheel must cover more distance than the inner. But there is a built-in penalty with stagger, because the handling advantage in the turns becomes a disadvantage on the straight sections where, with one rear tire larger than the other, more rubber tends to be scrubbed off an already thin tractive surface.

The concepts of progress and pragmatism have tended to play each other false at Indianapolis. Pragmatic Indy mechanics, once they have become entrenched with an *idee fixe* of what a racing car should be and how it should look, can become aggressively reactionary and alarmingly resistant to change. After "Black Jack" Brabham appeared at Indianapolis in 1961 with his forest green Cooper Climax and it seemed the rear-engine configuration was Indy racing's gateway to instant success, a great hue and cry developed. Stateside car builders resisted the changeover to the rear engine "funny cars," citing their fragility, their ugliness, and their un-Americanness. They had their reasons. First, a substantial number of oafish, front-engine Speedway cars were sentenced to sudden obsolescence. Second, a substantial number of mechanics were sentenced to preparing a radically different kind of car that they understood too little about. Said Clint Brawner about the coming of the rear engine revolution: "Most of the things I'd spent years learning were applicable no longer. Now I'd have to enroll in kindergarten and learn an all-new type of race car, the rear-engine or 'funny car.' Only I wasn't laughing."

Similar to the real or imagined threat posed by the rear-engine revolution was the coming of the turbine engine to Indianapolis competition in 1967. Chicago's controversial Andy ("Mr. 500") Granatelli entered the equally controversial STP Pratt and Whitney turbine racer with Rufus "Parnelli" Jones (the 1963 winner) as the driver. Accused of "sandbagging" (holding back on speed to mislead the competition), Jones qualified the car for sixth starting position, took the lead on the first lap, and led for a total of 171 circuits. Still leading on the 197th lap, a gearbox bearing failed, putting the car out of the race with a little more than two laps remaining. He eventually finished sixth in the race.

Andy Granatelli's 1967 Pratt & Whitney turbine driven by Parnelli Jones.

David Knox

A year later, the Speedway's entry list contained nine turbine-powered cars. One of them crashed in the southwest turn, killing the British driver Mike Spence. Another, driven by Joe Leonard of San Jose, California, set new one- and four-lap qualification records during time trials and started the race on the pole. With world driving champion Graham Hill at the wheel, a third turbine car started the race on Leonard's right, in the middle of the front row. The only other turbine in the race, piloted by Oregonian Art Pollard, started the race back in fourteenth position. Although none of the turbines won the race, they managed to inflict fear on the competition. Leonard finished twelfth after having broken a fuel pump drive while leading on the 192nd lap. Finishing behind Leonard in thirteenth position was Pollard, who, running in sixth place on the 189th lap, was also sidelined with a broken fuel pump drive. Hill, in fourth position on the 111th lap, came to a sudden stop when he lost a wheel in the southwest turn.

The message was clear. Turbine cars had to be gotten rid of. In 1967, USAC set the maximum allowable inlet annulus for turbine-powered cars at 28.5 square inches. In 1968, this was reduced to 15.999 square inches, and by 1969 the maximum was 11.999 square inches, effectively rendering the turbines uncompetitive. The so-called silent screamers were at last put to rest. Despite Granatelli's convincing arguments in favor of turbines — that they cost little more than other current racing engines, that they lasted 120 times as long, and that they spewed neither water nor oil — the game was over.

But for other than turbine cars, the game continues. To the unpracticed eye, the outward design of current Indianapolis cars may seem anything but dissimilar, inasmuch as all have four wheels situated around a wedge-shaped body equipped with a small wing in the front and a large wing, with a maximum width of thirty-six inches, centered between the rear wheels. The overall impression that one gets is that of a huge mechanical grasshopper or a lady's slipper. The driver, his head encased in a large, space-age helmet, is in a 30° semi-reclining position amidships, with his legs out toward the nose of the car where his feet touch the accelerator, clutch, and brake pedals. He is held securely in place by a harness over each shoulder, and a seat belt which spans the pelvis beneath the anterior superior iliac spines. At his sides are two crashworthy fuel tanks carrying a maximum methanol (wood alcohol) capacity of forty gallons, not more than twenty of which are contained on the right side. To inhibit fuel from sloshing in the tanks, car constructors divide each into a series of interconnecting cells.

Present United States Auto Club (USAC) rules for Indy cars call for an automobile with a maximum length of fifteen feet, a maximum width of eighty inches, and a minimum (dry) weight of 1,500 pounds for cars with supercharged engines, 1,425 pounds for cars without supercharged engines. The cockpit opening must be at least 500 square inches. The general configuration of current Indianapolis (otherwise known as "championship") cars is that sketched in USAC's book of *Official Competition Rules:*

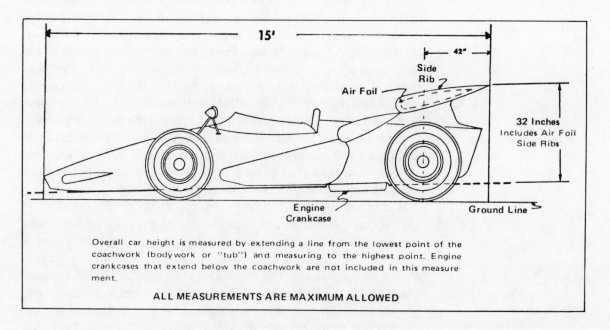

Overall car height is measured by extending a line from the lowest point of the coachwork (bodywork or "tub") and measuring to the highest point. Engine crankcases that extend below the coachwork are not included in this measurement.

ALL MEASUREMENTS ARE MAXIMUM ALLOWED

Whereas the novice spectator may recognize color only as the main difference between one car and another, racing car configurations at Indianapolis are modified to some extent during and after each season. The more familiar designs —

Coyotes, Wildcats, Lightnings, McLarens, Parnellis, Penskes, and Eagles, in addition to ingenious hybrids — are never exactly the same the following year. The fundamental notion behind the design of each car, however, is to slice through the atmosphere at speeds well over 200 miles per hour with as little interference as possible. To that end (and whether they be all so pragmatic or not), racing car designers are all but obliged to seek out the use of a wind tunnel such as the one available at Purdue University.

Virtually all Indy cars are constructed to have a frontally downward pitch, which creates an immense aerodynamic downforce over the entire automobile, pressing it to the track with ever greater force as speeds increase. It has been pointed out repeatedly that the total design of a championship car comes in the form of an upside down airplane, the object being to keep it fixed on the ground rather than to carry it aloft. As a consequence, a car that executes an inadvertent 180° spin on the race track will tend to lift as it moves backwards.

That immense downforce that acts to advantage on the turns acts to disadvantage on the track's straight parts, where the car would run faster if it could shed its wings and accelerate freely without being quite so earthbound. Were airfoils to be removed entirely (as a good many Gasoline Alley philosophers indeed advocate) the result would be higher straightaway speeds and reduced corner speeds. In the golden age of wingless cars and narrow tires, the driving technique at Indianapolis was very different. Today, the driver remains "on the gas" and at the same speed virtually all the way around the course, easing up very slightly to "breathe" the engine as he enters a turn.

The greater the speed, the greater is the resultant downforce. Shock absorbers, all four of them surrounded by a kind of Hobson's choice of stiff coil spring, are pressed very nearly to the quick, almost turning the racer into an unsprung go-cart at high speed. At the same time, the car comes perilously close to bottoming-out on the race track. The downforce (which engineers call "negative lift") that tends to hold the car to the track's surface in the turn also produces drag, which retards forward motion, labors the engine, and endangers the 1.5-mile-per-gallon fuel efficiency minimum necessary if the car is to travel 500 miles with a total fuel allotment of a little more than 333 gallons.

Despite Indy cars' very low center of gravity, the problem of weight transfer from left to right as the car makes left hand turns is another insuperable dilemma facing the car builder, mechanic, and driver. Predictably, opinions vary widely on how best to deal with the car's tendency to slide off the track in the turns. Although Indianapolis racers weigh more on the left than they do on the right, the difference is never enough to compensate for total weight transfer at speed through a turn. Not even Smokey Yunick's 1964 Hurst Floor Shift "side-car," part of the purpose of which was to shift increased weight to the left side of the automobile, was successful in this respect, nor were subsequent efforts to achieve weight offset. Car builder Dan Gurney's 1977 Eagle, which, in Gurney's words, "tried to offset things to the left for a biased weight distribution" of its 1,500 minimum allowable poundage, was none too successful, either, having qualified ninth fastest at Indianapolis in 1977 and having finished in fifteenth position after its engine failed at 156 laps. Chief mechanics speak of "jacking weight" from one wheel to another, whereas they are not jacking weight at all, but adjusting spring tension instead. If, for example, a chief mechanic uses a coil spring with 500 pounds of tension on the right rear, he may use a lesser tension (perhaps 475 pounds) on the left rear, taking driver weight and fuel load into consideration.

The technical evolution of Indianapolis racing engines is a long and complex story. When twenty-seven-year-old California fruit vendor Kelly Petillo won the 1935 Indianapolis 500 in an Offenhauser-powered Gilmore Speedway Special, it was the first of twenty-seven Offy victories at the Brickyard, the last of which was Johnny Rutherford's 1976 triumph in a car known as the Hy-Gain McLaren. The involved history of the Offenhauser reaches back to the dominance of the Duesenberg engine at Indianapolis in 1922, 1924, 1925, and 1927. According to the venerated engine specialist Leo Goossen, who died in 1974, drivers Tommy Milton and Ira Vail purchased an eight-cylinder Duesenberg, borrowed between $4,000 and $5,000 in development funds, and delivered both the engine and the money to the Los Angeles shop of Wisconsin-born development engineer Harry Armenius Miller, whose carburetor factory was a gathering place for racing clans in the teens and twenties. Incorporating what he believed to be the better points of not only the Duesenberg, but also of the Peugeot and the Ballot, he produced the famous Miller Eight, which won at Indianapolis on eleven occasions between 1923 and 1938. When Harry Miller departed his bankrupt racing engine business in 1933, it fell heir to Fred Offenhauser, a Los Angeles native who had worked with Miller since 1913 and who had risen to become Miller's plant superintendent. Between 1931 and 1932, Offenhauser reworked the Miller Eight, and with the engineering skill of Goossen, transformed it into a four-cylinder powerplant which became known as the Offenhauser. It was not until April 1946, only a month prior to the resumption of Indianapolis racing after World War II, that Offenhauser sold his engine business to three-time Indianapolis winner Louis Meyer and his partner Dale Drake, a valve manufacturer who had been part of the original Miller organization. While retaining its identity, the Offenhauser then became known as the Meyer and Drake. Finally, in 1965, Drake assumed full control of the company, which still manufactures the Offenhauser in Irvine, California despite Drake's death on July 11, 1972. Beloved in its pre-supercharged days for its mellow sound and alleged reliability, the Drake Offenhauser is a 160-cubic-inch-displacement, four-cylinder, sixteen-valve, double overhead cam, dry sump, turbocharged engine which sells for $27,000. For customers with only $25,000 to spend, Drake Engineering also offers the Sparks-Goossen-Drake, yet another 160-cubic-inch-displacement, four-cylinder, sixteen-valve, double overhead cam, dry sump, turbocharged engine.

But today, trouble brews in Offyland. Between 1965 and 1978, Indy's checkered flag fell on eight-cylinder cars eight times in fourteen starts. When the Ford Motor Company descended on Indianapolis, it produced three wins in a row (1965, 1966, and 1967), skipped a year, and then enjoyed three more victories in 1969, 1970, and 1971. By 1977, when Foyt won with his made-over Ford V-8, the Drake Offy was also in imminent danger of being superceded by the Cosworth, an eight-cylinder engine of English manufacture. Both engines are turbocharged, meaning in principle that some exhaust energy is harnessed to a rotor which in turn forces more air and hence more oxygen into the engine's intake manifold. Although turbocharging results in dramatically improved horsepower ratings, its penalty is higher engine temperatures and poorer mileage. It is imperative, therefore, to monitor very carefully the amount of *boost*, or turbocharger-induced intake manifold pressure, lest the car use its entire fuel issue before the race ends. One Indy crew chief calculates that two laps run under the yellow flag (when drivers are obliged to reduce speed drastically because of some hazard on the track) equal about one lap under the green flag (when drivers are running at competition speeds). Some, but not all, Indianapolis cars have a cockpit boost control which allows the driver to increase turbocharger effectiveness at will by "turning the screw" to a USAC-mandated intake manifold pressure not to exceed fifty inches of mercury for V-8 engines, sixty inches for four-cylinder engines, and fifty-six inches for normally aspirated stock block engines. Although supercharged engines are anything but new in automotive engineering, the contemporary turbocharger has been developed by AiResearch of Los Angeles and by unsmiling Herbert ("Herbie Horsepower") Porter, who spends the better part of the year in Gasoline Alley's adjoining garages 68 and 69.

The growing preference for an eight-cylinder Cosworth DFX (itself an outgrowth of the Cosworth Engineering Formula I Grand Prix engine) over the four-cylinder Offy is in the growing realization that at the rate of turbocharger boost, the Cosworth reportedly generates approximately one hundred more horsepower. While there are rational explanations for preferring an eight over a four, relatively few members of the racing establishment can say, with much technical accuracy, what they are. A. J. Foyt, who purchased the Ford Motor Company's remaining inventory of V-8 racing engines in 1969 and then undertook development work of his own with them, has enjoyed tremendous success with the Ford engines that he has renamed "Foyt" and sells for the same price ($30,000) that the Cosworth DFX does. Asked during a press conference about the merits of an eight-cylinder car over a four, his reply seemed curiously vague: "You know the rule of thumb and I really don't have a degree from college, but it always takes an eight-cylinder to outrun a four, takes a twelve-cylinder to outrun an eight, takes a sixteen to outrun a twelve." Another pragmatist, a respected Indy car builder, put it this way: "An engine's nothing but a goddamned stove. If you take the same amount of firewood, you can't heat a room with one stove as well as if you put the same wood into two smaller stoves. You'll be better off still if you put the same wood into four stoves, and better yet if you put it into eight." Whether or not the analogy holds, it seemed to satisfy him. George Moore, an automotive commentator for the *Indianapolis Star*, puts the explanation into still different terms. "The V-8 has better volumetric efficiency due to having smaller chambers than a four," he writes. "The engine breathes better and extracts more power per pound of fuel." Others feel that the more cylinders an engine has, the greater its revolutions per minute and the greater its power.

After eight-cylinder cars won at Indianapolis in 1977 and 1978, eulogies were orated often for the passing of the late, lamented Drake Offy. George Bignotti, one of the more senior, more outspoken, and without any doubt more successful old-line Indianapolis car builders (having prepared six Brickyard winners), expressed himself with characteristic directness: "Anyone who enters a four [cylinder car] next year [1979] is an idiot or doesn't have anything else." Indeed, eight-cylinder engines were responsible for wins in all but two (Trenton and Phoenix) championship car races in 1977, and when the 1978 Indianapolis 500 was history, eight of the first thirteen finishers (including the first two) were cars powered by eight-cylinder Cosworth engines. Not since 1940, when Wilbur Shaw won the race in a Maserati, had a foreign-built engine come home first at Indianapolis.

"In one recent racing season," *Car and Driver* magazine reported, "only three new four-cylinder blocks were sold" by Drake Engineering. To save the company from extinction and to preserve its reputation, company president John Drake enlisted the talents of Hans Herman, a Danish engineer formerly with BMW, to develop an entirely new belt-driven eight-cylinder powerplant called the DT-160 to compete with

Master car-builder George Bignotti.

the Foyt and the Cosworth. Its weight (roughly 365 pounds) compares favorably with the Cosworth's 390 pounds and the Drake Offy's 420 to 430 pounds, although its price ($32,000 to $35,000) exceeds that of the competition.

In the meantime, two other eight-cylinder purveyors have entered the racing scene. The more developed engine is by National Engineering Company of Signal Hill, California; it is an American Motors stock block that markets for a modest $20,000 to $25,000 and supposedly produces the same horsepower (800-850) as the Drake Offy, the Drake DT-160, the Foyt, and the Cosworth DFX. The less-developed engine is an aluminum, flat eight cylinder, the handiwork of Bruce Crower and Bob Bubenick of Chula Vista, California.

Specifications for cars and engines at Indianapolis are a constant source of controversy. The pre-September 1978 fuel limitation of 1.8 miles per gallon had resulted in a marked tendency to "blow" engines whose fuel consumption had been leaned out to its limits. Fuel limitations had also resulted in cars not finishing races because of their having used their entire allotment. When the maximum allowable number of miles per gallon was "raised" from 1.8 to 1.5, there were more engines saved from destruction and more cars finishing races. Specifications and regulations are always somewhat arbitrary, but rule adjustments made by the United States Auto Club's board of directors in the September conclave appeared to pacify the racing constituency to some extent. "I think the board did the right thing," George Bignotti commented afterward. "They did as good as they could. You can't keep everybody happy." During the same meeting, the maximum rear wing width was reduced from forty-three inches to thirty-six inches. Whereas the maximum manifold pressure, which had been set at eighty inches of mercury for qualification runs only, had been imposed for both qualifying and for racing. But once the agreed upon specs are established, however tentatively, it remains to be seen whether all of the various racing components will function to everyone's satisfaction.

At Indy, you *swallow* a valve, you *throw* a rod, and you *lose* a wheel, but you hope, at the very least, that those things don't happen to you on the same day, particularly if it is race day. In spite of elaborate race day preparations, there is invariably one car that resists starting, and a succession of others that fall apart a few minutes after the race is underway. Engines blow up like grenades. Turbochargers fizzle. Clutches lose their grip. Crews pack their tools away while their drivers walk dejectedly back to the showers vowing to return to Indianapolis next year.

Next year.

Chapter 3

TALES OF A TURN:
THE SOUTHWEST

At the close of the Second World War, the government-imposed ban on automobile racing was lifted and the manufacture of racing rubber resumed at the Akron, Ohio, Firestone plant. Prewar racing cars, retired from Speedway action between Pearl Harbor and the war's end, were rolled out of storage, dusted off, and returned to life. By May 1946, subsequent to dapper Anton Hulman's purchase of the track from warrior-celebrity Eddie Rickenbacker (who had in turn purchased Eastern Airlines), racing cars and racing people made a long-anticipated reappearance in decrepit Gasoline Alley. The Bowes Seal Fast Special that Rex Mays wheeled to second place in 1941 was pressed back into service, along with Jimmy Snyder's record-setting car from 1939. Floyd Roberts' 1938 winning Wetteroth was resuscitated, as was the 1941 pole-winning Maserati that fractious Mauri Rose had driven for master car builder and former driver Lou Moore.

Those of the racing fraternity who had survived military service were eager to resume the frenzied freedom of motorized competition. Out in balmy California, an exciting new generation of brash, on-the-make youngsters like Johnnie Parsons, Bill Vukovich, and Rodger Ward — each of them accorded at least one eventual Indianapolis win — strapped themselves into the narrow confines of midget racers, sometimes every day of the week, and raced the short, floodlit tracks up and down the Pacific Coast. Frank Kurtis, the most prolific and successful car builder of the postwar period, opened his shop on East Colorado Street in Glendale and fabricated racing cars by the hundreds as others arrived from all over the country.

Drivers earned a reputation for being a fearless, nothing-to-lose band of Gypsies who asked little more out of life than to be footloose in 1940s America, armed with helmet, goggles, and roadmap. They earned their way to Indianapolis as they still often do, by gaining experience and name on the sometimes grubby quarter-mile and half-mile tracks, but virtually always with the ultimate intention of driving in the 500-mile race.

The injury odds in those days were grim. Of the thirty-three men who competed at Indianapolis in 1950, nine eventually died as a consequence of racing mishaps. On July 29, 1951, racing's Black Sunday, the fraternity lost three cherished members on the same afternoon. Time trialers Cecil Green and Billy Mackey sailed backfirst over the low, first turn railing at the paved half-mile bowl near rural Winchester, Indiana; and Walt Brown perished after a deceptively innocent-looking brush with the wall at the muddy Williams Grove dirt oval in Pennsylvania. Racing clans continued to sacrifice a substantial number of their promising young men in the 1940s and 1950s until gradually they became aware that precautions like fireproof driving suits and roll cages could reduce injuries, fatal and otherwise, to a fraction of what they had been. Said one grizzled survivor of the postwar racing scene, "We felt that if a driver thought he needed all kinds of safety paraphernalia, he probably had no goddamned business in a race car in the first place."

Although American oval track racing car drivers have tended to be temperamentally somewhat the same over the years (independent, fun-loving, egocentric, and assertive), they have in recent years been more inclined to appear as well-coiffed sporting gentlemen. Drivers with a glossy, public relations mentality have, in general, won the privilege of driving the more classy, potentially winning machinery at Indianapolis, orating at respectable suburban high schools and Rotary Clubs, and decorating cocktail parties underwritten by corporate megadollars. But with the passing of the front line drivers with gritty fingernails and oily overalls went much of the theatrical aura of postwar, roadhouse campishness, when big time motor racing in America (such as it was) was still more genuinely an individual, rather than a corporate, effort.

One very curious human holdover from racing's postwar phase is Travis "Spider" Webb, who today is more a survivor than a contemporary. A native of Joplin, Missouri, Webb now resides in Norwalk, California. He won the American Automobile Association-sponsored "big car" championship in the Middle West in 1948 and consumes almost as much beer and utters nearly as many expletives now as he did then. Webb drove at Indianapolis on six occasions between 1948 and 1954, finishing no better than nineteenth. Today, he holds forth from the back door of a white camper where he remembers the postwar scene at Indianapolis vividly. "You know, we had very little money to spend in those days. My car owners, Lou and Bruce Bromme, would call on Meyer and Drake and gather up whatever used parts for our engine that they could. If somebody left a bad set of pistons or a crankshaft that they thought was going to break, why, we'd buy them and use them in our car. We came to the Speedway with only one engine, and that meant that we would run it as little as possible. I'd take two practice laps in the car and then try to qualify it. If you call yourself a driver," Webb continues, "you don't need more than five laps of practice at the most. You don't get paid for practicing at Indianapolis, or anywhere else. We'd put the car in the race and run the little humper for as long as it would hold together." Webb, however, was beset with more unsuccess than most of his contemporaries who ran there as often as he did. In 1949, for example, his temperamental red and black Grancor Special failed to leave the starting line under its own power, resulting in a last place finish and a paycheck amounting to $1,555, which had to be divided several ways.

Spider Webb will tell you that the legend of the Indianapolis race is written in the Speedway's four turns. The front and back straightaways are places where the experienced driver need only keep his car pointed straight ahead (albeit at very high speeds), away from the walls, and away from the competition. In the turns, it is different. Sideforces come into play. The racing car, particularly in Spider Webb's day, has a nasty tendency to break traction and head toward the outer retaining wall. The running groove narrows, and there is a very limited width to the track that is usable at speed. The closer a driver comes to the wall in the north and south chutes, the more track he uses and the faster he can go. The scenarios enacted on Indy's four turns have sometimes been ugly, sometimes glamorous, sometimes merely enervating for driver and spectator alike. While all the track's a stage, the footlights seem to shine brightest where the track bends and develops its maximum pitch, and where the cars that have moments ago run as much as three abreast on the straights must now knuckle under, accommodating each other by falling into a whirlwind beeline as they skim through Indy's corners.

More eyes have been fixed on the action deep in the number one turn, the southwest, than in any of the other three corners of the track. At the end of the main straight, this is the turn closest to the Speedway's busiest pedestrian gate, located at the corner of West Sixteenth Street and Georgetown Road. On race day as well as on time trial days, so many bodies pass through this portal that as many as ten ticket-takers are kept well occupied. After World War II, grandstands B, E, and D faced the track directly at this juncture on the course. During the ensuing years, B and E were removed and reconstructed, while grandstand D was replaced between 1966 and 1968 with a huge aluminum stairstep called the Southwest Vista. Across the track, trailing along the infield grass, is an ageless, elongated sign that warns, A BOTTLE ON THE TRACK MAY CAUSE A SERIOUS WRECK WATCH YOURS. Behind the sign in the infield lies the infamous Snake Pit, a product of the turbulent, hallucinogenic, countercultural 1960s.

Before the construction of massive new grandstands in turn one, the view from the starting line was much different. Looking south over the roofs of grandstands B and E, you had a reasonably clear view of the great phallic Prest-O-Lite stack spewing noxious black smoke toward downtown Indianapolis.

The southwest turn.

David Knox

Traditionally, so the story goes, many an anxious driver thus ascertained (or thought he ascertained) the direction and force of winds prevailing from the west, the winds being a crucial factor to consider when attempting to navigate the track at high speed. The Prest-O-Lite stack is still there today, but it emits much less smoke and is much less visible, obscured as it is by the gigantic fried chicken amphitheatre that curls around the southwest turn.

Until 1956, when fresh asphalt was layered on the turns at Indianapolis, there was a unique problem in turn one. At the entrance to it there was (and still is) a crossway used by pedestrians and motor traffic when the track was closed to racing activity. At that time, motor traffic had worn a scarcely perceptible dip in the race track itself. Although you could not see the dip, you felt it more and more as you passed over it at ever-increasing speeds in a racing car. Former driver Freddy Agabashian of Walnut Creek, California remembers it well: "You had to watch yourself in turn one because of that bump in the track," he recalls, "and once you passed over it, there was still another dip in the track just a little bit ahead." If you can locate some 1940s Movietone newsreels of cars rounding the southwest turn, you can see racing cars heave as they make their way around the corner. But to Spider Webb, that same heave could be played to advantage: "I would let up on the throttle as I came through there. It would sound as if I was off the gas entirely at that point, but that's not true; I was just easing back a little bit. I tried to drive through there in exactly the same place every time. I'd catch that bump, which always pitched the rear end of the car out toward the wall. If you came into the southwest in just the right way, it would cock your front wheels to the left and help set you up for the turn."

If Spider Webb actually did use the dip in turn one this way, he was one of the few who had perfected the technique, for that same dip caused a number of his predecessors and successors untold grief. Earl Cooper crashed there while leading the 1925 race, and in 1927 car owner Henry Kohlert, taking over for his driver Freddy Lecklider, hit the wall in the southwest turn after colliding with Cliff Bergere. Bergere continued on to ninth place, while Kohlert overturned and was thrown on the track with serious injuries.

Webb began his eventful racing career in 1928, the same year that a young California mechanic named Louis Meyer won the first of his three Indianapolis victories. Twenty-nine sad-looking cars started the race that year, when the trackside pit area consisted of groin-high wooden enclosures that resembled pig pens at the Chicago stockyards. Benny Shoaf, who had started the race in twenty-sixth position, also finished in twenty-sixth position after his Duesenberg banged the wall very hard in the southwest turn on his 35th lap. Fortunately he sustained only minor injuries. Ira Hall's Duesenberg also came out second best in an argument with that same wall on his 115th lap. Earl DeVore in a striking chrome-plated car (appropriately called the Chromolite

Special) was the next turn one casualty when he connected with the concrete after 161 laps.

Louis Meyer enjoyed his somewhat unanticipated second Indianapolis win in 1933. One of the forty-one other cars chasing him, a Studebaker-powered Universal Service Special driven by Westville, New Jersey's Malcolm Fox, slowed momentarily behind another car in the southwest turn on Fox's 123rd lap. Riding behind Malcolm Fox was Les Spangler in a Miller Special owned by driver Harry Hartz, himself now enshrined securely in the pantheon of racing immortals. Spangler's machine drove over Fox's right rear wheel, bolted through the air, and came to rest right side up on the turn one apron. Wrote *Motor* magazine's Harold Blanchard after he returned from the accident scene, "Spangler and his mechanic, G. L. Jordan, were so badly crushed and mangled that their friends had some difficulty in telling which was which." Fox's passenger-mechanic Bert Cook, meanwhile, spun several times and climbed the wall also, sustaining a fresh round of relatively minor injuries. "It might have been us," said Fox after the accident, "but I guess we were lucky."

Blanchard the scrivener was back at the Speedway with a *Motor* magazine gig in 1934 when, during one practice session, driver Peter Kreis and his riding mechanic Art Hahn, driving still another version of a Miller-Hartz Special, cleared the southwest turn retaining wall and wrapped themselves around a tree that blossomed just off of West Sixteenth Street. Only the tree survived. Said the speculative Blanchard (who surveyed the two remaining pieces of the car after they were returned to the garage compound), "Members of Gasoline Alley at the Speedway have been greatly mystified as to the cause of this accident. Kreis was a capable driver, steering parts had recently been X-rayed, and were assembled by unusually competent mechanics. In consequence, there is uncertainty as to whether something went wrong with the car or did Kreis faint?"

Allegedly because Wilbur Shaw's Lion Head Special lost the better part of its six-and-a-half-gallon oil capacity on the track during the 1934 race, even the early stages of the contest were run over a decidedly slippery track. Participating in his fifth consecutive Indianapolis 500, Chet Miller and his mechanic

Eddie Tynan were running well behind the leaders when their poorly handling gold Bohnalite Ford began to spin through the southwest turn. After having looped once toward the inner wall, it left the apron and spun twice more, finally moving up and over the outer wall. Witnesses reported that the car executed a complete somersault in the air and then landed right side up about fifty feet east of the Stevens residence where, during the month of May, drivers enjoyed a sumptuous twenty-five-cent home-cooked lunch. Chet Miller remained all the while in the car's cockpit, but Eddie Tynan was thrown into a tree where miraculously he received what one reporter described as "a few minor scratches." Miraculously also, the Bohnalite Ford was reported to be only "slightly damaged" in spite of having its hindquarters disengaged. The Stevens's lawn was minimally disrupted.

A little less than a year later, on May 21, 1935, Stubby Stubblefield and mechanic Leo Whitacker ramped the southwest wall on a time trial run and were both killed. The attentive reader will recall that prior to the 1936 race, the Speedway management had altered the configuration of the turns, the outer margins of which had been banked more steeply than the brick running groove. The original idea, evidently, was to provide a little catch-banking to aid any unfortunate competitor who might swerve so far out of the groove that he needed it. Although this supplemental banking was paved with good intentions, it was bordered with a retaining wall of nine-inch-thick reinforced concrete extending thirty-three inches above the race track. The wall, alas, was perpendicular to the ground, but not to the contour of the turns. The mishaps involving Malcolm Fox, Les Spangler, Pete Kreis, Chet Miller, Stubby Stubblefield, and a fated group of other unfortunates were abetted by a ramp effect on the periphery of the turns, and by the retaining walls that encouraged cars to careen like airborne buzz bombs out of the track, rather than to remain on it. By the 1936 race, however, the banking on the turns had been rendered uniform in slope, striking a maximum pitch of nine degrees and twelve minutes. New reinforced concrete walls were placed in front of the old ones, and made to tilt toward the track itself. Meanwhile, the inside retaining walls, which had triggered more problems than they had solved,

**Left to right: Ted Horn, Bill Holland, Mauri Rose.
Receiving awards at the drivers' meeting prior to
the 1948 race.**

Craig Collection

were removed and replaced by an oiled dirt safety apron. In
1937, all turns were surfaced with asphalt for the first time,
and the original Culver Brick was obscured. Even so, the new
asphalt surface did not prevent Frank McGurk, reaching for
his second Indianapolis start, to crash his Belanger Special in
the same southwest turn. Mechanic Albert Opalco died.
McGurk sustained serious injuries, returned in 1946, and
crashed again.

Perhaps no Indianapolis 500 has been rerun as many times
as the 1947 event, which developed into an epic duel between a
disagreeable little man named Mauri Rose and his smiling
teammate, rollerskating Bill Holland. Both men drove metallic
blue cigar-shaped Blue Crown Spark Plug Specials. It was the
year when Rose scored the second of his three wins at the

Speedway, and the day I listened to the drama unfold over my postwar Detrola radio while I lounged in a hammock, recovering from what I believed to be a terminal case of the mumps. According to what I could learn over the radio, however, rookie Holland was in the lead with Rose in second place when Moore flashed an ambiguous "OK" pit sign to both drivers, evidently instructing them to hold their positions and finish one-two. Moore then erased the "OK" and replaced it with an equally ambiguous "E-Z." Holland took his directive seriously and eased back, while Rose continued to forge ahead, overtake Holland, and win the race, much to Holland's eternal regret.

There were thirty cars in the 1947 race, however, and Holland had started in eighth position, in the middle of the third row. Directly in front of him, starting fifth, was William "Shorty" Cantlon, the second place finisher in 1930, who was making his eleventh and final start. A compulsive worrier and a popular underdog, the aging Cantlon confided to reporter Russ Catlin before the race, "I'm going to win this one." Ominously, his car stalled twice as it tried to leave the starting line and join the pack.

Holland, too, had every intention of winning, and was in the lead when thirty-nine laps were down. But as he made his arc into the first turn on his fortieth circuit, he momentarily lost control and slid into the grassy area below the track's inner white line. The mud and turf flew as Holland, an experienced Pennsylvania dirt tracker, fought for control and darted back on the track directly in front of Cantlon. Although the two cars did not make contact, Cantlon took evasive action by turning to the right. His orange number 24 Automobile Shippers Special, a Detroit-owned front drive Miller, struck the wall head-on, then spun and hit tail-first, leaving orange impact marks on the white retaining wall. When the ambulance arrived, Cantlon was slumped over the wheel with a crushed chest and a broken leg. He became the fifteenth driver to die at the Speedway. Curiously enough, his car remained on the track for the balance of the race.

Among the thousands present on the afternoon that Shorty Cantlon died was driver George A. Metzler. Those who recall his presence in Gasoline Alley remember him best as a

**George Metzler at Indianapolis in 1947. Behind him,
Jack Dixon, the car's builder and owner.**

slender, likable, long-laboring man.* They remember him also
as a mediocre driver, a man sometimes ruefully referred to as
a "fill-in" at the Boondock big car roadshows sponsored by the
American Automobile Association where there were not
enough front-line drivers to fill the field on a humid
midwestern Sunday afternoon. But the important thing is that
Metzler possessed a certain attitude, a mentality not at all

---

*The reader is reminded, however, that racing people seldom agree on much of
anything. According to Jack Dixon, who, as we shall see, played a role in Metzler's
coming to the Speedway as a driver, Metzler was slender, but certainly not likable. "If
you want to know the truth," says Dixon, "he was both overbearing and bull-headed."
Long-laboring? Perhaps. But Dixon recalls Metzler's installing left hubs on the right
side of the car, and right hubs on the left side: "If he had driven on the track that way,
the wheels would have come off."

unrepresentative of hundreds of similarly inclined young men who come to the Speedway with visions of dollars and golden accolades dancing in their heads. Metzler wanted to race at Indianapolis in the most obsessive way that a man can. But for him, alas, the story was to end amid noise and confusion in the southwest turn.

St. Joseph's Cemetery is located on South Meridian, the heavily travelled thoroughfare that divides east from west in Indianapolis. Close to the intersection of South Meridian and Pleasant Run Boulevard lies the unmarked grave of George Metzler, scarcely a hundred feet from the motor traffic that snarls this section of Indianapolis' foundering South Side.

Metzler's life reveals a good deal about the racing mentality in America. A local boy, he was born into a working-class German-Catholic family in 1912, the year that Joe Dawson won the second running of the 500-mile race. As a ten-year-old, Metzler stood in the Speedway infield as Jimmy Murphy, driving his own number 35, dominated a field of twenty-six cars, composed mainly of Duesenbergs and Frontenacs, to win the race from the pole position. After eleven years of public education, Metzler followed the example of his uncle Edwin Metzler, himself once a riding mechanic, who had in his later years devoted himself to preparing cars for the great race. In 1935, during the waning of the Depression, Metzler was twenty-three years of age, married, and determined (by a combination of economic necessity and temperamental inclination) to try his luck at racing automobiles. One week before he saw Kelly Petillo set a new 500-mile race record of over 115 miles an hour, he persuaded car owner Dale Chastain to let him drive his big car on the half-mile tracks of Ohio and Indiana. Lacking wheels and tires, Metzler appealed to his friend John Byrne, an Indianapolis machinist who stabled racing cars of his own, for a loan of the needed parts until Metzler earned enough to replace them.

In the thirties the International Motor Contest Association in Chicago and the Central States Racing Association in Dayton, Ohio, maintained a cluttered calendar of niggardly paying county fair races (known in the business as "kerosene" or "pumpkin" dates) for their nomadic entourage of race-bitten camp followers. It was also in those days that Metzler became the father of a son and sought to improve his bank account with earnings from such ill-conceived dirt tracks as those at Scottsburg, Bloomington, Columbus, and Franklin, Indiana. The worst of the tracks was Jungle Park, an infamous course located a few miles north of Rockville, Indiana. This was roughneck, rock-flying, dusthole racing at its most primitive and treacherous. Known throughout the country as "The Track With 1001 Turns," Jungle Park was a thoroughgoing nightmare. "Whoever laid out the track originally," wrote Jerry Miller of the Marion, Indiana *Chronicle-Tribune*, "was either a comedian or a sadist. Just looking at the oblong half mile of hard brown dirt convinced you it was the devil's work. Every foot of the track was bad, first twisting up, then down, then to one side, with uneven, pitched turns at each end."

By December 7, 1941, Metzler had been divorced and remarried. His new bride was a quiet, red-headed Indianapolis girl named Marjory. At the outbreak of the war, he was drafted into the United States Army, where he survived both the Japanese and a bout with malaria. Returned to Indianapolis in 1945, George and Marjory Metzler rented an apartment in an aging, two-story frame dwelling at 32 South Dearborn Street. Behind the house loomed the P. R. Mallory electric plant where, in spite of an overwhelming number of employment applications from other returned servicemen, he found work as a machinist.

Metzler had returned from the Pacific with the residual effects of his malaria and with an army cash bonus. While the former prevented his immediate return to dirt-track racing, the latter enabled him to purchase a big car, which he hired fellow driver Cliff Griffith to race on the half-mile tracks. By the spring of 1946, however, Metzler registered with the American Automobile Association and competed in what is reputed to be the most difficult of all racing circuits, the one the AAA had organized in the Midwest, with its most frequent ports of call at Dayton and New Bremen in Ohio, and Salem and Winchester in Indiana. Predictably, he found the going difficult. The competition, dominated by such pop heros as Elbert Booker, Johnny Shakleford, and Spider Webb, was as arduous as it was dangerous. But because the AAA was then the autocratic governing body for the Indianapolis 500 (and would remain so until the United States Auto Club superceded it in 1955), Metzler had little choice other than to join the party and become visible in AAA racing circles by demonstrating that if he could not win races, he could at the very least worry the competition.

By all odds, Dayton, Salem, and Winchester were (and still are) the most terrifying of the tracks, perhaps as much for the spectator as for the contestant. All of them were paved half-mile saucers with fearsomely steep banking on the turns, where the upright, spindly cars rocketed a squirrely path around those tracks on narrow wire wheels at dizzying speeds with precious little protection for anybody on the premises. Today, Spider Webb remembers George Metzler on a hot day at Winchester in 1946: "Johnny DeCamp [another driver] and I had walked over to the infield at the bottom of the first turn to see how the other cars were running that Sunday afternoon. We hadn't been there long before Metzler came over to us with his hands in his pockets and said that he hadn't too much experience on the high banks. Then he asked us what the best way of driving the track was. I just told him to put his foot down hard on the accelerator and hold on real tight. He nodded and walked back to the pits."

Affable Jack Dixon of Indianapolis had driven at Winchester in 1918, crashed, was sent home on a freight train with his teeth knocked out, his thumb nearly severed, and his leg badly broken, and had long since given up car piloting in favor of car building. He and his partner Fred "Skinny" Clemons had built an Indianapolis car in 1941, but the war had prevented their racing it. Clemons had died in 1945, and Dixon brought the automobile out of storage in the winter of 1946-1947 with the intention of running and selling it at Indianapolis in 1947. Dixon accepted the recommendation of fellow car owner Harry Wade and hired Metzler to be his driver. Dixon submitted the $125 entry fee ($100 of which was to be refunded to the entrant by the Indianapolis Motor Speedway if the car made a bona fide attempt at qualification) by the April 15, 1947 deadline. The Speedway's official entry blank pledged a total of $75,000 in prize money, with $20,000 to the winner and $10,000 to the second place finisher. Among the 1947 rules was a continuation of the long-standing proviso (prudently instituted in 1930) that "the Chief Steward [the person who, more than any other individual, supervises the conduct of the race] shall have the right to require drivers to prove their ability to drive on the Indianapolis Motor Speedway. "These demonstrations," the supplementary regulations continued, "shall be for a distance of at least ten laps at each of the following speeds: 85, 95, 105, 110, and 115 miles per hour."

The chief-steward-designate for the thirty-first running of the 500-mile race was articulate Tommy Milton, eight times a starter and twice (1921 and 1923) a winner at Indianapolis, who ultimately took his own life in Mount Clemens, Michigan in 1962. One of Milton's paramount concerns was the screening of rookie drivers in his own rookie year as chief steward. "The problem of educating drivers to make safely the jump from hot rods or midgets to major league racing," Milton wrote in one of his AAA postrace reports, "is both serious and difficult." Part of Milton's way of dealing with George Metzler and his fellow Indianapolis freshmen was to dispense with the stern lectures that he referred to as "chalk talks" in favor of what he called "the personally conducted tour plan." The idea, said Milton, was to invite "four or five candidate drivers" for a passenger car tour of the track. The chauffeur was to be "a top-flight driver whose Indianapolis record would engender respect and confidence."

Metzler and Dixon towed the number 55 unsponsored car to Gasoline Alley behind a prewar pickup truck and deposited it in garage 24 where, owing to Dixon's illness, Metzler singlehandedly performed most of the mechanical work. He took his personally conducted tour with three other rookies. When the track opened on May 1, he logged as few laps as possible for fear of damaging the only four-cylinder Clemons engine that Dixon owned. Metzler began the ritual driver's test, successfully completing the 85, 95, and 105 phases without apparent difficulty. After one lap in the 110 range, however, strange and wondrous sounds developed in the engine. Both it and Metzler were through at Indianapolis 1947, although they raced part of the balance of the championship season on borrowed parts, finishing forty-third in the point system contrived by the American Automobile Association.

Metzler and Dixon were still at the Speedway when Rose won the 1947 race and a traditional Victory Lane kiss by Mrs. Horace Schmidlapp (actress Carole Landis) who, with reluctance, came to Indianapolis to publicize her latest Hollywood epic, entitled *Out of the Blue*, with George Brent and Turhan Bey.

On the second Sunday following the race, Metzler time trialed at a slow 27.28 seconds over the high-banked Dayton Speedway in his own number 56 Fronty-powered car, which he had rechristened the "Dixon Special." Feeling an obligation to redeem his inauspicious Indianapolis debut of the previous month, Metzler was out to rescue his damaged reputation. The skies over Dayton, Ohio were heavily overcast when he took hold of a tow-rope for the start of the first, eight-lap heat race of the afternoon. Lined up with him on the track were Spider Webb, George Connor, Norm Houser, and veteran campaigner Elbert "Grandpappy" Booker, the forty-five-year-old 1946 AAA Midwestern big car champion who appeared to be not a day under sixty. Booker, who had made an unsuccessful attempt at Indianapolis in 1946, worked at a place called the Briggs Body Company in Detroit and came to the race tracks with his wife and three children. When starter Ken Fowler (retired from racing after his last Indianapolis start two weeks before) green-flagged the first heat, Booker fell into place behind Metzler and began threading his way through the noisy traffic ahead. Moving alongside Metzler at the midpoint on the backstretch, the two brushed wheels, sending Booker's number 34 Jewell Special into the guardrailing. Booker sailed an estimated one hundred feet through the air, finally coming to rest with his car on top of him. He was dead at the scene. Metzler, unscathed, loaded his car back on its trailer and started back toward Indianapolis on Highway 40.

Racing people have always placed great value upon resilience, watching and waiting for one of their number to buckle back into a racing car after a serious accident. How long would it take? Metzler was behind the wheel of the same car one week later at Winchester, where he won the fourth ten-lap heat of the afternoon. Returned to Winchester again on August 10 and September 21, he placed out of the money on both occasions. On October 12, he was at the Dayton Speedway, placing eighth in the ten car feature event. On December 18, Metzler's shop, containing his racing car and $10,000 worth of machine tool equipment, went up in flames. He was uninsured.

Over the winter of 1947-1948, Jack Dixon sold the car to Lee Glessner (then a used car dealer and pinball czar in Wheeling, West Virginia), who hired mechanic Bob Johnson to remove the Clemons engine and replace it with a very used, 270-cubic-inch Meyer and Drake. In the spring of 1948, Glessner returned the $125.00 Speedway entry fee at the same time that his driver George Metzler became the father of another son. Short of money and mechanical assistance, Metzler again resumed the responsibility for the car's preparation, but not with any success. Mechanical problems developed, and the car never took to the track. Glessner disposed of the car, brought Metzler to Wheeling, and set him to work repairing and selling used cars. Metzler was to get one final chance at Indianapolis in 1949.

The 1937 winning Gilmore Special that Wilbur Shaw had driven came back to the Speedway six more times and finished in the first ten on a total of five different occasions. Originally a two-seater, the car, known in Gasoline Alley as "Catfish," was rebuilt by driver Mark Light after World War II so that it would accommodate only the driver. George Barringer drove the car in a 1946 dirt-track race of 100 miles at Lakewood Park in Atlanta, where an accident claimed his life and the life of 1946 Indianapolis winner George Robson. When Glessner purchased it for George Metzler to drive at Indianapolis, its ownership had changed three times. Metzler enlisted his temporarily unemployed uncle, Edwin, to act as chief mechanic, while Metzler himself concentrated upon passing the elusive driver's test begun in 1947. Soon after Glessner submitted the now doubled ($250) entry fee to the Indianapolis Motor Speedway, Ed Metzler resigned before he had begun to work. Master mechanic Cotton Henning had died the previous winter, leaving the three-car Maserati team (owned by a group of Indianapolis businessmen known as Indianapolis Race Cars Incorporated, or I.R.C.) in need of a team manager as well as a chief mechanic. As the stresses of the month of May wore on, differences developed between Ed Metzler and the I.R.C.

organization that led to his abrupt departure. It was too late, however, for him to be of much aid in readying his nephew's car for the 1949 race, and the mechanical burden fell once more on George Metzler himself.

Uppermost in his mind was the driver's test. Putting as little stress as possible on the Meyer and Drake, Metzler resumed his testing on May 5, 1949, a Thursday. The 1949 rookie class at the Speedway was unusually abundant with talent. Norm Houser, Johnny McDowell, Tommy Mattson, Ralph Pratt, George Fonder, Kenny Eaton, Bayliss Levrett, Dick Frazier, and Jimmy Daywalt all passed inspection. So too did eventual Indianapolis winners Troy Ruttman (1952), Pat Flaherty (1956), and Jim Rathmann (1960). The remaining rookies encountered problems of various kinds. Byron Horne crashed on the south chute on the eighth lap of his 115-miles-per-hour test, sustaining injuries so extensive that attending Speedway physicians scarcely knew how to evaluate his condition. He finally survived. Randall Banky failed to complete his test, as did Leroy Warriner, Bill Taylor, Lindley Bothwell (an old man in a 1914 twin-seated Peugeot), and Frank Burany, the Milwaukee midget racer.

When Metzler's turn came, a corps of experienced drivers took their places at various points around the course to assess his every move on the track. Among his examiners were some of the most notable names then on the racing scene: George Connor, Billy Cantrell, Billy DeVore, and the great Rex Mays, who was destined to die that same summer on the mile dirt horse-racing track at Del Mar, California. They were assisted by two others who would one day finish first at Indy: Lee Wallard (1951) and Sam Hanks (1957).

Metzler was required by Chief Observer Ike Welch to rerun the entire test. He eased through the 95-miles-per-hour portion, passed, and took the car to 105. Passed again. He cleared the 110 phase with ease and increased his lap times to 115 miles per hour, then to a single lap at 119. Signalled back into the pit area, Metzler was informed by Welch (after minutes of muffled deliberation with his men) that he had passed the first ritual hurdle that a rookie at Indianapolis must make.

But George Metzler had meals to eat and bills to pay in the meantime, making it necessary to race big cars over a few short tracks before the running of the Indianapolis 500. Time spent on the short tracks, however, was time spent away from the listless Glessner Special, which would have to improve by another seven miles per hour if it were to run (even shotgun) at Indianapolis in 1949. On Sunday, May 8, he appeared at Winchester in the number 25 Ray Beasley Hal (an engine fitted with a sixteen-valve conversion). Turning the track at 23.175, Metzler was assigned to the third heat race of the afternoon, and retired from competition after five of its eight laps had been run. Back to Indianapolis.

The month grew frantic for George Metzler. Despite changes of the Glessner car, it would not exceed the 119-miles-per-hour lap recorded during the driver testing program. The front end pushed. The engine balked. The rains came, as they do so persistently during an Indiana May. Missing the opening of qualifications on May 14, Metzler stood alone in the grassy area in the southwest turn as Duke Nalon posted a four-lap average of 132.939 in a screaming eight-cylinder Novi Special to win the pole position for the thirty-third running of the Indianapolis 500. Joining Nalon on the front row were two other Californians, Jack McGrath and Rex Mays. On May 15 the rains fell, again washing all track activity away. It was clear the following day, a Monday, and Metzler returned to the track, but with no improvement in his lap times.

Only one more weekend of qualification rounds remained. When Saturday, May 21 arrived, the car was still not delivering speed. By the final day of time trials, Sunday the twenty-second, Metzler had despaired. Another big car race, this one at Salem, was on the AAA schedule. Beasley and Metzler loaded their car under a black Indiana sky and drove southbound to Salem over State Route 31. Arrived at the track, Metzler made a qualification run of 24.97 seconds over the steeply banked half-mile saucer, and before the day ended his earnings came to a grand total of $50: $15 for the heat race, and $35 for the consolation race. Beasley waited at the Salem paywindow for the money, and returned to find Metzler brooding in the front seat of his pickup truck. Back to Indianapolis they went.

By the time the pair had reached Columbus, the rain began to fall on the truck's windshield. At Indianapolis, as they were shortly to find out, it had been raining all day. For the second time that month, time trials were washed out. Tommy Milton had issued an official AAA bulletin and had posted it in Gasoline Alley: Qualification runs would be resumed on Wednesday, May 25 and again on Saturday, May 28. Metzler had two more days to make the race.

More discouragement. On Monday and Tuesday, his speeds did not improve. Still no luck on Wednesday morning. He watched as other drivers attempted qualification runs. On Thursday, he padlocked his garage, packed a suitcase, and drove straight east to Wheeling, West Virginia, for an eleventh-hour conference with Glessner, who listened sympathetically to Metzler's story of how the engine was not pulling and how a new set of pistons might provide the seven or so miles per hour necessary to make the race. Glessner dispatched his driver back to Indianapolis early on Friday morning with instructions to buy the pistons from Meyer and Drake and install them overnight. He promised to be at the Speedway on the morning of May 28 to lend whatever support he could toward Metzler's qualification run.

Metzler arrived at the Speedway late on Friday afternoon after five hours on the road. He took the four new pistons to a grocery store in Speedway and weighed each of them on a butcher's scale. At ten that evening, his old friend and retainer John Byrne looked in on Metzler's Gasoline Alley garage. "He had that car in a blue million pieces," Byrne recalls nearly thirty years afterward. "They were all over the garage floor. I mean *everywhere*. George told me that he had to get the pistons in by morning, that it was his last chance ever to run at Indianapolis. He said that if he didn't make the race this time, nobody would ever hire him to run there again. I thought that he was a pretty decent mechanic, but he was working alone. I felt sorry for him. I finally went home to bed, but George kept working."

Metzler got no sleep on the night of May 27, 1949. He had left Gasoline Alley at about one in the morning to commiserate with some night-owl friends over a round of beer at Mates White Front, and then returned to finish reassembling his engine. When Metzler lowered the Meyer and Drake back inside car 67, it was nine in the morning. An abundant crowd had by this time poured through the Speedway gates. Tommy Milton had decreed that the track should open at ten for a final practice session prior to the end of qualifications for 1949. AAA observers were dispatched to their posts around the two-and-one-half-mile course.

Down in the southwest turn, sitting at a green trackside observer's table situated between grandstands B and E, were Paul Johnson of Anderson, Indiana, and his companion Harold Murphy of Chicago. Both men, fitted out with radio communications, were in touch with other such observation posts around the Indianapolis Motor Speedway. A wind prevailing from the northeast blew the smoke from the Prest-O-Lite stack toward St. Joseph's Cemetery. It also ruffled a printed directive from Tommy Milton that lay in front of Johnson, who secured it to the green table with an empty Coca-Cola bottle. "Don't use the word *tire* in your reports," Milton's instructions read. "It may sound like FIRE."

The 500-mile race was a short two days away, and the final five positions in the Memorial Day classic were still open as several cars took to the track for this final practice session. Rookie Bill Cantrell motored his number 74 Kennedy Tank Special into the first turn, followed by Freddy Agabashian (replacing Hal Robson) in the I.R.C. Miller number 15. In the infield, a Hollywood crew busied itself filming some footage for Mickey Rooney's *The Big Wheel*, to be released later that year. Cincinnati's heavyweight boxing champion Ezzard Charles roamed the pit and garage areas signing autographs. For Indianapolis television, this was Day One, as WFBM-TV broadcast some forty minutes of final Speedway qualifications.

For George Metzler, the pressure was on. Not having slept in twenty-eight hours, he still had not found his speed at Indianapolis. Lee Glessner, just arrived from Wheeling, stood by in the pits as Metzler grimly donned his helmet and gloves for what would be the final time. Metzler's Meyer and Drake engine came to life and warmed its oil for a minute and a half. Moving out of the pit lane slowly, Metzler guided the car low in the southwest turn, where he waved quickly to Johnson and Murphy. After three warm-up laps, Metzler moved the Glessner car out into the groove, turning laps at 112, then 118, then 120. Glessner himself flashed the pit board. Other cars were turning the track faster. Levrett was lapping at close to 130 miles an hour, easily enough to qualify for the race, while Emil Andres was running in excess of 126. Other entrants had resorted to tricks that were causing speeds to climb. Some had lowered their rear axle ratios for greater acceleration as they exited the turns, while others had replaced their carburetors with fuel injection systems that showed a great potential for improving laptimes. Metzler, however, found himself lacking straightaway speeds, and was attempting to compensate by driving harder and deeper into the turns, especially the southwest, where the gap in the track's surface caused him to lose control momentarily each time he passed over it.

Paul Johnson glanced at his watch. It was now 10:49.

On Saturday evening, when qualifications were complete and the field filled for the running of the 1949 Indianapolis 500, Ike Welch wrote a summary report of the day's activities. Levrett, Cantrell, Agabashian, Andres, and Manuel Ayulo had earned starting positions in that order. Welch continued his report to the AAA Contest Board: "May 28th at 10:50 A.M. driver George Metzler lost control while passing hump in turn #1, headed toward apron, over-corrected, and struck wall twice, seriously injured, car wrecked badly."

The 1949 Oldsmobile Rocket 88 pace car sped to the accident scene bearing an anxious contingent of American Automobile Association officialdom that included Milton, Welch, and metallurgist Sol Silbermann. Lee Glessner ran on foot to the southwest turn, followed by an ambulance and a bevy of newspaper reporters and cameramen. At the accident site was Speedway Superintendent Clarence Cagle and a safety patrolman. Metzler had hit hard. Unconscious, he was lowered carefully on a rolling stretcher and hurried to the infield hospital, where Marjory Metzler waited. The number 67 Glessner Special, its front side flattened and its body buckled as far back as the driver's cockpit, was towed by a wrecker back to Gasoline Alley.

Inside the Speedway press room, a reporter for the *Indianapolis Star* hurriedly composed the Metzler story in time to make the Sunday morning edition. "The grim battle for places in the field took its toll," he wrote. "Metzler took his car to the track a few minutes before qualification runs to nudge just a few more miles per hour out of it so he could go to the starting line later. The car skidded down into the dirt in the inside of the track and then darted up and almost head-on into the wall as Metzler fought for control."

At the infield hospital, Dr. E. Rogers Smith, an Indianapolis neurologist who would supervise the activities of some 237 physicians and nurses on race day, waited for Metzler's arrival. Despite his recognition of Metzlers injuries (a crushed right chest, severe brain damage, and probable ruptured spleen), Smith predicted "a fifty-fifty chance to recover" to *Star* reporters in front of the hospital gate after Metzler had been hurriedly transferred to Indianapolis' downtown Methodist Hospital. Metzler's critical condition notwithstanding, the Sunday *Star* reported that "his injuries were not as serious as those of Byron Horne of Scenery Hill, Pa., who crashed a few hundred feet from the same spot on May 2 and is still in the hospital." In Gasoline Alley, the talk of the morning centered upon a *Star* allegation that Metzler "had been riding without a safety belt," an allegation denied by Glessner, who had seen him drive from pit lane on his final run.

*   *   *

Metzler remained unconscious and in critical condition on Sunday, May 29 at Methodist Hospital. At the Speedway, Tommy Milton and Wilbur Shaw conducted the annual drivers' meeting, admonishing all thirty-three to exercise every possible caution on race day. Hydroplane racer and perennial Indianapolis 500 buff Guy Lombardo arrived with his Royal Canadians for a dance engagement at the Indiana Roof. "Race fans from the East have been rolling in on Highway 40 in a steady stream," wrote Wieland Brown of *Speed Age* magazine. Out on West Sixteenth Street, a sideshow featuring "Hitler's personal armored pleasure car" drew the abundant prerace crowd inside its tent. When darkness descended on the Speedway, Brown observed "pickpockets, prostitutes, professional gamblers, and other practitioners of frowned-upon vices."

No report was made on Metzler in the Indianapolis dailies

The start of the 1949 race. Duke Nalon assumes the lead over front-runners Rex Mays (middle) and Jack McGrath (outside).

on race day, May 30. At four in the morning, just after daylight, a bomb exploded high in the atmosphere over the Speedway, signaling the opening of the public gates and rattling window panes over Speedway City. Said one incredulous onlooker from atop the Chinese pagoda, "As the gates open, some two or three hundred motorcycles charge through Gate Five and vehicles, vehicles, vehicles surge through the six tunnel lanes under the track and a dozen lanes over the track into what can best be described as a reenactment of the opening of the 'Cherokee Strip.' " Thirty-three cars were pushed into position on the track prior to the playing of "Taps" and the singing of "Back Home Again in Indiana"; one-third of them were to be driven by rookie drivers. By day's end, forty-one-year-old Bill Holland, the roller-skating rink owner from Reading, Pennsylvania, would win the Indianapolis 500, collecting $51,575 in first place money after having taken the lead at 150 miles in a Blue Crown Spark Plug Special.

Metzler died Friday, June 3, at 1:22 A.M. His funeral began at 8:30 A.M. the following Monday at G.H. Herrmann Funeral Home and continued at St. Catherine's Church, where a priest averred that because Metzler had devoted his life only to pleasure, he had reaped the penalties. The priest did not accompany the funeral party to St. Joseph's Cemetary, where Metzler was buried in a number 30 Monarch Vault in Lot 17. One of the pallbearers was Cliff Griffith.

On Thursday, June 23, Carroll F. Durrell of the AAA Contest Board disbursed a $1,500 death benefit claim check to Marjory E. Metzler at 32 South Dearborn, Indianapolis, Indiana.

*   *   *

George Metzler was neither the first nor the last casualty of the southwest turn, although he is assuredly one of the lesser known. Others were to follow in his wake. In 1953, for example, fifty-three-year-old Chet Miller, who had hurtled the wall there in 1934, died at the southwest turn during a practice run in one of the ill-fated, ghost-white Novi Specials. He had been an enormously popular, graying senior driver at Indianapolis and the proprietor of an upholstery shop in Glendale, California. Miller, who had driven in sixteen Indianapolis races, the first of which was in 1930, found himself in the same kind of fix that George Metzler had experienced: sliding low on the track, seeming to over-correct, and catching the wall almost head-on. The track was closed in his memory during his May 19 funeral, after which Speedway activity resumed with full force.

With only two minutes of practice time remaining on the eve of time trials in 1955, four-time race veteran and postwar California standout Manuel Ayulo, the mechanic and driver of Peter Schmidt's bright red number 88 roadster, drove into the wall in the southwest turn without having made any apparent effort to turn left. He was not wearing a seat belt at the time of the mishap, and he died the following day. The specific reason for the Ayulo accident has remained a mystery, like so many other situations at the track. One educated Gasoline Alley guess was that the steering had failed in his Kurtis roadster somewhere along the main straightway. An experienced driver, the thirty-three-year-old, 150-pound Los Angeles-born son of a Peruvian diplomat had begun his racing career in hot rods and midgets on the Pacific coast. The same John Byrne who had looked in on George Metzler on the eve of Metzler's fatal accident, had also looked in on Manny Ayulo. "I found Manny doing about the same thing that I had found George doing," he recalls. "There were parts all over the garage floor. It was an unholy mess in there. Manny was getting ready to put his engine back together again, and like George, he didn't seem to have anybody helping him. The next day, he was dead."

Twice an Indianapolis also-ran, Charles Rodeghier was an ex-marine from Blue Island, Illinois, who enjoyed considerable success racing midget cars in the Midwest under the name of "Chuck Rodee." Misnegotiating the southwest turn in 1966, his number 92 Leader Card Special slammed the wall, making Rodeghier the first qualification fatality since Stubby Stubblefield's 1935 accident in almost precisely the same place. At the time of the mishap, Rodeghier lived in Speedway City with his wife and two children, one of whom turned up in the role of a pit man at the Speedway years later.

In the 1968 race more drama unfolded in the southwest. After Carl Williams bumped the wall on the second (southeast) turn on his 164th lap, his Sheraton Thompson Special finally rolled to a stop in a burst of flame. Williams was uninjured. In the meantime, Joe Leonard, at the wheel of one of Colin Chapman's four-wheel-drive STP turbines, was in front and showed every indication of remaining there. The yellow flag was displayed while the wreckage of Williams' car was removed from the course. As Leonard passed the starting line on his 190th circuit, starter Pat Vidan reached for his green flag to resume competition on the next go-around, and STP public relations man David Blackmer located Leonard's wife in the terrace tower grandstand and began to usher her toward Victory Lane in anticipation of Leonard's winning the race. But as

Veteran Gordon Johncock at speed, 1978.

Vidan waved the green flag at the beginning of Leonard's 192nd tour, the turbine unaccountably lost all power. Leonard raised his hand to signal drivers behind him, and then pulled into the grass in the southwest turn, where an anonymous reporter wrote his impressions: "It's unbelievable! The stands go crazy, everyone goes wild as Leonard limps down to the infield in the first turn and off onto the grass just a few feet from Victory Lane. Blackmer and Mrs. Leonard stop right at the pit gate, turn around, and walk slowly back. Leonard sits motionless in the car for several moments before climbing slowly out."

Gordon Johncock, the 1973 winner, had the misfortune to repeat Leonard's act in the 1977 race. Leading (in still another STP-sponsored car) at 184 laps, Johncock also came to an unexpected halt in the southwest turn when a faulty valve spring caused his Bignotti-prepared Patrick Racing DGS Wildcat to move from first to eleventh in the final scoring. Exhausted from stress and intense heat, Johncock lifted himself slowly

Gordon Johncock pit stop, 1977.

David Knox

from the car, sat on the side of it momentarily, and teetered thirty feet toward Ditch Creek, where he anointed himself with muddy water as A. J. Foyt streaked past him to an unprecedented fourth Indianapolis win.

Chapter 4

ROUNDING THE SOUTHEAST TURN: BACKSTAGE AT THE FOLLIES

*E*xcept in the force and direction of prevailing winds, turn two (the southeast) is theoretically no different from turn four (the northwest). In both cases the driving emphasis is aimed more at getting out of it than at getting into it. Besides the ever-present danger of running into something (such as a concrete wall or another automobile), the driver concentrates on exiting the southeast swiftly and cleanly and setting himself up for the 3,300-foot straightaway that lies before him. While there is a fairly well-established, tire-blackened groove that points the way out of turn two, negotiating that (and every other) turn is not a simple matter of following the leader. An attentive spectator can recognize that different drivers strike a different driving pattern while at competition speeds on the track; some tend to pinch their cars to the inside, while others tend to use more of the race track, very nearly brushing the wall midway through the chutes and at the exits to turns two and four. Still others follow a middle course between the two extremes. Less-experienced drivers are inclined to be less consistent, appearing at times to let the car drive them.

Regardless of the specific pattern a driver elects to follow through the southeast, part of his objective is to push the automobile to the limits of its traction, always riding the ragged edge beyond which the car seems all too ready to break into a dizzying, tire-smoking spin. Unusual indeed is the turn two spectator who does not tense at the prospect of a car's circling the course at the limit of its tractive possibility. At its most artful, the rounding of the southeast is a marvelously graceful, delicate, and dangerous feat, demanding the driver's utmost sensitivity to the nuances of both car and track. Even the handful of men who have apparent mastery over the course lament the extreme difficulty of "putting all four turns together," or rounding each turn perfectly in a single lap. A well-turned lap at Indianapolis, like a perfectly executed play on the football field, can be a source of great satisfaction to anyone perceptive enough to appreciate its subtleties. In the hands of a substantial, top-line Indianapolis driver, a racing car appears to be coursing the turns as if it were comfortably and securely mounted on rails. The racer's turbocharged engine howls to the extent that it can be heard blocks away, and it is a good, clean, solid, pleasing sound that (unlike the cloying dissonance of a teenager's hot rod) satisfies aesthetically.

To appreciate fully the beauty of a 180-mile-an-hour left turn requires a practiced eye. During the month of May, drivers themselves saunter on foot to the south end of the Speedway, where they scrutinize the way their fellow competitors are managing themselves in the turns, taking careful note of the "line" that the other drivers are using, along with the timing and extent of brake and throttle use. I, too, like a closer look as one of the limited number of people who come to roost in the southeast turn for tens of hours. The location affords me a different and, in certain ways, better perspective on the Indianapolis scene. My preference, among the virtually limitless possibilities for vantage points, is the apex of an aluminum structure called the southeast Vista, erected with geometric precision high above the number two turn between 1971 and 1973. The perspective is something like that of a person who swings precariously from a trapeze dangling from the uppermost peak of a circus Big Top.

When I first took my young son to the track, he (having a gifted imagination) believed fervently that, once the racing cars were out of visual range over in the southeast turn, they performed some bizarre, mystic, supernatural gyrations; that they looped-the-loop, dove precipitously beneath scented subterranean tunnels of love, rushed upward through the Arden Forest, traversed the Land of Cockayagne, and then returned to the race track for another swift Speedway go-around.

At least part of the intrigue at Indianapolis, to be sure, is the part that you cannot see. What you cannot see, you conceptualize. Brightly painted cars whiz by, but fail to whiz by a second time. Where have they gone? Are they stranded motionless at some remote point on the course? Are they stalled in the pits? Crunched against a wall somewhere? Up a tree? Under a rock? In 1958, for example, when youthful Pat O'Connor was the principal casualty in a multi-car first lap collision of drastic proportions at the north end of the track, only about three-fourths of that fateful morning's starting field survived the smashup; those who did survive did not prevail altogether unscathed from the melee, dribbling around as they did with crunched nose cones, black tiremarks, leaking fuel tanks, and other imitations of egregiously foul play.

If I had been here in what I consider to have been the old days, the view from the southeast Vista would have been different in a good many respects. Almost directly in front of me would have been a spectator catwalk across the track, and well beyond it an airplane landing strip. Behind me would have been a garage and an airdrome a few feet away from West Sixteenth Street. The friendly looking Superintendent's residence which was there then is there still: a veritable oasis of privacy.

To learn about the past, every true Indy buff has filed next to the old family Bible a copy of a moldy-looking, red and black tome entitled *Floyd Clymer's Indianapolis 500 Mile Race History*. Even when new, it appears to be liberally thumbed and prematurely yellowed. Somewhat incoherent though it may be, it has within its covers a gallery of seemingly ancient photographs of men in knickers and sketchy glimpses of days long past when the titans of the Speedway reigned invincibly and when it seldom rained in Indianapolis except after the race had ended and everyone had gone back to work.

A reporter for the New York magazine entitled *The Horseless Age* indulged himself the night prior to the 1912 race at Indianapolis's Claypool Hotel, itself a lingering remnant of the Gilded Age, and was impressed by the lavishness of pre-race revelry. The Claypool, he said, "resembled some of the hotels on Long Island. Almost everybody of prominence in the automotive industry could be found within a stone's throw. Gay parties were many the night before the race, and it is safe to say that there were a large number that did not see a bed at all."

Those still awake when the sun rose over race day 1912 soon found themselves confronting traffic that congested the five miles between the Claypool and the Motor Speedway. An hour before the start of the race, the twenty-four contestants lined their cars on the track in four rows five abreast and a fifth row of four cars. Among those assigned to the third row was driving veteran Bob Burman, adorned like his crew in an impeccably starched white shirt with "Wolverine Motor Club" printed across the back. Burman's number 15 Cutting was entered by the Clark Custer Auto Company of Jackson, Michigan. It was a two-seater with barely sufficient room for Burman and his riding mechanic Harry Goetz. After the race was flagged off, Burman worked his way methodically into first position, troubled all the while by a grossly unbalanced right rear wheel. Having stopped in the pits on seven different occasions, he was riding third as he began his 157th lap.

As Burman rounded the southeast turn at ninety miles an hour, both rear wheels parted ways with the Cutting and the car went into a spin. The man from *The Horseless Age* made his way to the southeast to record the details of Burman's mishap: "The machine skiddled and turned turtle," he reported. "It was thought that Burman and his mechanic had been killed, but when a rescuing party arrived at the scene of the accident they were both standing beside their upturned car." Burman and Goetz were bloodied about the neck, shoulders, hands, thighs, and knees, but not so severely that they did not return later that same afternoon to the pits to join their friends in seeing the finish of the race, which was won by Joe Dawson, a resident of the local YMCA. Dawson, who had driven an Indianapolis-built National, had assumed the lead when Ralph DePalma's Mercedes came to a sudden, altogether unanticipated stop on the backstretch after 495 miles. As Dawson returned to the YMCA on a streetcar, the mobs that lingered around the Indianapolis Motor Speedway seemed to regret DePalma's luck. At the time of DePalma's unforeseen departure from competition, wrote the anonymous man from *The Horseless Age*, "a moan went up from the spectators, who appreciated the misfortune of the Italian."

The 1912 race lasted six hours, twenty-one minutes, and six seconds, after which Burman gathered up his driving togs and caught a ride back to downtown Indianapolis, where he took to his bed at the Hotel English to nurse his wounds — but not for long. More reporters soon knocked at his door, and Burman received them at his bedside with cordiality. "I never had anything happen to me so quickly in all my experience," he exclaimed. "I thought that I surely would be killed and I was rather surprised that I was alive when it was over." Burman, who planned to set out shortly for another automobile race in Philadelphia, shrugged off the horrendous accident on the southeast turn only a few hours earlier. "It would take a worse spill than that to stop me," he told reporters confidently. According to Burman's own account of the accident, he had hung tenaciously to the steering wheel as the Cutting rolled over. Seatmate Harry Goetz, however, was tossed some twenty-five feet out of the car. Goetz, Burman explained, had been wearing Burman's stopwatch securely around his waist to calculate lap times during the course of the race. When the dust of the mishap cleared, Goetz brushed himself off and ran back to Burman with the assuring news: "Bob! I didn't break your stopwatch!"

On the morning after the 1912 race, the principal topics of discussion in Gasoline Alley were Dawson's win, DePalma's disappointment, and Burman's wreck. Evidently wishing to reassure Indianapolis residents about the legitimacy of motor races at the Speedway, the morning paper gave the previous day's race some good press. "There has been no better mannered gathering in Indianapolis," the readership was informed over its morning coffee. "There was no pushing, no crowding, no profanity, no discourtesies." Too much to believe? Perhaps. Elsewhere in the paper the assessment of the second running of the 500-mile race differed. A Cincinnati woman of dubious character, it reported, had converged on the Speedway with a well-drilled team of twenty pickpockets recruited from dark alleyways across the Middle West. Before the day ended, the ring had been rounded up by hoosier gendarmes and checked into the city jail for the night on charges of vagrancy.

Those involved in subsequent turn two accidents at the Speedway through the years were not altogether as fortunate as Bob Burman and his airborne riding mechanic Harry Goetz. It was in 1919 that French driver Louis LeCocq and his mechanic-rider both succumbed in their gray and blue Duesenberg on their ninety-sixth lap as they rounded the southeast turn. Darwin Hatch, managing editor of *Motor Age*, was at the scene: "The gasoline tank exploded, the car overturned, and the two men were killed instantly and their bodies cremated under the burning car." Although Germany's signing of the Versailles treaty was still nearly a month away, the Speedway had scheduled the running of the 1919 race after two successive years of war-imposed cancellations. "Prophecies that motor racing never would come back into popular favor were adequately disproved by the attendance and enthusiasm at Indianapolis," one news release reported. "Estimates of attendance varied all the way from 75,000 to 125,000. ...Whatever the actual number of spectators the turnout was sufficient to show the interest in the public, in general, and the delegations from other cities by train and motor indicated that it was in no way localized." Johnny had indeed marched home, and in his wake had come a contingent of speed-demon Frenchmen eager to have a fling at Indianapolis. Among them had been LeCocq, whose scorched racer came to rest pointed the wrong way against the old retaining wall on the southeast turn, where it remained for the rest of the afternoon.

A decade passed before there was another race fatality at the Motor Speedway. The year was 1929 and the location was the same as it had been for the LeCocq accident. This time the trouble came on lap nine, when twenty-four-year-old Bill

Spence of Los Angeles spun into the wall and flipped over. His lavender and black Duesenberg slid upside down through a considerable stretch of the southeast turn, leaving Spence behind on the track with a fractured skull. Although Joe Caccia and his mechanic Clarence Grover died during a practice run through the southeast in 1931, the Spence accident, as it turned out, was curiously prophetic of a now fabled 1933 mishap involving another purple-hued Duesenberg, and in virtually the same track location. The driver this time was Mark Billman, the twenty-seven-year-old son of an Indianapolis golf course groundskeeper who lived with his parents on Villa Avenue. Billman, an employee of the Ford Motor Company, had driven his first race at the old Hoosier Speedway, a half-mile dirt track once located slightly northeast of Indianapolis on Pendleton Pike, and had competed on the board track at Altoona. Five years before coming to race at Indianapolis, Billman had partially crippled himself in a big car accident on Indiana's treacherous Jungle Park oiled dirt track. He started the 1933 Indianapolis race in twenty-second position in an overflow field of forty-two cars. His was the ill-fated Kemp-Mannix Special that weighed a hefty (but hardly unusual) 2,100 pounds dry. The car had persistent difficulty with the right front shock absorber, which had occasioned a pit stop after the first fifty laps of the race. In the cockpit with Billman was another first-year man, mechanic Elmer Lombard, a daredevil in his own right, who had become increasingly uneasy over the track's growing slickness as the race wore on. The Speedway's solution to greasy conditions in the turns in those days was to station on the sides of the track what appeared to be leftover World War I doughboys with buckets of sand which they had license to throw (with some abandon) across the track's running groove. It was the same khaki-clad militia that disposed of any stalled or otherwise wrecked cars that came to a stop anywhere nearby.

One driving veteran of the middle thirties recalls track conditions at Indianapolis with great vividness: "If there was an oil spill, the state militia would have pails of sand behind the retaining walls on the turns. They'd pitch it right out in front of you. They didn't particularly care who was coming along the track at that moment. And if your car stalled, they didn't send a tow truck after you, or fool around with you at all. If you were on the outside of the track, the men picked your car up bodily and pitched it over the wall. If you were on the inside of the track, the same thing. About fifteen guys would slip two-by-fours under your car, and it was all over. Goodbye, Charlie."

The chief steward for the 1933 race was W. D. "Eddie" Edenburn, who, after the contest had been run, advocated an abrupt end to the use of sand on the Speedway. "Throwing the sand on a dry track," he said, "produces a condition for the drivers similar to driving on ball bearings or marbles, and further, the sand pits the glass of the goggles and obscures the vision of the drivers." There was ample sand and oil in turn two on the seventy-eighth lap of the 1933 race when Billman and Lombard had just overtaken future (1935) winner Kelly Petillo. As they rounded the southeast turn on the following lap, the car began to slide out of control on the inner apron of the turn and then drift up the banking. AAA observer Tom Mulligan noted that something evidently went wrong with the car's mechanical condition just prior to the accident. The rear wheels had apparently locked while Mark Billman wrestled with the steering wheel to bring the Kemp-Mannix back under control. Instead, however, the machine continued its slip up the banking until it crunched a large V-shaped portion of the concrete wall. The car then bounced high in the air, eventually coming to rest with the rear of the automobile on the wall and its front still on the race track. Bouncing along the wall another forty feet, the racer hurled mechanic Lombard eastward over the wall and well out of Mulligan's vision.

Ironically, Lombard's injuries were comparatively slight. Forty years later, from the living room of his retirement home in Venice, Florida, he seemed to relish the opportunity to relive the accident. "Neither Mark nor I wore seat belts. It was all a question of whether you wanted to stay with the car in an accident situation, or whether you wanted to part ways with it. There were no roll bars or anything like that, and most of us figured that it would be better to leave the car than to stay with it. I don't know what would have happened if we *had* been buckled in, of course. The newspapers had me listed as seriously injured, but there was no truth in the report. I went flying over the wall about where the Southeast Vista now is, and landed in the middle of Pop Myers's tomato patch. Pop was vice-president of the Speedway at that time. I was burned and cut a little, and I think that the accident gave me a bad eye. Really, there wasn't anything much the matter with me. I let them take me to a hospital anyway. He remained there for three weeks.

Mark Billman was not so fortunate, however. As the number 64 Kemp-Mannix straddled the wall in a shower of sparks, he was thrown forward and caught beneath the car as it continued along the top of the retaining wall. When the car finally came to a stop, the right front wheel was resting on Billman's body. And after the passage of some twenty minutes, when militiamen lifted the car over the wall and allowed it to roll down the embankment outside of turn two, Billman was more dead than alive. His left arm was all but severed, and his legs were both fractured. His internal injuries were still undetermined. At the infield Speedway emergency hospital, doctors completed the amputation of his arm and made a determined effort to preserve Billman's life with repeated blood transfusions, but their efforts failed. The Billman-Lombard accident transpired at 1:59 P.M. on May 30, 1933. Seven minutes later the race was on again, except at the south end of the track, where yellow caution conditions prevailed until the debris was cleared for the resumption of racing.

Amid threatening rainclouds, the winner of the 1938 race was Floyd Roberts, living at that time in Van Nuys, California, driving a Burd Piston Ring Special. Far behind Roberts, finishing in twenty-ninth position, was an exceptionally tough and determined Emil Andres of Chicago. Andres, along with constant companion and racing competitor Jimmy Snyder, another Chicagoan, was the proprietor of a watering hole called the Jockey Club (later The Speedway Cocktail Lounge) which became one of the few Windy City racing hangouts in the 1930s. While Snyder finished an eventual fifteenth place in 1938, Andres fared infinitely less well after a curious turn two incident that sent him to a hospital and another man to a morgue. Andres's car was a six-cylinder, 272-inch, Brisco-powered, black and white upright racer designed primarily for dirt-track competition.

With one pit stop behind him, Andres was moving through the southeast turn when a wheel collapsed, sending the car into an uncontrollable 400-foot slide toward the inner safety apron and through the inside guardrailing, slicing off several wooden posts at ground level as it did. Once through the railing, Andres dove into a wooden culvert where the car began a series of northbound barrelrolls. His left front wheel was sheared off and sent bounding high in the air. Andres was hurled from his car, which travelled another 200 feet before it came to a stop. Gathered up unconscious by an ambulance crew, he was dispatched to Methodist Hospital with a concussion, a broken nose, and chest injuries. Like Elmer Lombard, however, Andres was alive and eager forty years later to retell the story:

"1938? I remember it all. I lived at the Riley Hotel, just across the street from Methodist Hospital. We all paid our own way. There was no such thing as a retainer fee for a driver in those days, and the money for room and board all came out of my own pocket. We could go to Indianapolis for the month of May before World War II for $250 and play the big wheel role. On the other hand, we weren't exactly what you would call flush in the middle thirties, either. [Duke] Nalon, [Paul] Russo, [Tony] Wilman, [Jimmy] Snyder, and I always had a buck in our pockets, though. We'd go out and buy a couple loaves of bread, a couple hocks of ham, a couple quarts of milk, and a can of beans. We'd have lunch for three bucks. And it was fun! We called it bunching for lunch. My 1938 car which was called the Elgin Piston Pin Special wasn't too much fun, though. It was a huge, six-cylinder machine, and there was always something squirrely about the chassis. I never knew what it wanted to do, because it sort of had a mind of its own. On the forty-second lap my right front wheel folded under. We were using wire wheels in those days, and they had a certain lifespan to them. The ones I was using must have been pretty old at the time. When the wheel gave way I took a long, looping spin into the infield. I went through the inside railing and was dumped out, remained unconscious for ten days at Methodist Hospital. On the eleventh day I woke up for the first time, and they wanted to keep me longer, but I was a pretty young bull, and I told the hospital people that I was leaving. About the time that I was packing my clothes, Mauri Rose came to visit me and wanted to know what the hell I was doing out of bed. He finally drove me back to Chicago in my own car. It was a sorry thing to do, because by the time we got to Lebanon, Indiana I started to bleed out of my nose and mouth, and I was about ready to turn back. But we drove on to Chicago, and by the time we got there I was feeling a little better. We were pretty brave in those days. You either had to drive a car and make a buck, or you had to get a job somewhere. So four weeks later I was back driving midgets again, turned upside down, and got a black eye out of the deal."

The tragic consequence of the Andres accident escaped the immediate attention of most onlookers, whose eyes were on Andres himself. Indeed, most of the turn two crowd failed to follow the course of Andres's wheel as it soared 125 feet through space, falling with all its force squarely on the head of one Everett Spence, a thirty-three-year-old Vigo County, Indiana, probation officer and the father of three children. Spence had been observing the race from his perch atop the cab of a truck parked in the second row of vehicles lining the safety fencing on the inside of turn two. Chaos reigned for several minutes before rescue teams realized that Andres was not the only injured party. Twenty-two years would pass before any other spectators would suffer fatal injuries. It was in 1960 that a spectator-constructed thirty-foot scaffolding toppled in the direction of the backstretch during the pace lap, killing two and injuring about seventy others. Scaffolding was thereafter banned, and no further spectators succumbed to injuries in the intervening years.

Having taken home a sizable portion of the $91,075 Speedway payoff in 1938, and having established a new 500-mile race record of slightly more than 117 miles per hour, popular Floyd Roberts was eager to stage a repeat performance in 1939. The jovial, slightly obese thirty-nine-year-old Californian derived a kind of perverse pleasure from thwarting the generally superstitious tendencies of his driving companions at Indianapolis. He adopted a large, ominous black cat as his Gasoline Alley mascot, and posed good-naturedly with the beast before the lenses of news photographers dispatched from across the country. Back at the Speedway in 1939, Roberts had the same, mean-looking ebony cat and the same car that had carried him to victory the year before. The racer, which was a 270-cubic-inch Offenhauser mounted in a magnificent upright Wetterroth chassis, was entered once again by Lou Moore and sponsored by Burd. Although the car's red, black, and silver color scheme was unchanged, the car's number was altered from 23 to 1, emblematic of Roberts's having won the prestigious AAA National Driving Championship during the 1938 season.

During the 1939 Speedway qualifications, Roberts ran the car more than three miles per hour faster than the previous year, but was nonetheless relegated to start the race far back in twenty-third position. Starting twenty-first was Emil Andres, back for another try at the 500-mile race after his horrendous accident on the southeast turn the year before, driving this time for his friend and business partner Jimmy Snyder. Roberts was far more confident than Andres, however. On the night prior to the race, Roberts confided to his friend Henry McLemore, "I have the car that can do it. Tomorrow night I'll have twenty grand in my kick, and you won't hear any more about a driver not being able to win two in a row."

Whereas Roberts had triumphed the year before under threatening skies that had dropped rain during his 192nd lap, race day in 1939 dawned bright and hot. When the race got under way at eleven, Roberts could do no better than to dice with the latter half of the thirty-three-car field. The pace was terrific, with straightaway speeds exceeding 150 miles an hour. California midget ace Bob Swanson, who left the race after nineteen laps with rear axle problems, roamed the pit lane offering his services as a relief driver. After exhausted veteran Ralph Hepburn relinquished the seat of his steamy Hamilton-Harris Offenhauser on his 107th lap, Swanson donned his helmet for the second time that afternoon and climbed into the sweltering cockpit without having had previous experience behind the wheel of the car. Leaving the pit area in an inordinate rush, Swanson rapidly escalated to racing speed by the time he had reached the south chute. As he moved into the southeast turn, the car began to spin. It was now 2:19. In the AAA observation stand at the outside of turn two, Tom Mulligan was back from the year before when he had reported on Emil Andres's accident. At his side was another Detroiter, former driver Gene Haustein. Bob Swanson was sideways in the running groove in turn two when the Burd Piston Ring Special driven by Floyd Roberts appeared.

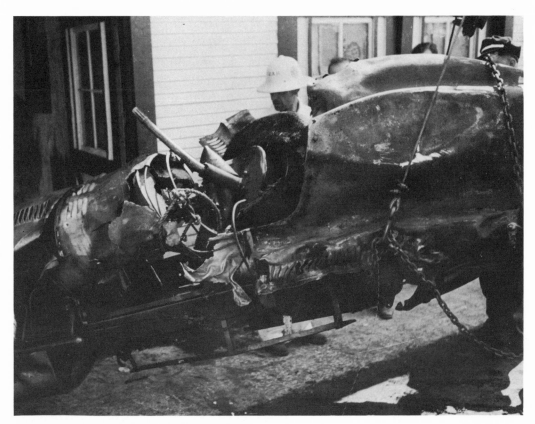

The wreckage of Bob Swanson's Hamilton-Harris Special following Floyd Roberts' fatal accident in 1939.

Roberts's immediate reaction to the crisis before him was to attempt to slip between Swanson's car and the retaining wall. The attempt was unsuccessful, and Roberts crashed broadside into Swanson's automobile. Within a second, both machines had exploded, and Swanson's number 25 reacted from the impact with three rapid rollovers, coming to rest on the outside of the track opposite old Gate Five. Swanson, having been thrown from the car, lay helpless in the middle of the track with his back and hands burned severely.

Roberts was not nearly so lucky. After broadsiding Swanson's Hamilton-Harris Special he plowed through some twenty feet of guardrailing beyond the point where the concrete wall ended at the exit of the southeast turn. Roberts's momentum carried him another 150 feet and sent him through a section of Carl Fisher's original "tight board fence" toward what is now a golf course, where his car continued to burn. Rushed to Methodist Hospital, he was found to be nearly pulseless and died forty-five minutes later from injuries sustained at the base of his brain and the upper regions of his spinal cord. Because emergency crews chose not to deliver the injured to the emergency hospital in Speedway infield, friends and relatives of the injured drivers did not know immediately what had become of them.

Moments after Mulligan and Haustein had flashed the yellow caution light, a third car entered the wild melee. This was car number 3, a maroon, Chicago-owned Boyle Products Special driven by Chet Miller. When Miller prepared to round turn two, he found Bob Swanson still lying in the middle of the track, his car in flames against the wall, and a gigantic hole in the outer guardrailing where Floyd Roberts had exited the Speedway for the final time. To avoid running Swanson over, Miller veered to the left, missed Swanson by a matter of inches, then slid across the track, through the safety apron, and through the inner guardrailing, ripping out two lengthy board sections. Miller's number 3 flipped over on the grass in the infield some thirty feet from the track, hurling Miller out of the car and eventually into the hospital for a six-month convalescence. In ceremonies the following year, Miller was awarded a gold watch for his selflessness and bravery in the incident.

Wilbur Shaw, the eventual winner of the race, drove past the accident scene moments later: "Actually, I didn't know Roberts was involved at the time. I could see the Swanson and Miller cars, but Floyd's car had rolled down an embankment and was out of my range of vision, although the smoke and flames from it were very much in evidence." Shaw, whose win that day was his second of three eventual Indianapolis triumphs, did not take the second turn accident any less lightly than anyone else on race day in 1939: "I guess every race has its gruesome side," he reflected later. "I would just as soon not talk about it other than to say that Floyd Roberts, in going out, died the way he lived, thinking of somebody else. He was avoiding hitting Bob Swanson when he crashed to his death."

Emil Andres shared Wilbur Shaw's high regard for a fallen comrade: "I was out of the 1939 race before Floyd had his accident, and I didn't see it. I remember Floyd as being just a big farm boy from South Dakota. A terrific, fantastic guy, and honest as the day is long. He really didn't have a chance to win the 1939 race, though, with that four-cylinder Offy he was driving, because the Maseratis that Wilbur Shaw and Jimmy Snyder were driving were just about unbeatable that year. There was no way to get around those two unless they quit running."

But Roberts, Swanson, and Miller were not the only persons to suffer injury during the three-car crash. For the second year in a row, spectators were involved in turn two accidents. Mrs. Bruce Millikan of Thorntown, Indiana, sustained a broken leg after having been struck with a piece of flying debris probably originating from the outer guardrailing. Martha Ponclite, visiting the track with friends from Collinsville, Indiana, was hit about the head and shoulders with flying timber. Two men who were part of the on-track rescue team were also hurt. One of them, Glen Wills of Indianapolis, suffered burns on the head and neck. Another track attendant, William Allen of Brandenburg, Kentucky, paid a prolonged visit to the infield hospital with a forearm lacerated at the scene of the three-car accident in the southeast turn.

Harry Bennett, one of a number of AAA observers stationed around the course on race day 1939, rapidly transcribed a series of notes during the Floyd Roberts wreck. As the yellow caution light flashed, two-thirds of the track width in turn two was enveloped in flames from Bob Swanson's spilled fuel. at 2:20 P.M. One minute from the onset of the accident, Bennett wrote, "Three cars are in a mess, can't tell numbers, [need] help on job." The continuing sequence of his written impressions tell the story.

2:21   Fire apparatus arrived O.K.
2:24   Fire is in general path of cars on back stretch.
2:25   Fire not reduced any in last three minutes,
        another fire truck on apron. . . not much progress
        in reducing fire, seems same intensity on track
        and rail zone.

2:20	Car #3 [Chet Miller] on inside of guard rail, upside, #1 [Floyd Roberts] on outside of track, and #25 [Bob Swanson] is burning. Lots of water on straightaway from fire trucks.
2:30	Fire raging quite badly.
2:31	Fire broke out new on rail, really going again, appears worse than at any time.
2:33	Fire is out, track flooded with water, very bad.
2:37	One driver just taken across track on stretcher.
2:39	One driver dumped onto track, then fire broke out.

In all, thirty-one minutes were required to clear the track of debris, fire, and water. The green light flashed at 2:50 P.M. and the race was on again.

But the saga of the southeast turn was not over for 1939. Three-time race winner Louis Meyer, looking for his fourth win, was discontentedly riding in second position with three laps remaining in the race. Determined to catch leader Wilbur Shaw, Meyer came within ten feet of Shaw's elusive maroon tailfin as the two swept through the track's dangerous south chute. Meyer took the high groove in an effort to move around Shaw's Boyle Maserati. Whether the southeast turn was still showing the effects of the Swanson-Roberts-Miller accident of an hour before is difficult to say; but as Louis Meyer entered turn two he lost traction, rapped the wall, and began to spin up the backstretch, taking a long, diagonal slide against the inside guardrailing. Miraculously, the car remained upright as it hurled Meyer in the grassy safety area that insulated the backstretch spectators from the track itself. Also, miraculously, Meyer was uninjured. Having spun earlier that same afternoon in the south chute in his quest to overtake Wilbur Shaw, Meyer wisely interpreted two Speedway incidents in the same day to be a true and certain sign that he should retire from driving. His illustrious career, highlighted by three Indianapolis wins, was at an end.

It was anything but the end of turn two racing accidents, however. In the following year, when Argentinian champion Raoul Riganti started his third Indianapolis 500, he finished last after a particularly nasty-looking tailspin as he prepared to exit turn two on his twenty-fourth lap. His bright blue and yellow sixteen-cylinder Maserati was demolished totally after it plowed through thirty-five feet of low wooden inside guard-railing. Riganti, like so many other accident victims of that beltless era, was thrown clear. He too escaped serious injury.

In 1941, the grief fell on lanky Sam Hanks, a likable, twenty-six-year-old resident of Alhambra, California, who eventually made a distinguished Indianapolis record for himself with one first-place finish, one second, and two thirds in a dozen starts. But 1941 was not one of his better years. On May 29, the eve of the last race prior to the Second World War, the track was closed for a general cleanup and a flurry of eleventh-hour repairs. One final practice period for cars that had qualified for the race was designated in the early evening between six and six-thirty. Anticipating his second try at Indianapolis the following morning at eleven, Hanks took one final practice spin in his red number 28 Tom Joyce 7-Up Special, a conventional but cumbersome upright dirt-track machine with a 270-cubic-inch Offenhauser mounted in a Kurtis chassis. Making his way through the southeast turn at 6:15 P.M., Hanks felt the engine seize and the car drift into a slide. The car careened through the inner railing at the bottom of the second turn, and the impact threw Hanks halfway out of the cockpit. Hanks fell out completely as the racer turned on its top and moved through the railing a second time. It eventually came to rest on the safety apron. Listed in serious condition with a concussion and a left leg injury, Hanks's body was as badly bent as that of his car. Returned to Indianapolis after the war, Hanks was forced out of the 1946 race after eighteen laps in a car sponsored by musical madcap Spike Jones. He then took over for Reading, Pennsylvania's full-blooded Cherokee Indian driver Joey Chitwood and finished fifth in the Noc-Out Hose Clamp Special that had won the 1941 race with Mauri Rose and Floyd Davis taking turns at the wheel.

There was more unforeseen and undesirable excitement in the southeast turn during the 1946 practice runs when Swiss driver Rudi Caracciola, referred to by automotive historian Floyd Clymer as "a fearless driver of great ability," lost control of his Thorne Engineering Special and was heaved out of his car on his head, sustaining serious injuries from which he managed to recover. Only five minutes prior to the accident, wealthy car owner and sometime driver Joel Thorne had engaged in an altercation with AAA Chief Observer Ike Welch over whether Caracciola should be permitted on the track with a silk helmet instead of the usual fortified racing headgear. Welch held his ground, and the use of a more conventional helmet may well have saved the European driving champion's life. Reports from the scene of the accident indicated that Caracciola had been struck in the goggles by a low-flying bird, which blinded him temporarily and set the mishap into motion.

Today the tight board fence has disappeared. So have the guardrailings through which so many out-of-control cars went in the 1930s. Even so, the same white retaining wall is still there, and the southeast turn has the same bias and contour that Floyd Roberts knew. Inevitably, racing cars still experience trouble there occasionally, while others sail through it with repetitious grace and precision in quest of the prizes and prestige that accompany a thoroughgoing assault on speed at the world's most celebrated race course.

Chapter 5

FROM THE BROWNSBURG CARWASH TO THE NORTHEAST TURN

*F*rom a spectator's point of view, the least-examined section of the Indianapolis Motor Speedway is the portion of the track that curves through turn three, the northeast. Until an enlarged version of Grandstand L was constructed on the outside of the track in 1964, a relatively small contingent of the May racing crowd ventured over there. Even now, when the typical race-viewer prefers to situate himself along the main straight, turn three remains a somewhat less preferred region of the raceway. Because the approach and contour of the northeast is theoretically the same as the southwest, the only ostensible difference between them is to be found in the force and direction of wind gusts, always a critical consideration on high-speed tracks like Indianapolis. Like the other turns, however, the northeast is a nearly blind corner with very restricted driver visibility. And although the presence of warning lights around the course will keep a driver apprised of any especially hazardous situation that may lie ahead, the flashing of a red or yellow signal may come too late to prevent another mishap.

Turn 3 (near) and turn 4 (beyond), northeast and northwest respectively.

David Knox

Not always with the benefit of a sophisticated warning-light system, Egbert "Babe" Stapp competed in thirteen Indianapolis races between 1927 and 1940, earning a grand total of just under nine thousand prewar dollars. Born in San Antonio, Texas, and raised in California, Babe Stapp has not only been a driver, but a mechanic and a promoter of races as well. Today he lives comfortably and tidily, adjacent to the Brownsburg Carwash, which he owns and manages in the center of Brownsburg, Indiana, roughly five miles west of the Indianapolis Motor Speedway. Stapp is a witty, pleasant, and principled man. Auto racing in general, and the Speedway in particular, has been, more than any other influence, the controlling passion in his long eventful life: "In 1927, when I came back to Indianapolis, I paid a guy twenty-five dollars to let me ride in the rumble seat of his Chrysler from Los Angeles to the Speedway. It took us seven days, and it rained on me four days out of the seven. Four days! Everybody said to me, 'Boy, you must have been nuts,' and I said I was. Absolutely nuts. I wanted to drive that Speedway beyond anything else. I didn't care what. I would have walked there if I had had to. That Speedway was, and still is, the pinnacle of all."

Babe Stapp was at Indianapolis in 1930 for his fourth try at the great Memorial Day classic. Despite the social and economic ravages of the Depression, the race's attendance was estimated at 170,000, an increase of about 12 percent over the previous year. Gate receipts, according to one estimate, were up by 20 percent. At numerous landing fields and airports in the Indianapolis vicinity, aeronautics authorities anticipated about 150 aircraft bearing race fans from across America for the eighteenth running of the 500-mile race. A party of youths from Flora, Illinois copped first-in-line honors out on West Sixteenth Street near the Speedway's main pedestrian gate. The party, consisting of a dozen post-Jazz Age men all under the age of twenty, positioned their automobiles in line on Monday, and devoted the remaining part of the week to frolicking before Friday's race day.

Meanwhile, Indianapolis was all abuzz with the heartrending story of the Rain Baby, an infant abandoned by the side of Bluff Road at eight o'clock one rainy, cold evening, and not discovered until four-thirty on the following morning. The child was taken to an Indianapolis hospital for care and treatment, while police managed to solve the mystery of the child's origin, tracing it to a twenty-one-year-old divorcee from Bloomington, Indiana, who told reporters that she left the child because she had no home, no food, and no money. Two days later, a second infant was found abandoned in the back seat of an automobile parked behind the Indiana Theatre, where a traveling vaudeville troupe entertained the mounting pre-race crowd. Elsewhere, the Bandbox movie house featured a "Men Only" double bill consisting of *Pitfalls of Passion* and *Does White Slavery Exist?* The admission price — twenty-five cents.

Babe Stapp, unconcerned with white slavery and passionate pitfalls, resided with his wife at the Pennsylvania Hotel, from which he departed on race morning barely after daybreak. His car was a number 8 Duesenberg; all of the automobile—body, frame, engine, everything—was manufactured in Indianapolis. Both Stapp and his car were crowd favorites, although there were seven other Duesies in the thirty-eight-car field.

When the Speedway opened on race morning, 1930, the boys from Flora were among the first to enter the infield, followed by a huge race day contingent. Since two o'clock that morning, there had been nonstop bus service to the track available for ten cents in carfare, while trains shuttled passengers to the track from Indianapolis's Union Station for thirty-four cents, round trip. The city streets were alive with motor traffic. Wrote one reporter, "Nobility, society, and labor rubbed elbows at the eighteenth running of the American auto derby delux." Nobility at the Speedway? Definitely. "Nobility came to Indianapolis for the race," wrote still another scribe, "in the person of Baron Rothschild." The weather was clear as Speedway owner Eddie Rickenbacker appeared at the front gate at the wheel of an imposing, well-polished sixteen-cylinder Cadillac. He rolled his window down long enough to issue a statement to the waiting press: "Ninety-five miles an hour will win the race," he said confidently, almost arrogantly. Up went the window as Rickenbacker motored into the track's infield.

The area in and around the Speedway was amply stocked with law enforcement officers in quest of illicit booze. "Hip flasks, kegs of beer, and iced quarts will be targets of dry enforcement agencies at the Speedway Friday during the 500-mile auto classic," Police Chief Jerry Kinney announced. "The police will watch bus, railway, and traction stations, and the unloading terminal across from the Speedway entrance." The *Indianapolis Star* also warned that "federal agents probably will follow their usual custom of wandering about the grounds pursuing riotous parties."

As the cars that comprised the starting race line-up were pushed into position along the pit wall, Stapp's racer attracted attention with its striking blue and silver paint. Said pit lane stroller Norman Isaacs, "Babe Stapp's Duesenberg is one of the most beautiful jobs ever turned out by the local plant. And whoever said a Duesie wouldn't run? They're still running when the cows come home." Another of the eight Duesenberg drivers entered on this day was Chet Gardner, starting fifth in a green Buckeye Special. Amid the usual pomp and ceremony, all thirty-eight cars left the starting line promptly at 10:00. They were led by a stately front-drive Cord pace car driven by Wade Morton as they prepared to take Grantland Rice's starting flag the next time around. Babe Stapp recalls the situation clearly:

"We came down there for the start, and up toward the front of the pack was Chet Gardner, who had never practiced with a full tank of gas in his car. When you took your foot off the throttle with a full tank, the car just kept on going. That's what happened to Gardner. He flew down into that first turn, lost it, and hit the inside wall. Everybody missed him. Not a soul hit him. I don't know *how* they missed him, but they did.* Then on about the third lap I broke a throttle spring. I came into the pits, and the boys didn't have any spares, because nobody ever figured that we'd break one of those. So we bent it and straightened it out, and I went for about five more laps and it broke again. This time I told the crew, 'go get the spring off Chet's car.' They did, and I went back out and was running real good. In the meantime there were two new cars that Fred Duesenberg had built, great big old two-man cars. I called them 'portable bungalows,' and Fred got mad at me for saying that. You could have put a locomotive engine in them. Pete DePaolo was driving one and Bill Cummings the other [DePaolo came into the pits on his eighth lap, complaining that the car was unmanageable, and turned it over to relief driver Red Roberts, an Illinois dirt-track racer who had driven relief for Billy Arnold the year before at Indianapolis.] Pete came in and said that he couldn't drive that big old blunderbuss. I was gaining on Red Roberts all the way up the back straightway. He was maybe six car lengths ahead of me when he went into turn three with his tail-end coming out. He went down on the track, then started coming up again. I figured that the only thing I could do was to move down under him, which I did. But he started back down the track just as I got there at the 'psychological moment.' I hit him with my right front wheel, which drove my front axle clear back. It knocked me this way and him that way."

The ensuing six car pileup in turn three occurred on leader Billy Arnold's twenty-third lap. Roberts, driving DePaolo's

*Said one philosophic race reporter, "There is no criticism of Gardner; he was simply the accidental victim of one of the hazards of racing."

Duesenberg (reputed to be longest, if not the worst handling, car at the track) went into a skid coming out of the northeast turn, moving in the direction of an overhead bridge that was there then. On Roberts's final spin, Stapp hooked the rear end of Roberts's Duesenberg, which threw him into the outside and Roberts into the inside. Next on the scene was affable Johnny Seymour in a yellow and black front-drive Miller; he first plowed into Stapp and then into the wall. A Duesenberg piloted by Deacon Litz hit both Stapp and Seymour, parted ways with a left front wheel, and slid along the inside wall for more than five hundred feet. The fifth participant was car 54, driven by Marion Trexler, which smashed into Roberts beneath the overhead bridge, pushing its Lycoming engine through the radiator. Participant number six was Lou Moore at the wheel of a Coleman front-drive Miller, who executed a skid, punched into the outside wall (removing a large portion of it), and finally came to rest with both of his right side wheels perched neatly on the wall. Roberts was also atop the concrete retainer, his car balanced precariously.

Billy Arnold, who won the race that afternoon and who led for 198 of the 200 circuits, collided with one of the cars momentarily, but survived the brush with only a damaged left rear hubcap. Jimmy Gleason's number 7 Waverley Oil Special then picked up somebody else's spring leaf in the spokes of his right rear wheel. The leaf not only divested Gleason of his spokes, but stripped his timing gears. When the leaf dislodged, Gleason somehow coasted around to the pits, through for the afternoon. The yellow flew as damaged cars were towed from the track. Babe Stapp recalls the incident with faint ironic amusement: "I got my left hand scratched a little bit. I didn't know it at the time, but one of my knuckles must have jammed against something. But nobody had any serious injury at all. We all got out and walked away from it, you see. But that's an awful mess, to be sitting there looking the wrong way down the race track and seeing everybody spinning and coming right at you. It's just like the Hollywood Freeway." The accident, however, was not altogether trouble-free for the men who were involved. Deacon Litz left the Speedway that evening with his right wrist in a splint, and was prevented from competing in the next AAA championship race on the one-mile dirt oval at the Michigan State Fairgrounds at the Eight Mile Road in Detroit on June 6. Mechanic Johnny Apple, riding with Babe Stapp that afternoon, was treated for contusions on his right leg, as was Ted Everrode, the riding companion of Jimmy Seymour.

Whatever the explanation might have been, the Speedway's northeast turn may have proven more consistently troublesome in 1930 than at any time before or since. On the lap following the Roberts-Stapp-Litz-Seymour-Trexler-Gleason-Arnold mixup, still another car had trouble in turn three. "Waltz me around again, Willie," shouted an infield spectator. "There goes another one." It was unheralded Charles Moran, a rookie driver from Long Meadow, Massachusetts, sharing the cockpit of his cream-colored DuPont Motors Special with mechanic Gene Reed. After the boxy machine "kissed the wall," as one reporter expressed it, the occupants of the racer were injured only slightly. But the worst was yet to come on the northeast.

At the age of twenty-eight, Cy Marshall was the proprietor of a garage on Fort Wayne Avenue in Indianapolis. Twice married and the father of two children, Marshall had driven relief for Earl Devore during the 1928 race and finished eighteenth after a skirmish on the southwest turn. He had passed the race by in 1929 and returned in 1930 at the tiller of a green Duesenberg entered by George A. Henry, then a member of the Indianapolis City Council. As a local driver entered in a local car by a local politician, Marshall found special favor with the local press; one paper referred to him as "an Indianapolis boy, especially well-liked, and considered a good driver."

Qualifying tenth at a speed of 100.846 miles per hour, Marshall had given in somewhat reluctantly to his brother, thirty-four-year-old James Paul Marshall, Jr., who wanted to be his riding mechanic. Paul, a widower of three months, supported his four children by working as a carpenter and house painter in Detroit. Although Cy Marshall had acquired a middling reputation on Indiana dirt tracks, his brother had never set foot in a racing car, much less at Indianapolis. It was soon after the start of the 1930 race that, having somehow avoided Chet Gardner's first turn, first lap spin, the brothers experienced clutch trouble that necessitated a prolonged, sixteen-minute

Equipped with
Winfield Carburetor

CY MARSHALL, Driver -- Paull Marshall, Mech.
In DUESENBERG SPECIAL
Indianapolis Motor Speedway May 1930.

28385
KIRKPATRICK
619 W.WASH ST.
INDPLS.

Cy Marshall and Paul Marshall in Duesenberg Special, 1930.

Indianapolis Motor Speedway

pit stop. At the time of the accident involving Red Roberts, Babe Stapp, and the others, the Marshalls were several laps off the pace set by Billy Arnold. Returned to the track with their clutch problem tentatively corrected, the two entered the northeast on their twenty-sixth lap. As they came into view of the six-foot section missing because of the earlier accident, Cy Marshall may have been using as much throttle as he had with his clutch slipping, or the clutch may have ceased functioning altogether.

Whatever the explanation, the brothers felt their car begin to slide out of control and head toward the inside wall. Wrenching the steering wheel to the right to correct the slide, Cy Marshall succeeded only in pointing the Duesenberg toward the outer wall, loosening it for more than thirty feet.

The Duesey then veloplaned over the wall, fell about fifteen feet, nose-first, and then hurtled for another one hundred sixty-five feet before stopping. Cy Marshall, whose headgear offered little protection, lost his left ear, fractured his skull and jaw, and sustained numerous cuts and bruises. Both Marshalls were rushed to the infield hospital, where waiting physicians worked diligently to save both lives. Only Cy, who had been rescued from beneath the wreckage of his car, survived. Unaware of his brother's death, he pleaded with the medical staff to "fix Paul up first."

At City Hospital on the following day, Cy had recovered sufficiently to ask about his brother's condition and to request a newspaper. The question went unanswered and the request was denied. Marshall eventually recovered, and, after a hiatus of seventeen years, he qualified at Indianapolis once more, logging 197 laps in a supercharged Alfa-Romeo, and finished eighth.

Stylish Billy Arnold's winning speed in his front-drive Miller-Hartz Special was 100.448 miles per hour, a new record for 500 miles. With his winnings amounting to over $20,000 of the $97,600 total purse paid out to contestants, Arnold was in an expansive mood following the grind. "I'd been confident of winning for days," he announced triumphantly in a post-race interview. When the subject turned to the Marshall accident, which was the only fatality of 1930, Arnold was unequivocal. "Here's the way I see it," the Indianapolis champion speculated. "You're going to get it sometime. No matter where you are — walking down the street, standing in a building, or tearing down a race track. When your time comes, you go. So why stop racing?" Arnold, with the grandest pay check of his life, seemed similarly cavalier about the disappearance of his svelte Chrysler roadster, which had been sacked from the 1500 block of North Illinois Street on the day before the race. "Tell the guy (who stole it) to come around to my room and I'll give him the certificate of title," said the new reigning idol of Indianapolis. The invitation was never accepted, for while Billy Arnold made the rounds of post-race parties, police found the missing car at Twentieth and Meridian streets, and returned it that same evening.

In retrospect, seventy-four-year-old Babe Stapp reflects

often on the sport that has taken more than one close friend. As racing people, Stapp says, "we are associated with death. We know it, we accept it, and there's not much that we can do about it. Losing friends in racing hurts a lot, especially if they have been real close. I quit racing for a time after Bill Spence got killed in 1929. He and I were very close. You hate to lose a friend, regardless of whether it's in racing or not, but when the friend is racing, he seems a little bit closer to you. Some sports writers and editors condemn automobile racing because someone gets killed. But if a steelworker falls from a building, they don't make any big story about it because he's been doing something that's constructive; everybody can be a part of it, and use it, and appreciate it. There's a different attitude in sports, though. In horse racing, jockeys now and then get killed. Football players get killed. A race driver is out there racing because he wants to, or he wouldn't be driving in the first place. There's not much that can be done about it."

*   *   *

Indianapolis, 1931. Morning papers were on sale outside the gates along West Sixteenth and up Georgetown Road. SPEED-MAD FANS POUR INTO CITY FOR ANNUAL 500-MILE RACE TODAY. Leslie Seaward, a fireman from Savannah, Georgia, had pedaled his red bicycle 900 miles to see the race. He was the guest of the Indianapolis Fire Department at downtown headquarters, where he was given a bunk. Asked about his pending return to Georgia, Seaward told his fellow firefighters, "I'll not go so fast this time. Just take it easy and enjoy the way." The celebrated gate-crasher, none other than the inimitable One-Eyed Connelly, made his annual appearance and was up to his old tricks again at one of the Speedway gates. He feigned a fit and was chauffeured to the infield for medical attention. Left alone for a few minutes in the hospital, he devoured a bowl of apples designated for the race day medical staff. After being treated and advised to rest on a cot inside the hospital, he mysteriously disappeared minutes before the race was to begin. But Connelly's timing was off this year. The skies over Speedway were ashen gray and rain-laden. The race was delayed. The National Broadcasting System moved its air time from 2:15 P.M. to 4:15 P.M. Pre-race activities went on as scheduled, however, and as the crowd waited restively for skies to clear, Speedway's long-anticipated 1500-piece marching band proudly strutted up the homestretch to the tune of "Betty Coed."

Once the race began, however, the event was rife with excitement. "The race was remarkable because of the number of serious spills from which the drivers emerged almost unscathed," said one commentator. "Wilbur Shaw, in his 60th lap, while driving Phil Pardee's Duesenberg, skidded and climbed the outer wall." By pre-race arrangement, Shaw had agreed to relieve Pardee once the race was under way and join mechanic Walter "Otto" Hannowsky, who was all but hidden in the cockpit. Having had no practice time in the car, Shaw first sat behind its wheel as he was dispatched into competition after early race traffic had thinned itself out. With no regulations governing the addition of oil to cars during the race, the track was impossibly greasy. Pardee's Duesenberg, an unusually ornery, ill-handling missile, behaved even worse on a slippery track. "Weighing almost 2,400 pounds," Shaw said in his autobiography, the car "rode like a baby buggy." At 1:50 P.M. while Shaw and Hannowsky were in their sixteenth lap, the Duesenberg got out of shape on the northeast turn, spun, and went over the wall farther up the track, sailing at least twenty-five feet and taking out a considerable footage of telephone wire strung on utility poles anchored outside the turn. Landing on its wheels, the car rested momentarily in a cloud of dust before Shaw and Hannowsky crawled out. Shaw was unhurt, but Hannowsky's forehead was cut.

At the time of the mishap, Freddy Winnai in a Bowes Seal Fast Miller had swerved to avoid Shaw, drove through ten feet of outer wall a short distance from the Shaw accident, and landed upright with slight injuries to his back and leg. All three men were taken to the infield for medical scrutiny. Ambulance drivers "darn near killed us as they tried to set a new record for the trip to the emergency hospital over some of the roughest terrain ever navigated by a four-wheel vehicle," said Shaw, who had his superficial cuts and scrapes dressed with iodine before setting out for the pit area once again. Once there, he put on his helmet and goggles and reentered the race, relieving Jimmy Gleason at the controls of yet another orange and white Duesenberg which Shaw proceeded to pilot to sixth place. The victor, however, was toothy and diminutive Louis Schneider, a former motorcycle cop, driving his own Bowes Seal Fast Miller, a twin to the car that Winnai had put over the wall in the northeast.

The northeast furnished more undesirable race day excitement in 1932 as 1930 winner Billy Arnold ramped the wall on his fifty-ninth lap, rolled his gray and blue Miller-Hartz, and broke his shoulder blade. Mechanic Spider Matlock suffered a fractured pelvis. The incident turned out to be a curious reversal of the previous year, when it was Matlock who broke his shoulder and Arnold his pelvis in a northwest turn incident to be mentioned later.

But by 1933, however, a May 28 time trial mishap on the northeast had infinitely more serious consequences. The Brady and Nardi Special with thirty-two-year-old Bill Denver (William Orem) of Audubon, Pennsylvania, at the wheel spun out at about 110 miles per hour, sprang to the top of the banking, and catapulted down the embankment on the outside of the track. According to one observer, the car "spent its force against a tree." Denver and his mechanic Hugh "Bob" Hurst were hurled out as the car ruptured its tank and exploded in flame. Neither man survived. It had been on the Monday previous that driver Al Aspen and rider Mitz Davis both failed to survive a wreck in the same car when it struck the retaining wall on the inside edge of the southwest turn. Crews had worked uninterruptedly to restore the car for Sunday qualification runs, when Denver and Hurst were to have placed the machine in the field for the twenty-first running of the 500-mile classic.

On the occasion of the twenty-second running of the race in 1934, the atmosphere at the Speedway seemed ironically felicitous in contrast to the morose economic depression that had cast its pall over virtually every aspect of American life.

SEX ADDS TO SPEEDWAY COLOR was the headline for one reporter's impressions of the 1934 crowd that assembled at West Sixteenth Street and Georgetown Road: "Gay little ginghams and seersuckers, piqués and batistes went to the race today and won out in a big way in the fashion sweepstakes." Elsewhere in the news, Clyde Barrow, designated by the FBI as Public Enemy #1 in the Southwest, was killed in Louisiana after riding into a police ambush with his cigar-puffing gun moll, Bonnie Parker. Closer to home, Indianapolis police acknowledged that another fugitive had been sighted in the area: He was John Dillinger, destined to be lowered to his eternal rest beneath the sod of Indianapolis's Crown Hill Cemetery on West Thirty-eighth Street.

Over on West Sixteenth, however, the 1934 race was paced to a start by former relief driver William "Big Bill" Rader, latterly a Detroit automobile man, in a LaSalle. In the early going, Bill Denver's 1933 accident in the northeast was brought to mind once again when George Bailey, thirty-two, of Detroit, driving a beautiful tan, black, and white Studebaker-powered Scott Special, cleared the wall on the northeast, incurring injuries to his left wrist, along with numerous body bruises. His companion, Jim Johnson, sustained injuries to his head, occasioning a bloody nose and the loss of four teeth. Swathed in bandages, he was able to leave the Speedway hospital not long after being admitted.

Oily conditions were a menace during the 1934 race. Shaw noted in his autobiography that "it wasn't unusual for a car to use fifty or sixty gallons of oil in the Indianapolis event, and 80 percent of it was on the track during the late stages of any race. Every time a car stopped for fuel and tires, it also took another ten or twenty gallons of oil." Owing partially to oily conditions on the track, driver Gene Haustein's eight-cylinder Hudson spun around three times in the northeast turn while Haustein and riding mechanic Ed Beaudine were on their fourteenth lap. Their orange Martz Special eventually lost its momentum against the outer wall, with the car's nose pointed toward the inside of the track. According to reports, most of the oil in turn three had come from Shaw's Red Lion Miller, which had deposited the contents of its crankcase there. "Here again," said a local reporter, "is demonstrated the courage and sportsmanship of the drivers, in their desire to prevent further accidents, when Haustein and his mechanic braced themselves against his car and kept it from rolling down the track, thus preventing further accidents. For this courageous deed, Haustein was awarded the Julius Wark annual trophy, consisting of a Swiss timer."

But the incident was not yet over. Eager to rejoin the race, both driver and mechanic eased the car to the track apron and then attempted to restart their engine by pushing the bulky 2,100-pound speedster back into life. As the car gathered momentum, Haustein tripped the ignition switch and threw the racer into gear. As the Hudson began to sputter, Beaudine heaved himself on the tail of the car and prepared to crawl back into the passenger seat. Along came Doc MacKenzie in a tubby 2,559-pound orange Studebaker; he plowed into them, tearing out the tail of Haustein's car and hurling Beaudine back on the track. Paradoxically, no serious injuries resulted from the fracas.

In the 1934 race, only a few drivers wore helmets worthy of the name. The rest wore jaunty, tight-fitting, aviation-inspired cloth caps that fastened around the chin and were, in an accident, the next best thing to worthless. In 1935, however, hard helmets became a requirement, although the AAA mandate was hampered by an insufficient inventory of approved headgear. Some of the helmets, like those worn by Bob Sall and Jimmy Snyder, caused the driver's head to resemble a twenty-five-pound jellybean, and afforded little protection around the temples or at the base of the skull.

AAA Eastern Dirt Track Champion Johnny Hannon, a twenty-five-year-old Norristown, Pennsylvania, rookie at Indianapolis in 1935, needed every bit of the protection he could find. On May 19, while establishing a new one-lap record of 40.61 seconds on the one-mile dirt track at the Wisconsin State Fairgrounds in Milwaukee, Hannon crashed through the inside fence and rolled his car twice in an immense cloud of dust without injury to himself or any spectators. Undaunted, his next stop was Indianapolis, where he had been offered his first Speedway ride in one of Leon Duray's red, white, and black Bowes Seal Fast cars. Hannon arrived in town with his long-suffering mechanic Oscar "Shorty" Reeves, an Indianapolis native who had ridden with Hannon for five years on the dirt tracks and had the scars to prove it. Both Leon Duray and driver Tony Gulotta insisted, however, that they each take practice runs with Hannon to familiarize him with the track before they set him free on the bricks with Reeves as his riding passenger. Hannon agreed. Duray and Gulotta cautioned Hannon not to take much liberty with the turns at Indianapolis, nor to underestimate their potential peril.

The weather was clear on Tuesday morning, May 21, when Gulotta eased behind the wheel of the car for his final practice session, turning in a lap at 117 miles per hour. He returned to the pits, where Hannon and Reeves were given the go-ahead to practice on their own. Reeves, an employee of Indianapolis's Sugar Creek Creamery by day and a dance band drummer at the local Alpine Inn by night, gamely joined Hannon in the Bowes cockpit. Whereas even experienced Indianapolis drivers work up to speed gradually, methodically becoming accustomed to both car and track, Johnny Hannon took no such precaution. Taking to the track with his right foot hard on the throttle, he roared into the first turn, the second turn, and up the back stretch at what sounded like full bore. But at the approach to turn three, the car began to zig-zag and skidded toward the inside wall without making contact. It then made an abrupt turnabout and headed into the outside wall, where it removed a yard of concrete as it left the track entirely. Hannon was thrown an estimated fifty feet, suffering head and chest injuries that took his life. Reeves survived.

Although the excitement in turn three during the running of the 1935 race was less serious, there was excitement nonetheless. The protagonist was Junior Oldham, aged thirty-six, of Louisville, Kentucky. He allegedly arrived the Wednesday prior to the Friday race, somehow entered the infield unnoticed, and climbed a very tall tree near the northeast turn. He was supposedly still in the tree during the running of the race, but fainted when the contest was about half completed and became wedged between two large branches sixty feet from the ground. The crowd below him summoned patrolman Plez Oliver of the Indianapolis Police Department, who summarily borrowed a hundred-foot length of rope and enlisted the services of Renciel Williams, described by newspaper reporter Robert Early as a "Negro tree climber, 1850 Peck Street," who assured Patrolman Oliver that he could "shinny up a tree like a cat." After Williams had scaled the tree, tied the rope around Oldham's chest, and given a signal to the resourceful Oliver, Oldham was lowered gingerly to earth. "When Williams had scrambled to the ground," wrote Early, "spectators praised him, slapped him on the back, and showered him with coins," after which Williams "gathered them in his hat and ambled away. . ."

*　　*　　*

It was 1941. Sam Hanks had destroyed his Tom Joyce 7-Up Special and injured himself in a final practice run on the day before the race. He was scored in thirty-third and last place in the race that was yet to be run. On the following morning, the weather was overcast and foggy, with light rain falling. At 6:10 A.M. a fire broke out in mechanic Eddie Offutt's Miller garage, where electric heaters had been trained on oil cans to warm their contents. A mechanic placed an oil drain pan on car 35, to be driven by George Barringer. The pan exploded in flame. Offutt's other Miller, car 12, to be driven by Al Miller, was hurriedly removed from the garage before it too caught fire. Not until 8:00 was the conflagration under control. With Hanks's and Barringer's cars out of commission, the 1941 field was reduced to thirty-one starters.

With five laps down, attention was on the northeast again, where Emil Andres in a yellow and red Kennedy Tank Special fitted with a six-cylinder Lenki engine spun as he prepared to exit the turn. He was struck by twenty-six-year-old Joel Thorne, a controversial millionaire from Burbank, California, driving his own car. Andres was hit on the left side and spun still another time, after which he hit the wall and rolled to the center of the track. Out of turn three came Louis Tomei in a black, front-drive Offenhauser, making his eighth bid at Indianapolis. Tomei collided with Thorne, and survived the mishap with his right front innertube unaccountably wrapped around his axle. Continuing around to the pits, he replaced his right front wheel and charged back on the track to finish all 500 miles in eleventh position. Thorne and Andres were unhurt, and their cars were towed off the course. Starter Seth Klein displayed the yellow for the next 75 miles of the race while incidental debris was cleared from the track.

* * *

After World War II, during which the Indianapolis Motor Speedway clearly showed the ravages of neglect, the green AAA observation platforms located at points outside the track were made only somewhat less unwieldy when flat stones were eased beneath their legs to render them less wobbly. Occupying the observation stand in the northeast turn in 1946 were three Chicagoans, Jimmy Thompson, Harry Lynch, and Bill Vanderwater. Between 1954 and 1961 Vanderwater was to become the chief starter for the 500-mile race, succeeding Seth Klein, who had held that assignment since 1934. Vanderwater, the regular flagman on the AAA midget car circuit acquired a reputation as a natty dresser and an accomplished tippler.

The resumption of racing at Indianapolis after the war brought with it some monumental problems in track restoration, driver relations, and traffic management. A unionist aggregation of drivers who called themselves ASPAR (American Society of Professional Automobile Racing), with driver Ralph Hepburn as its spokesman, threatened to strike unless promised that they would be offered 40 percent of the Speedway's gate receipts. The threat of a strike was ultimately averted through the use of an intermediary, sportswriter Bill Fox, Jr., who negotiated an arrangement between the dissident drivers and the Speedway management that permitted the race to be run as originally contemplated.

The orderly movement of race day crowds in 1946 was perhaps a less contemplated problem, however. "As the thirtieth renewal of the 500-mile race started here today," wrote Fox after the race had been run, "thousands of persons were milling outside the gates, victims of the worst traffic jam in the city's history." He continued, "Several squads of police fought traffic at Union Station as race-goers waited in line for the railway facilities to the Speedway. All along the route which I followed in reaching here in exactly three hours time, people were leaving their cars, running ahead to farm houses, and grabbing buckets of water to pour into overheated motors."

With a significant proportion of the spectators still outside the track, the race got underway at 11:00 A.M. as scheduled. At sixteen laps, Paul Russo had crunched his Fageol Twin Coach twin-engined number 10 against the wall at the northeast turn, breaking a leg as he was thrown from the car. Russo had dipped below the inner white line, slid into some soft infield dirt, and then hit the wall practically head-on. A loud explosion sounded as Russo's front tires burst from the impact. While this was taking place, car 31, an orange and black Automobile Shippers Special driven by English-born Henry Banks, slid deeply into the track's inner apron opposite Russo, finally coming to rest with his rear wheels mired in the dirt. Eased out by a wrecker, Banks's car continued around the course under its own power.

At 12:50 that same afternoon, exactly thirty minutes after the Russo accident, Mauri Rose, in a number 8 Blue Crown, banked his car against the wall in the northeast, amid a sizable cloud of dust and debris. This was Rose's fortieth lap, during which he had slid through turn three just as a rescue truck was preparing to remove Russo's rumpled Fageol. Rose's Blue Crown piled into Russo's wreckage, and Rose himself was dumped on the track. Having crawled to the outer wall, he was assisted over by track attendants and made to lie down on the wall itself. Rose's mishap was not altogether unanticipated by Thompson, Lynch, and Vanderwater, however, inasmuch as they had observed him execute two shorter slides through the northeast on earlier laps. In twelve minutes, the track had been cleared and the race was on again.

When another English-born driver, thirty-seven-year-old George Robson of Maywood, California, crossed the finish line first in 1946, eight other cars were still cruising around the track, with ninth place finisher Bill Sheffler some sixty-one circuits behind Robson himself. Most of the remaining twenty-four cars, predominently prewar reruns, had fallen victim to numerous categories of mechanical failure. Robson collected $42,350, an around-the-world airline ticket, and a gratuitous year of dining at Wheeler's restaurant. His career cut short by a double fatality with George Barringer the following September at Atlanta's Lakewood Park dirt track, Robson did not survive long enough to enjoy his Indianapolis winnings fully.

In 1947, a northeast turn incident was a curious reminder of the year before, when Henry Banks had spun his orange Automobile Shippers car. Recently discharged from the Navy, thirty-three-year-old Frank Wearne, a 200-pound driver from Pasadena, California, spun another orange and black number 31 racer entered as the Superior Industries Special. Although the machine was not the same that Banks had driven, the ownership of the car was. Wearne's short wheelbase Offenhauser had once dominated competition at the Pike's Peak hill climb, and its stubby upright Miller chassis appeared to be far more suited to dirt tracks than for a realistic threat at the Indianapolis 500. Wearne looped the car on his 138th lap without hitting anything. In this, his seventh consecutive race at Indianapolis, he motored on around the track and into the pits, where he called for relief. Veteran Louis Tomei took over the driving chores, finishing fourteenth. Wearne, who had finished in the first ten of five occasions, had made his final Brickyard appearance.

Ralph Hepburn had fifteen Indianapolis starts behind him in 1948, having made his Speedway debut in a Miller Special in 1925. Out of competition since 1946, when he piloted a Novi to fourteenth place, Hepburn was fifty-two when he replaced Cliff Bergere behind the wheel of one of Lew Welsh's two Novis. Bergere had spun during a practice session and declared that the Novi to which he was assigned was indeed unsafe to drive. Hepburn, in the meantime, had arrived at the track with one of Don Lee's supercharged twelve-cylinder Mercedes-Benz racers. When Welsh offered him the seat of Bergere's vacated Novi, he agreed immediately. Referring to the Novi, he told his historian friend Charles Lytle, "That's my baby." One of the most admired of competitors at Indianapolis, Hepburn had raced motorcycles as far back as 1915, and had as his goal a win at the 500-mile race. With a third-place finish in 1931, a fifth in 1935, a second in 1937, and a fourth in 1941, Hepburn had repeatedly come within striking distance of realizing his ambition.

When Bergere's Novi was repaired and deemed trackworthy, Hepburn posed for photographers shortly before he took to the track for a shakedown run on May 17. It proved to be his last. Having turned one practice lap at 133 miles an hour, the front-drive, supercharged Novi slid sideways as Hepburn attempted the northeast turn on the following lap. Pointed toward the bottom of the track, the car dipped below the white line and onto the grassy infield. As Hepburn applied throttle to regain control, the car swung 180 degrees, headed back on the track, and shot toward the wall, where it connected at an angle of 45 degrees to the track itself. Hepburn's helmet and goggles flew off from the force of impact, as Hepburn himself went momentarily out of the cockpit and then back inside it once more.

According to Wilbur Shaw, not another car took to the Speedway that day, as a pall descended over the track and its occupants. The tragedy prompted Chet Miller to withdraw as the driver of the other Novi and to be superseded by perennial Speedway favorite, Dennis "Duke" Nalon, who guided the car to third place in the 1948 race. *Motorbook* publisher Floyd Clymer was part of the huge funeral entourage that descended on Glendale, California's Forest Lawn Cemetery. It was a double funeral service, Hepburn's eighty-three-year-old father having succumbed four days after his son's death. The elder Hepburn, according to reports, had never been notified of his son's passing.

Articulate Duke Nalon, one of nine children born into a working class Chicago family, had risen to eminence in the American racing scene by distinguishing himself in every kind of racing car on every kind of track, including the kind fabricated from boards. He spent his autumnal years as a driver in Sherman Oaks, California. Perhaps more than anyone else, he was to become firmly identified in the public mind with the famous and infamous Novi racing cars after the death of Ralph Hepburn, and returned to Indianapolis during the ensuing six years without improving on his third-place finish in 1948. There were times, however, when Nalon seemed certainly on the verge of a long-sought victory at Indianapolis. Establishing a new four-lap track standard of 132.939 miles per hour, the fabled "Iron Duke" placed his Novi on the coveted pole starting position for the thirty-third running of the Indianapolis 500 in 1949. Sharing the front row that year was teammate Rex Mays in another Novi, while sophomore starter Jack McGrath occupied the outside starting position in a dirt-track car whose appearance could hardly have been more dissimilar.

Race day in 1949 was to become the most memorable day in the life of Duke Nalon, not only for what happened to him on the track, but for what happened off it. Minutes before the start of the race, Novi owner Lew Welch ordered his garages cleared of all persons except himself and his drivers Nalon and Mays. Once the door had been closed securely, Welch's message was as direct as it was surprising: as long as both cars were running competitively, one car was forbidden to pass the other for the lead. Furthermore, said Welch, whichever of his drivers was ahead at the end of the first lap, was to remain ahead; the other driver was not to overtake him. On the remote chance that the Novis were to finish the race in the first two positions, the prize money was to have been divided equally, and Welch (in Nalon's words) "did not want Rex and me to be running through our rubber trying to pass each other." Both drivers, nevertheless, were aghast. Any violation of this pre-race understanding, said Welch, would result in the guilty driver's being black flagged (disqualified) and fired from the Novi racing team.

The twin front-drive Novi racers with their supercharged eight-cylinder engines were not the twins that they were alleged to be. Both machines were equipped with three forward speeds, but the gear ratios in Mays's car were all in a lower range than those in Nalon's car. Side by side on the backstretch on the pace lap, Nalon (having thrown kisses to the crowd) heard Mays rev his engine and slip into second gear. Nalon assumed Mays would race him to the starting line in this intermediate gear, and then make a determined effort to remain ahead at the conclusion of the first lap of the race. At the north chute, Nalon pulled somewhat ahead of Mays, revved his own engine, and made an obvious gesture of slipping into his own second gear. It was, however, no more than a gesture, and Nalon intentionally held his car in low. Mays, assuming that his second gear would out-drag Nalon's felt confident that he would reach the starting line first, and that he would be able to take the lead and hold it for the crucial first lap. For Duke Nalon, the ruse worked; laying his foot down hard on the throttle, he wound the Novi's engine to its uppermost limits, floating its valves, and reached the starting line first. At least four cars crossed the line ahead of Wilbur Shaw's Oldsmobile pace car. Shifting into second gear and then into third, Nalon held the lead by several yards on the backstretch. On the first lap of the race, Detroiter George Lynch spun his Automobile Shippers Special in the first turn, rapped the wall, and ended in the infield. In an accident that could well have ended more seriously, he suffered only a broken ankle. After Seth Klein's green flag appeared again, Nalon turned a record race lap of 126.564, establishing still another record for the first twenty-five miles of the race. At the fifty-mile mark, he continued to hold the lead, with Mays trailing.

His racing luck, however, was brief. Moving up the backstretch into turn three, Nalon's left rear axle snapped. The Novi's weight loaded on the right-hand side of the car, and the left rear axle and wheel had come detached. Riding behind Nalon was Mauri Rose, who had won the previous two races and recognized the problem before Nalon did. On this, Nalon's twenty-third lap, the ensuing accident was unfortunately reminiscent of Hepburn's accident the year before. Nalon began to spin toward the base of the northeast turn, while the departed left rear wheel rolled to the outer edge of the track and rebounded off the wall, as Nalon himself would do momentarily. As the car backed to the top of the track, its fuel tank ruptured, igniting almost a hundred gallons of fuel, a mixture of 90 percent methanol and 10 percent benzol. A fiery trail followed the white Novi as it skirted the contour of the retaining wall, backwards. When the car came to a stop against the wall, both left wheels were missing, and the car had deposited an eight-foot-high wall of flame down the track. The force of the explosion had blown the seams out of his driving uniform and Nalon was burned extensively. He unbuckled himself and left the wall. His fate was to spend the next four months in Methodist Hospital, where painful skin grafts were performed. So tightly were the grafts applied to the backs of his hands and fingers that Nalon's ability to achieve a tight grip

Dennis "Duke" Nalon in 1969, twenty years after his crash in the northeast and northwest turns.

David Knox

on the steering wheel was seriously impaired. Back in Gasoline Alley following the 1949 race, Welch denied that the Nalon accident had been triggered by an axle failure, although a photo sequence of the mishap clearly contradicted his denial. After his dismissal from Methodist Hospital the following September, Nalon recovered sufficient strength to make a courageous return to the Speedway the following year, but failed to qualify his Novi for the 1950 race.

In the rain-abbreviated 1950 classic, Troy Ruttman and Jim Rathmann (both eventual winners at Indianapolis) spun in the northeast as rainwater flooded the track almost instantly. In 1952, when the 245-pound Ruttman won the race at the age of

1953: the hottest 500. Early going with Tony
Bettenhausen, Jim Rathmann, Pat Flaherty and
Gene Hartley in turn 1.

twenty-two, the victory had seemed securely in the hands of
hard-charging Bill Vukovich, then in his second Indianapolis
appearance. His car, a mouse-gray fuel injection roadster
entered by Californian Howard Keck and prepared by Jim
Travers and Frank Coon, developed steering problems on
Vukovich's 192nd lap. Vukovich had been hampered by the
steering wheel's tendency to twist rightward as he ap-
proached the Speedway's third turn in the middle of the track
rather than in the running groove. His car veered to the right,
scraped the retaining wall, bounded off, and scraped it a
second time before it ceased running at 3:45 P.M. in the afternoon. A thoroughly disgusted Vukovich climbed out of the car
unhurt, glanced beneath the hood, and hopped the wall to
safety. Refusing to check in at the Speedway hospital,
Vukovich stayed with his stalled car at the northeast turn for

the remaining eight laps of the race as Ruttman inherited the lead and crossed the finish line waving his bare right arm in triumph. Vukovich's wife, Esther, in the meantime, waited at the hospital in a state of near hysterics, believing that her husband had suffered injuries during the mishap. Vukovich was indeed injured, but not physically so. "What a dirty lousy break!" he exclaimed back in Gasoline Alley. "That Ruttman never won an easier one!" As Ruttman declared that he could drive still another five hundred miles that same afternoon, Vukovich vowed to return to the Speedway in 1953 a winner.

Duke Nalon's difficulties in the Speedway's northeast turn were still not over, however. During the latter stages of the 1953 race, track temperatures reached 130°F. Relief driving, gone well out of fashion in later years, was at a near record as drivers found themselves physically incapable of tolerating the suffocating heat of the day in addition to the sweltering fumes that blew back in their cockpits from overheated engines. Tony Bettenhausen had patted himself on the helmet during the race, indicating to his crew that he required relief. He was replaced by his teammate, 1952 AAA National Driving Champion Chuck Stevenson, who in turn surrendered the wheel of car 98 to youthful Gene Hartley, a second generation midget car standout from Roanoke, Indiana. Hartley, who had spun earlier that afternoon in another car, spun for a second time in what was Bettenhausen's Agajanian dirt track machine. The accident occurred as the cream and red Kuzma chassis was on its 196th trip around the northeast, where Hartley guided the car in serpentine fashion, finally contacting the wall on the north straightaway. Nalon, back for still another assault on Indianapolis, spun his Novi into the grass in an effort to stay out of Hartley's path. Neither driver was injured as the yellow caution light flashed for fifty seconds before Seth Klein's red flag brought the day's racing to a halt, partly because spectators had broken down a section of the fencing at the north end of the track and had converged on the area of the Nalon-Hartley accident.

Bill Vukovich, well accustomed to the sun that fell with scorching intensity over the grape vineyards of Fresno, California, was the winner. The loser was Carl Scarborough of Clarkston, Michigan, who had made an obscure reputation for himself in mostly non-AAA sanctioned big car races, and who gave his age as thirty-eight. Scarborough died of heat exhaustion at the infield hospital while Californian Bob Scott continued in his his mahogany and copper hued McNamara Kurtis Draft dirt track car for 190 laps, finishing twelfth. As the race ended under the red flag, the liberal supply of eligible relief drivers had been exhausted, and more than one racer capable of continuing the 500-mile race was abandoned along pit lane, driverless.

The intense heat of the day had taken its toll in the northeast earlier that afternoon, as drivers doggedly continued to give their best under circumstances that would have destroyed men of lesser stamina. With three laps down, former prizefighter Andy Linden, of Manhattan Beach, California, spun twice. Jerry Hoyt of Indianapolis, yet another second generation driver spun his turquoise number 55 dirt-track car from Tulsa, Oklahoma, in an effort to avoid Linden. One hour and eight minutes later, Pat Flaherty, a red-headed Chicago bartender who had signalled his pit crew frantically on the previous lap, spun through the northeast and struck the outer wall, continuing for another 270 feet after the original contact. Not seriously injured, Flaherty found himself trapped temporarily in the car while crews struggled to free him, which they did in less than seven minutes.

Except for Vukovich, who collected $89,496.96 in prize money the following evening and enjoyed a kind of cosmic revenge on his miserable luck only a year before, Indianapolis 1953 was not a memorable occasion for most people present.

It was not until 1958 that the most complicated, most photographed, and most discussed of all Speedway mishaps in the northeast turn occurred. Instead of the usual practice of lining cars on the track prior to the start of the race, the 1957 and 1958 races had all thirty-three starters positioned at an angle along the pit wall, with each driver buckled in and prepared to go racing. The lining-up of starters in eleven rows, three abreast, turned into a monumental fiasco in 1958, as it had threatened to do the year before. Pole sitter Dick Rathmann, along with pugilistic Ed Elisian and Oklahoma's Jimmy Reece, anticipated the signal to fall in behind the Pontiac pace car, but moved in front of it instead. The result was that the front three cars were at one end of the track, while the thirty other contestants were at the other. Receiving contradictory signals and instructions from United States Auto Club officials on the one hand, and from pit crews on the other, the trio did not know whether to speed up and join the pack, or to slow down and allow the pack to join them. Three laps later, when 1957 Indianapolis winner Sam Hanks pulled the pace car off the track, the field was in relatively orthodox formation for the waving of starter Bill Vanderwater's green banner.

During the month of preparations that led to this most climactic of moments, Rathmann and Elisian had been locked in a battle for speed supremacy that had become an intense personal warfare of nerves. After one driver had turned in a rapid practice lap, the other followed with a still more rapid performance. In winning the pole position for the 1958 race, Rathmann had registered a four-lap average of 145.974 miles per hour on the electric eye. Elisian, who cultivated an unnerving way of dirt tracking his car through Indy's four turns, was only a tick of the stopwatch behind, with a four-lap sequence of 145.926. The cars were nearly identical Watson chassis powered by Drake Offenhausers. Johnny Boyd, from Fresno, California, who had qualified nearly two miles per hour slower, started in eighth position. He remembers ninth place starter Tony Bettenhausen's paying him a garage visit the day before the 1958 race. "Tony warned me," Boyd recalls, "that there was probably going to be trouble up front at the start of the race, and that I had better hang back in the pack with him until things got sorted out up there. That's pretty much what I did, except that after we got the green flag, I found myself leading one pack of cars on the backstretch, while Tony was a little farther back leading another group. I kept my eye on the third turn all the while, wondering if and when something was going to happen. Sure enough it did, and I headed for the infield grass, pretty much as I had planned."

Bettenhausen's prediction of trouble was, unfortunately, borne out. Elisian and Rathmann had charged into the northeast turn at full tilt, each seeming to dare the other to back off the throttle last. As Rathmann pulled his car behind Elisian's, Elisian began to slide out of control in front of Rathmann and the other thirty-one cars. Rathmann's roadster followed suit, and the two cars backed into the number three turn side by side. The chain of events that followed almost defies sequential description. Reece's was the next car to whirl around. He was struck from the rear by Bob Veith and shoved into the path of Pat O'Connor, who in turn rode over Reece's wheels. For an instant, the front of O'Connor's dark blue Sumar Special hung ominously over Reece's head. Then it rolled over, landed wrong side up, then righted itself. For several seconds, there were two cars off the track for every car on it. Jerry Unser's McKay Special ramped over Paul Goldsmith's yellow City of Daytona car and sailed over the wall. Unser sustained only a broken shoulder, making him the last man ever to clear the wall at Indianapolis. Drivers Len Sutton and Art Bisch found their cars too bent to continue. O'Connor was dead. His car was demolished, as were seven other racers. Veith, a hulking driver from Oakland, California, limped his Bowes Seal Fast car around to the pits with a leaking gas tank, thereby logging one full lap which finished him ahead of seven other contestants.

What had impressed me about the whole horrendous accident was having seen O'Connor early that morning in mufti, seeming fit and vivacious. He had paid one final visit to pit row for the purpose of giving his car a last check. Two hours later he reappeared in driving coveralls, and a half an hour later he was dead. When the day ended, I was struck by the fearsome contrast of a man living and a man not living.

Cigar-chomping Arizona cowboy Jimmy Bryan, whose racing exploits on dirt tracks accounted for the better part of his truly legendary reputation, managed to evade the O'Connor accident and win the race in a yellow Epperly chassis with a lay-down sidewinder Meyer and Drake engine. In second place was a car of virtually the same description, driven by Wisconsin's George Amick. Boyd was third, Bettenhausen fourth. After the race, Bettenhausen paid Boyd still another visit. "In a way," said Bettenhausen, "it was a good thing that there was trouble at the start over in turn three." Boyd asked why. "Because," said Bettenhausen, "you would have been the laughing stock of the Speedway, driving all over the grass that way, while the rest of us were on the track where we were supposed to be."

Boyd looked up. "What about you, Bettenhausen? You were down there with me."

Bettenhausen shook his head. "I stayed on the track where I belonged."

Boyd remembers the conversation with amusement, "I looked at the films of the wreck later," he recalls, "and Tony was mowing the grass down there with the rest of us."

Among the entries for the 1959 race was driver Bob Cortner, a rookie who had captured the Bay Cities Racing Association Midget Championship in 1957. He was assigned to car 51, the Cornis Engineering Special. On Friday, May 15, the car began leaking oil badly, necessitating the postponement of the final stages of Cortner's driver's test. On the Monday following the first weekend of time trials, Cortner finished the test to the satisfaction of his examiners. Almost immediately afterward, driver (and later car builder) Don Edmunds, of Anaheim, California, offered Cortner the seat of his Braund Plywood Special. Cortner asked for a day to consider the offer, and in the meantime, the car went to another Anaheim driver, Van Johnson. The following day, May 19, was extremely gusty and therefore unusually hazardous for drivers searching for speed at Indianapolis. Called into the pits to correct a faulty brake, Cortner was sent out for another round of practice laps in the Cornis car. In the northeast turn, the United States Auto Club's observer that day was Johnnie Parsons, winner of the rain-abbreviated 1950 race, who reported that a wind gust had evidently taken Cortner unaware, causing him to spin into the infield, then travel 138 feet into the wall. Unconscious, Cortner was removed to Methodist Hospital, where he lived until 6:50 P.M. that evening.

It was, all told, a bad year in the northeast. During the forty-fifth lap of the race itself, the McKay Special, with Illinois driver Chuck Weyant at the helm, went out of control and spun near the outside wall. He was struck by Mike Magill, who managed to wedge himself between Weyant and the wall. Magill stood his roadster on end for a moment before sliding over the upper regions of the track, upside down, for about 250 feet. He hit the wall again, and then slid into the infield. Weyant, meanwhile, parked in the middle of the track.

Texas dirt tracker Jud Larson came together with Indiana's

Richard "Red" Amick as they struggled to avoid Weyant's black and yellow car, joining Magill in the infield. Although he had served with the air force in the South Pacific in the Second World War, Magill had never been as imperilled as he was at this moment. He sustained a back injury that required a period of convalescence in a hospital and at the home of car owner George Walther in Dayton, Ohio. He returned to Indianapolis for another two years, failing to qualify for the race both times.

At 115 laps in the same race, Ray Crawford (who owned not only his Indianapolis racer, but a chain of supermarkets in California as well) crashed in the same northeast turn. The former P-38 pilot suffered injuries judged to be even more serious than those Mike Magill had suffered earlier in the day. Like Magill, Crawford managed a comeback to the Speedway for the next two races, but did not comprise part of the starting lineup either time.

In more recent years, the story of the Speedway's northeast turn has evolved through a succession of incidents with less serious overtones. Having spun on the previous circuit of the track, the loquacious racing comedian, Eddie Sachs of Center Valley, Pennsylvania, slid his Bryant Heating and Cooling Special, a front-engine Watson roadster, through the northeast at 181 laps in the 1963 race after having lost a left rear wheel. With characteristic flair, Sachs set out in search of the errant wheel, which he recovered and rolled a mile back to the pits, waving to an appreciative crowd all the while. Then, at the same location, Roger McCluskey spun through accumulated oil on his 198th lap while riding securely in third place with little more than two laps remaining. Having made a clockwise half turn, McCluskey hit the wall and came to a stop in the middle of the north chute.

On the day following the race, Sachs and McCluskey targeted their complaints at previous day's winner Rufus "Parnelli" Jones and at the reigning chief steward, Harlan Fengler. "One thing about him," Sachs said of Jones, "he sprays oil all over the track. I can't begin to tell you how many lives were in jeopardy because of it." He continued, "I went up the back straightaway, the whole straightaway, and to this day I don't know how I kept control." McCluskey agreed, say-

Turn 3. Mel Kenyon's Sprite Special after an accident on his tenth lap, 1971.

ing that his own spin had cost him between thirty and forty thousand dollars in potential prize money. The confrontation ended when Jones decked Eddie Sachs. Said Milt Dunnell of the *Toronto Star*, "The enemy had the oil. . . the losers lacked experience."

McCluskey found himself relief driving for Mel Kenyon in the 1970 race. His racer, a brilliant green car painted in the promotional colors of its sponsor's product (Sprite), spun again in the northeast, taking sportscar driver Ronnie Bucknam with him. Although Allen "Sammy" Sessions, Bobby Unser, and Jerry Grant were all involved in the mixup, there were no casualties. Race day crowd injuries continued to be the rule rather than the exception, however. At five that morning, when the Speedway's gates were opened to the public, three men were injured when they attempted to scream through a track underpass on two Harley-Davidsons. The result was a jumbled mass of twisted motorcycles, two men flown by helicopter to Methodist, and a third operated upon then and there by a team of Speedway physicians for a ferocious hematoma. Later that afternoon, a man with severely sunburned legs wandered into the track hospital requesting a pair of pants.

A curious replay of some 1970 third turn action presented itself in 1971. Kenyon, a born-again Christian, was back once more in a number 23 Sprite Special, although he had exchanged his Meyer and Drake from the previous year for a Ford V-8. Only ten laps of the race had been completed when Steve Krisiloff, of Parsippany, New Jersey, in a new, fluorescent red STP Gas Treatment car "lunched" his Ford engine which in turn divested itself of both oil and water through the northeast turn. Pursuing Krisiloff hotly, Kenyon inherited a well-oiled track which inevitably caused him to spin, trail the wall for a hundred feet, and stop with the car's rear quarters crunched against the wall. With firemen to his left and right, and with a third fireman en route, Kenyon extricated himself from the car at a leisurely pace until he spotted the orange number 7 Norris Industries car, Gordon Johncock aboard, driving straight toward his disabled racer. Kenyon, halfway out of his car, slid all the way back in again, and then some. Johncock went up and over the Sprite car as the three terrified firemen backed themselves as closely against the wall as possible.

It was, said veteran Kenyon, "the hairiest thing that ever happened to me." After removing his helmet, Kenyon discovered Johncock's black tiremarks across it. Cut slightly about the shinbone, Kenyon reported to the infield hospital, where he was told to be seated and wait his turn while victims of the pace car's having plowed into a portable photographer's stand were being treated. "Gordie came over to the hospital while I was getting sewed up and apologized all over the place," said Kenyon. "I told him to forget it. He certainly didn't mean to do it."

Chapter 6

TURN FOUR: A REMEMBRANCE OF THINGS FAST

My earliest recollection of the fourth and final bend in the track at Indianapolis comes not from having seen it first hand, but instead from having viewed seven or eight screenings of Mickey Rooney's *The Big Wheel*, retrograde (at best) Hollywood vision of motor racing. What a picture! The protagonist is a second generation oval track jockey named Billy Coy, son of the late and lamented "Cannonball" Coy whose life (so the story goes) was snuffed in the northwest turn at Indy. Billy Coy, as hard-bitten a racer as ever his father was, comes to Indianapolis on a shoestring and very nearly wins the great race in his first attempt. Rooney's part in the picture was filmed not in Indianapolis, but on the movie lots of Culver City. It was not until the picture made its inauspicious debut that Mickey Rooney paid a visit to the Speedway, and even then it was for promotional reasons.

Anyone who has viewed a reel of *The Big Wheel* will attest that if ever a picture needed promoting, this was it. Even so, certain footage had a curious romantic credibility about it. For instance, the camera turned upward every so often for a fleeting glimpse of a large sycamore (hardly an unusual sight in mid-America, granted) that flourished near the northwest turn until the middle sixties, when it was quietly sacrificed. But no matter: In the picture, the tree was rather effectively transformed into an ominous symbol of evil and destruction, the very marplot of Indianapolis. Its branches swayed insidiously from wind gusts out of the northwest that caused its massive trunk to bend. Billy Coy, meanwhile, is never so occupied with easing his bulky racer through the northwest that he has not a moment to glance furtively toward the tree with a fear and trembling so convincing that it shows right through his aircraft goggles. Hollywood had indeed come to Indianapolis (or had Indianapolis gone to it?), and for a person with a well-developed knack for suspending his disbelief, *The Big Wheel* might conceivably offer a few authentic moments, in spite of itself.

True, the northwest is Indy's final bend in the road. Every race day, attention focuses expectantly on that same turn. Regular as a cuckoo clock, a sincere-looking pace car bearing a terrified entourage of passengers hurriedly escorts all thirty-three contestants through that turn and down the main straightaway to the well-ritualized waving of the green flag. At a distance, the eleven rows of cars all three abreast are indistinguishable, darting out of turn four like a pack of field mice, and scarcely audible until they are close at hand. Clouds of dust and smoke hover in the air. The race is on.

Although the northwest turn, we are assured, is theoretically no different in contour from its counterpart, the southeast, the selfsame winds that ruffled Mickey Rooney's sycamore are a factor to be reckoned with on the track. Once a car is safely through the turn, the massive grandstands along the main straight afford a certain measure of protection from the sometimes erratic gusts that prevail in turn four. For the thirty years that I have spectated at Indianapolis, drivers have always cut themselves a generous arc through the northwest, using every inch of the race track that they possibly can as they enter and then exit the turn. But, like every other aspect of the Indianapolis scene, the northwest has to be seen first-hand in order to be appreciated. Rapid, incident-free high-torqued trips through Indy's fourth corner represent virtuoso performances to a practiced Speedway spectator.

But like every other bend in the road at Indianapolis, the northwest has a history and an ambience of its own that has grown out of a unique set of incidents, each of them related by both time and place. In 1914, the green Sunbeam factory team entry that French driver Jean Chassagne placed on the pole at Indianapolis with an average speed of 88.14 miles per hour (not the fastest among the thirty-car field that year) is scarcely recognizable as a racing car today. With a dozen cumbersome wooden spokes supporting each wheel, the car resembled a sporty touring roadster more than a roaring racer. Appearances to the contrary, however, the machine was competitive for the brief time it lasted at Indianapolis in 1914. Having been paced to a start by Carl Fisher at the wheel of a stately Stoddard-Dayton, and with twenty laps and slightly more than thirty minutes of racing time behind it, Chassagne's Sunbeam overturned on the northwest after having blown a tire and spun off the course. Although riding mechanic Samuel Morris was knocked temporarily unconcious, Chassagne thought the accident insufficient reason to drop out of the chase. "Chassagne had the car righted and expected to get back in the race," said one observer, "but found it necessary to withdraw." The same observer found the accident to be "a spectacular one," although the injuries fortunately proved to be minor, with Chassagne himself sustaining only a small cut beneath his left eye and another behind his left ear.

The French contingent, consisting of René Thomas, Arthur Duray, Albert Guyot, mechanic-driver Jules Goux (the champagne-guzzling winner from 1913), aviator Georges Boillot, and Chassagne himself, had carried $26,500 in prize money with them in their steamship voyage back to France after the 1913 event. Their appetites whetted, they returned in 1914, and found the greater part of mid-America engulfed in water, an inconvenience that forced Speedway officials to postpone the 1914 race from a Friday until the following Monday. In waiting for the race to be run, an army of devoted racing enthusiasts had made the best of it for the weekend, occupying every available hotel room in the city, and responding to the generosity of many Indianapolis residents by sleeping over in the homes of virtual strangers.

Whether it was all worth the trouble and inconvenience is a question, for when the 1914 race had finally been concluded, the press corps did not react lightly to the realization that the first four finishers were all French, and that all four Frenchmen had obliterated the previous 500-mile race record held by Indianapolis's own Joe Dawson. "Today has been a bad day for America," wrote Edward Schipper, the sober-minded columnist for *The Automobile.* "Our hopes have been crushed to earth one after another. . . our idols were shattered; one by one our chances faded." Of some faint consolation to chauvinistic reporters was the comforting realization that the Stutz that finished in fifth position had been driven by the American folk hero Barney Oldfield.

But the less than authentic response from the American press in 1914 was not necessarily shared by the immense, devil-may-care, holdover race crowd that had invaded the Speedway. "It must have been like this on the good old days of the Roman games," speculated Hector Fuller of the *Star.* "And while those daredevil drivers were risking their lives and making some of the fair sex among the spectators almost ill with the terrible risks they took, there were many others on the ground who calmly went to luncheon and to a bottle of beer on ice."

Partly because Chassagne and Morris were spared serious injury, their potentially disastrous accident received relatively little notice, although it was one of the first noteworthy mischances in a long series of incidents occurring in turn four.

After American automobile racing had taken time out for World War I in 1917 and 1918, attendance figures were unofficially estimated at 120,000 by 1920, a year when the northwest turn appeared to stand out from among the others in a motor race that otherwise seemed to be comparatively tame. "All in all," said Lambert Sullivan of *Motor Age,* "it was a great race, not spectacular in any sense of the word, but a real trial of the cars entered." Notwithstanding, the northwest turn was the site of what little unforeseen excitement there was in 1920. Roscoe Sarles drove his green Monroe into the fourth turn wall on lap fifty-eight. In the meantime, Art Klein, who had wrecked his Frontenac after forty-one laps, had relieved teammate Benny Hill, only to crash still another Frontenac in the northwest corner at 115 laps. His car plowed into the wall, destroying its entire front end, and eventually came to rest mid-track. Unhurt, Klein and his riding mechanic Clyde Tatman returned to the pits on foot while track attendants pushed their car, its radiator leaking profusely, off the track. A bridegroom of a few weeks, Klein was intercepted by his wife, who lost little time extracting a promise that he would (according to one eavesdropper) "quit the racing game." Klein held to his promise for one year, and then revisited Indianapolis in 1922 for one last try at the 500-mile race.

While Klein patiently sat out the 1921 race, Louis Fontaine's six-cylinder Junior became more unwieldy than usual through the northwest, ending the day straddled barely a few feet from startled spectators hovering near the inside wall there. Jimmy Murphy wrecked his confederate-grey Duesenberg Straight 8 later that afternoon in almost the same place, finishing fourteenth in a field of only twenty-three starters. One year later, when Murphy finished first in his own car, Jules Ellingboe at the helm of yet another Duesenberg Straight 8 whirled around three times in the northwest on his twenty-fifth circuit, slapped the wall, and destroyed his right rear wheel while he managed to prevent any injury to himself. News of Ellingboe's misfortune, slight as it was, was carried over the radio that day in 1922. Said one incredulous reporter: "They say that the radio fans who didn't join the great throng . . . may actually hear the hum of the engines as the speeding cars make the laps and that all the announcements will go whirring to their ears. How the world does move!"

With the proliferation of radios in Indiana came the escalation of miles per hour at the Speedway. Having piloted his own white Miller Special to a nineteenth-place finish in 1925 despite a crash in the Speedway's south chute, twenty-two-year-old Herb Jones returned in 1926 to be the youngest driver entered that year. He resigned from his job at the Haag's Drug Company in Indianapolis to pursue what he envisioned as a colorful and lucrative career as a racer of automobiles at the two-and-a-half-mile track in Indianapolis, where he had agreed to pilot fellow driver Al Cotey's blue Elcar. On May 27, a Thursday, Jones had registered one qualification lap at 105.67 miles per hour when he caught his left front wheel on the inner wall of turn four. The car rolled an undetermined number of times before it came to rest on the outer wall. He died before the first rescue party arrived. Although substantially demolished, the Elcar was reconstructed in time for still another qualification attempt, this time at the hands of substitute driver John Duff, who managed to start last in the twenty-eight car field, finishing ninth.

Popular Jules Ellingboe, however, had not seen the last of his problems in the northwest turn. Returned in 1927 in a supercharged front-drive car entered by retired driver Earl Cooper, Ellingboe staged a regrettable encore by crashing in the same place on the same (twenty-fifth) lap that he had in 1925. His low-slung Cooper Special, the body of which seemed oddly obscured between four huge wire wheels, was substantially destroyed. Beneath a headline reading "Spills and Thrills at Indianapolis," *Motor Age* magazine reported that the hapless Ellingboe "was so seriously injured that he was taken to the hospital as quickly as possible." It was his final appearance on the track at Indianapolis, and Ellingboe died in 1948 from causes evidently unrelated to his difficulties in the northwest turn.

Laps three and thirty-three were the fateful ones for two contestants in the running at Indianapolis in 1929. Cliff Woodbury, a leading contender for first place honors, had qualified his own Boyle Valve car, propelled by a smallish ninety-cubic-inch supercharged Miller, for the pole position with a run of 120.599 miles per hour, a mile and a half faster than the second fastest qualifier that year. It was Woodbury's ill fortune, however, to move from first to last in near record time. Riding in third position on lap three, his striking red, white, and blue racer spun in the northwest and eventually landed backwards against the outer wall with a collapsed right rear axle. While uniformed militiamen applied themselves to the arduous task of hoisting the crunched automobile over the wall with the use of board planks, Woodbury made a dash toward the pit area. Minutes later, teammate Billy Arnold arrived with his goggles shattered and his eye cut from a piece of flying debris. Subbing for Arnold, Woodbury drove six laps in the car before turning the wheel over to O. G. Roberts, another reliefer, who kept the car going until its 146th lap, when Arnold once again stepped into the cockpit. Woodbury, not wishing to let any grass grow beneath his feet that afternoon, then replaced Bob McDonough after thirty laps and drove the car for thirty-four additional circuits before the car's oil tank developed a pronounced leak. Woodbury's next stop was in the pit of Phil "Red" Shafer, where he relieved Shafer and was eventually flagged off the course at 150 laps, by which time Ray Keech of Philadelphia had finished the 500 miles a winner.

Although it had been an active day for Woodbury, he was by no means the only man in Gasoline Alley that evening who had spent a frenetic few hours. Jules Moriceau, who had driven an even tinier seventy-eight-cubic-inch Amilcar, had lost control on the northwest on his thirtieth lap, rammed the wall four times, and had demolished the tiny yellow and black racer without harm to himself. Even Harry B. Leslie, governor of Indiana, had had his troubles. After having invited Col. and Mrs. Charles A. Lindbergh to join him and Mrs. Leslie in the governor's box seats for the race, the newly wedded guests remained unaccounted for until shortly before the start of the race. To compound everyone's difficulties, temperatures on race day reached 89° F., although they seemed not to bother Keech, who had risen from the relative obscurity of dirt tracking and who had, only a year ago, hurled a racing car over the hot sands of Daytona Beach at well in excess of 200 miles per hour. On this, his second and final attempt at Indianapolis, Keech had improved upon his creditable fourth place finish the year before — he was greeted boisterously as the winner of the seventeenth running of the 500-mile race. Telegrams poured in from delighted radio listeners as far away as the chic resort hotels of southern Indiana, attesting that they had received reasonably good, static-free broadcast signals from the Motor Speedway itself.

Hell cut loose in the northwest in 1931, beginning with owner-driver Harry Butcher's orange Buick which, according to reports, went through (not over) the wall on lap six. Butcher, thirty-five, was all but unscathed in the accident. Joe

Russo, in the meantime, lost traction in his white Duesenberg and smashed its tail section while attempting to stay out of Butcher's path. Russo, a twenty-nine-year-old Indianapolis resident, brought his car under control and continued the chase for 109 laps before an oil leak retired him for the day.

Ahead by four laps, Chicago's Billy Arnold was on his 162nd go-around when his pit crew prepared to flash him a hastily scrawled chalkboard message reading "All's Well." In reality, all was anything but well; when Arnold next rode down the main straightaway, it was in an ambulance instead of a racing car. Having won both the Indianapolis 500 and the AAA National Driving Championship the year before, Arnold sported a huge blue number 1 painted boldly on his grey Miller-Hartz Special. As Arnold and mechanic Spider Matlock sailed through the northwest at 110 miles an hour, their car slid on the oily brick surface and headed for the outer wall. "The track was so soaked with oil," said Matlock after the race, "that it was almost impossible to control the car on the turns at any speed. We were lucky to get out alive."

Indeed they were. Their car had initially pulled toward the turn's inner wall where, because of the oil slickness, Arnold was unable to exert any control. When the racer suddenly changed direction, it sailed, willy-nilly, toward the outer wall, was struck by another car, and then climbed the wall in a terrifying explosion that produced an abundance of orange flame and black smoke. The impact threw both Arnold and Matlock out of the cockpit, tore a wheel off, and sent it rolling rapidly in the direction of Georgetown Road, which parallels the north-south direction of the Speedway's main straightaway. The wheel ripped through a refreshment stand (barely missing a woman patron) and sped roughly another 200 feet in the direction of eleven-year-old Wilbur Brink, a boy seated absent-mindedly on the runningboard of an automobile parked in the front yard of his home. The boy's body was fractured in numerous places. Rushed to the Speedway's infield hospital, he received two hours of attention from physicians before being sent on to City Hospital, where he failed to survive the night.

In the meantime, Billy Arnold's collarbone was fractured

and Matlock's pelvis broken.* But as both men were being transported to the infield for treatment, Arnold felt constrained to convince the race day onlookers that he was, in fact, essentially unharmed. Puffing defiantly on a cigarette, he made himself amply visible through the ambulance rear window. On the following morning, one newspaper headline read: ARNOLD, COLLAR BONE FRACTURED, PUFFS "FAG" IN AMBULANCE TO ASSURE CROWD. "Just a tough break, that's all," said the baby-faced Arnold from his cot at the Speedway's race day infirmary.

Billy Arnold was not the only man to suffer a tough break in the northwest turn that afternoon. Driving an orange and black Studebaker in sixth place, Luther Johnson spun his car to avoid Arnold, but instead drove over the top of Arnold's Miller-Hartz and landed upside down. Johnson and his mechanic William Richards emerged unhurt.

All was relatively quiet in the northwest until lap 167, when Tony Gulotta and mechanic Carl Rescigno lost a right rear wheel from their monstrous green and gold Studebaker entered in the race by a land speed record holder, the famed D. A. "Ab" Jenkins. Gulotta and Rescigno were holding second position when they, too, slid on the well-oiled northwest turn, obliterating a large section of the outer concrete wall as they passed over it. Although the men escaped with only minor cuts and bruises, their right rear wheel provided much of the consternation in turn four. It bounded into the outer wall, then into the inner wall, and finally came to rest in a gully a short distance from scurrying infield patrons.

In the 1932 event, the first two racers to drop from competition did so in the northwest. First to go was rookie Alan "Al" Gordon, the hard-drinking proprietor of Club Rendezvous in Long Beach, California. Gordon was at the controls of the number 26 Miller-powered Lion Tamer Special, with Horace John Booty of Indianapolis as riding mechanic. When the Lion Tamer "clicked hubs" (as one reporter had it) with another Miller driven by Stubby Stubblefield on the third circuit of the

---

*The reader may recall that in an accident in the northeast turn the following year (1932), it was Arnold who broke his pelvis and Matlock his collarbone.

race, the early race traffic was funneling through the northwest corner of the Speedway. The force of the accident sent Gordon's car through a wooden retaining rail along the upper homestretch. It slithered along the grassy strip between the race track and the front edge of old Grandstand H, where Gordon and Booty finally brought it under control at the north tunnel near the head of the straightaway. In the solemn judgement of AAA officials, Gordon himself was responsible for the unfortunate series of consequences that resulted in Horace Booty's multiple lacerations. "This accident can be traced to the fact that driver Gordon did not arrive until Friday previous to the race, had practically no time to practice, and did not understand that coming out of the northwest turn the car always drifts to the outside," the official AAA post-race report stated unequivocally. Gordon, who had failed to tame any lions at Indianapolis in 1932, finished at the end of the forty-car field assembled that year.

Al Gordon was followed out of competition by Gus Schrader, an aging Iowan who deserved his reputation as one of the country's more accomplished dirt-track jockeys, but who evidently found Indianapolis not at all to his liking. Both Schrader and his riding mechanic Fred Blauvelt, nattily attired in aircraft helmets, white driving uniforms, and black bow ties, lasted seven laps before their front-drive Miller ran into the wall at the north end of the track near the overhead bridge and climbed the wall with its left front wheel. Neither man was injured, although they were clearly out of luck for the balance of the day. Schrader, a World War I veteran, proceeded to ply his trade as a dirt-track specialist both in and out of AAA-dictatorially supervised races, but never again returned to the Speedway as a competitor. He continued to campaign until he paid the ultimate price at Shreveport during the Louisiana State Fair on October 22, 1941, in what was among the final automobile races prior to the outbreak of the Second World War.

The Bowes Seal Fast number 45 that bachelor Clay Weatherly of Harmon, Illinois, drove in the 1935 race had a decidedly checkered history. Johnny Hannon had lost his life in the same machine on May 21 while on a practice run. After the car was hurriedly rebuilt, Weatherly had qualified it in twenty-fifth position at a speed of slightly under 116 miles per hour. With the legendary Rex Mays leading the thirty-three car field on lap nine, Weatherly's Miller skidded 200 feet through the northwest turn, pierced the outer wooden guard-railing at the head of the straightaway as Al Gordon had in 1932, and scraped the protective wall in front of Grandstand H. Weatherly and mechanic Edward Bradburn were both pitched from the car as it rolled along the same grassy strip that Al Gordon had once inadvertently used. Weatherly died on his way to the infield hospital, while Bradburn was treated for a broken back and then sent to Robert Long Hospital for further treatment.

By lap seventeen of the race, the attention was once again on Al Gordon. On this, his third and final attempt at Indianapolis, the Speedway's fourth turn proved once again to be his undoing. Gordon's Cocktail Hour Cigarette Special, a racy cream and blue automobile with Frank Howard as riding mechanic, slid an estimated 600 feet through the northwest. The car made its way gradually from the inner to the outer wall and struck with force ample enough to split the concrete; it landed wrong side up on the wall itself. The mishap provided no substantial injury to either Gordon or Howard, although Howard was dumped from the car. "It just got away from me, that's all," said the plucky Gordon at the Speedway hospital. Mrs. Gordon, reportedly in a state of near collapse as she was brought to her husband's bedside found him sitting up, sucking on a large cigar, and declaring that he wanted to get back into the race. Instead, he returned to Gasoline Alley, where he and Howard convivially poured a drink for themselves and for movie idol Richard Arlen, who had passed the afternoon as a lap scorer in Lou Moore's Foreman Axle pit.

Al Gordon and Spider Matlock both perished the following winter, on January 26, when their Indianapolis racer went through the wall on the south turn at the Legion Ascot Speedway in Los Angeles. Wilbur Shaw had also been a contender that afternoon. "As far as sudden death was concerned," Shaw wrote later, "the racing fraternity was a hardened group." According to Shaw, it was Al Gordon himself who had responded to a recent outburst of criticism against automobile racing. "What difference does it make," Gordon was alleged to have remarked. "We all have to die sometime." The accident that took the life of Al Gordon precipitated a furor that closed racing activity at Legion Ascot permanently.

Wilbur Shaw had crossed the finish line a winner at Indianapolis in 1937, when rookie Floyd Davis of Springfield, Illinois (later a co-winner of the race with Mauri Rose in 1941), crashed in the northwest on his 190th lap. Earlier that afternoon, AAA observers had noted that the exhaust pipe on Davis's Thorne Engineering car had worked itself loose, and that riding mechanic Dee Toran was holding the pipe in place to forestall its falling off. When Davis and Toran spun, they struck the wall. Toran was thrown out and lay on the middle of the track not far from where the car itself came to rest. Davis and Toran were both momentarily unconscious, but Davis revived summarily and struggled to free himself from the stalled racer. After his co-win in 1941, Davis never returned to the Speedway as a driver. Toran, a veritable terror in midget cars after World War II, was eventually convicted of manslaughter in connection with the death of a rival Connecticut driver, Jeep Collkitt, in 1947.

When Davis and Rose triumphed in 1941, the annual mayhem at Indianapolis had acquired its now familiar carnival aura. If one were too weary of observing cars howl around the old track at West Sixteenth and Georgetown Road, there were other wholesome diversions around town. At the Fox burlesque theater, a well-publicized troupe of "25 Beautiful Baby Dolls" were featured throughout the month of May with their all new "Speedway Follies." And for theatrical patrons with somewhat different tastes in entertainment, the Riverview Amusement Park featured the inimitable Pasha Alexandra, the Egyptian Miracle Man who was buried alive nightly (twice on Memorial Day and on Sunday) before the eyes of awe-stricken tourists lately arrived in the big city, where they discovered a virtual cornucopia of entertainment possibilities, not the least of which was Horace Heidt and His Pot O'Gold Stars at the Lyric Theatre.

Out at the track on race day 1941, spectators in the northwest turn experienced a sobering moment late in the afternoon when three-fourths of the annual 500-mile race had been run. Everett Saylor, a relatively obscure thirty-one-year-old former public school teacher in Dayton, Ohio, spun his Cincinnati-owned Bowles Special on lap 155. The trouble began when Saylor dipped his car low on the apron of the turn; he continued through an inner guardrailing and then into a parking barrier wall situated well off the race course. After striking the concrete barrier, his red dirt-track racer rolled over and heaved into a parked car while frantic bystanders fled in every direction. For the critically injured Saylor, it was the end of the line at Indianapolis, and although he recovered in time, he never again returned for a rematch at America's premier motor race.

By the time that track crews had removed the wreckage of Saylor's car, Mauri Rose had wheeled Lou Moore's Noc-Out Hose Clamp Offenhauser into Victory Lane and was contentedly lighting his pipe and receiving the five-year-old Borg-Warner Trophy. Rose proceeded to pass the evening by taking his family out for a drive, at which time he called on battered Everett Saylor, who was liberally bandaged within the sanctimonious confines of Methodist Hospital. Seemingly unruffled by his first win at the famed brickyard, Rose (somewhat incognito) was dressed in a business suit the following morning at 7:30 when he left home for another routine day at the Allison plant in Speedway, Indiana.

"The 2½-mile brick Speedway with its patchy asphalt covering is no longer adequate in its present shape, contours and banking for the modern racing car," warned John Bentley of the British motoring journal *The Autocar* in 1949. "To misjudge the turns at Indianapolis," Bentley continued, "you may land on the inside apron, upside down, as Charles Van Acker's Redmer Special did this year, during the 11th [10th] lap, or you may end up facing the other way, with both left wheels ripped off, as did Duke Nalon on the 24th lap." While Bentley's admonitions proved to be at least thirty years premature, there was no gainsaying in 1949 that Van Acker, a jolly Belgian-born machinist from South Bend, Indiana, and sometime Notre Dame undergraduate, had indeed spun his wife's number 10 Redmer Special on the tenth lap as he prepared to exit the northwest. The stocky Belgian had slid through the track's inner safety apron, with the car's rear end threatening all the while to loop in a counterclockwise direction. The beefy, wire-wheeled car rebounded from the inner guardrailing about thirty feet from the north end of the track, spun, and struck the same guardrailing thirty-five feet farther down the track. After the car rolled one and a half times, it came to rest on the rail itself without crushing Van Acker. A posse of fast-moving firemen righted the car and Van Acker crawled out unharmed but understandably shaken. Once on his feet, he waved to the crowd. After this, his none-too-successful third Indianapolis start, Van Acker returned the following year in the same machine but was unsuccessful in bidding for a position in the 1950 starting lineup.

More than one racing notable experienced difficulty in the northwest in the years that followed. One of them was the remarkable Melvin "Tony" Bettenhausen, an otherwise immensely successful driver whose memorable eyes seemed curiously transparent. Bettenhausen drove in all but one Indianapolis 500 between 1946 and 1960, finishing in second position on two occasions before losing his life on the main straightaway in 1961 testing a car for old racing cohort Paul Russo. In 1951, Bettenhausen was a thirty-four-year-old Kaiser-Fraser dealer in Tinley Park, Illinois. His Indianapolis mount that year was a cigar-shaped, Offenhauser-powered Mobiloil Special entered and cared for by former driver Lou Moore. On Bettenhausen's 178th lap, the metallic blue racer executed a counterclockwise tailspin that carried him twenty-five feet into the grassy infield, where a disgruntled Bettenhausen unbuckled himself and prepared to exit the stalled racer. Attrition had settled in well at this point; Bettenhausen's closest competitor, Duke Nalon, another Chicago product, had stalled his temperamental Novi on the backstretch after 151 laps. Restarted with the aid of a tow truck, Bettenhausen drove back to the pits, where he remained for the closing minutes of the race while dark horse Lee Wallard drove a brakeless, deep-blue Belanger Motors dirt-track car to victory. Bettenhausen, meanwhile, was credited with ninth place; only eight of the original thirty-three starters were still running at the conclusion of the race.

Bayliss Levrett of Glendale, California, a way-back finisher in the 1949 and 1950 races at Indianapolis, had missed the 1951 race altogether, and appeared at the Speedway in 1952 in a dirt-track car (which he had constructed himself) sponsored by the Brown Motor Company, an auto dealership in Richmond, Indiana. On Saturday, May 10, Levrett lost control of the upright car as he came off the northwest turn. Norman Werking, a correspondent for *Automobile Topics*, was on the scene and reported that Levrett began his difficulties that day with "a long series of bumps against the outside retaining wall." Having scuffed the wall as many as ten times, Levrett began "bouncing back and forth like a billiard ball going into a pocket." The driver was thrown from the car and dragged for a hundred feet. The car then turned sideways in the center of the track while flames from its split fuel tank reached a height of twenty feet. Levrett frantically tore his flaming clothes away. Suffering first and second degree burns on his wrists and ankles, he announced his immediate retirement from the racing wars and managed to recover with surprising speed.

Part of the drawing card for the annual spring rites at Indianapolis in 1952 was the presence of Italian driver Alberto Ascari, a second generation grand prix driver who had prevailed in thirty-one international races dating back as far as 1937, and who had won the world driving championship in 1950 as a member of the Ferrari racing team. The likeable Ascari, who proved amenable to the press corps at Indianapolis, was also reputed to be, in the words of one commentator, the "greatest foreign threat in nearly three decades." After qualifying for the nineteenth starting position in a red Ferrari whose torque proved less than adequate to accelerate out of the turns at Indianapolis, the world champion driver demonstrated his skill behind the wheel by charging into eighth position at the end of the race's first fifty miles. Moving through the northwest turn at forty laps, however, Ascari became uncomfortably aware that the right rear wire wheel was about to collapse. In the meantime, the car began an 850-foot slide that brought it to the track apron and then onto the infield grass, where it spun in a clockwise direction, finally coming to a stop halfway on the apron once more. Although Ascari was reentered the subsequent year, neither he nor his car arrived for another assault on Indianapolis.

A year later, in 1953, forty-two-year-old Len Duncan from Germantown, Pennsylvania, a seemingly indestructable man with an interminable racing career who was once Harry S. Truman's European chauffeur, spun his Central Excavating Special in turn four on the final day of qualification runs. Although Duncan was uninjured, his racer was too badly creased to be repaired in time for another attempt at a starting position that year. During the race itself, quiet Don Freeland, a 190-pound California sprint car specialist from Redondo Beach, California, competing in the first of his eight races at the Speedway, grazed the wall on the northwest turn and spun crazily toward the infield, where he eventually brought his cream-colored Bob Estes Special under control.

The most outstanding of the 1953 rookie crop, however, was ectomorphic Jimmy Daywalt from nearby Wabash, Indiana. Daywalt, who adored public attention as much as any Speedway performer before or since his time, succumbed to cancer in April 1966. But never running worse than fourth at fifty-mile intervals in the 1954 race, visions of the Borg-Warner Trophy danced through his head until his 111th tour of the track, when he contacted the wall in the northwest, coming off turn four backwards and taking Pat Flaherty (relief driving for Jim Rathmann) with him. While there were no injuries to report, Daywalt returned to Gasoline Alley in tears, believing that his one chance ever to win at Indy had eluded him. He was, as it turned out, quite correct in his assessment.

By the time the 1955 Indianapolis 500 had been run, one-legged Cal Niday, a mustachioed ex-barber originally from Turlock, California, had more than thwarted expectations to deal with. With the tragic demise of Billy Vukovich in a complicated backstretch pileup that year, relatively little attention focused on Niday, a midget car expert, who struck the wall on the northwest turn slightly north of Grandstand H and ended up nose-down in a ditch. Niday contacted the wall in such a way that his head was pitched to the right side of the cockpit and into the wall itself. Listed in critical condition with head and chest injuries, Niday was also burned extensively after the car caught fire. He had been riding among the race leaders at 171 laps, and later expressed the opinion that, if it had not been for the crash, he might well have won the race. Like others who had experienced the violent crashes in the northwest before him, Niday did not attempt an Indianapolis comeback after his lengthy recovery.

Nor did Marvin Pifer, a Michigan driver whose racing background included a great deal of experience with the International Motor Contest Association, and who was among the 1956 Indianapolis rookie crop. Assigned to the red Commercial Motor Freight Special financed by Karl Hall of Orleans, Indiana, Pifer had turned laps in the dirt-track car in excess of 138 miles an hour, a speed that would still not have earned him a starting position at Indianapolis that year. It was on May 10 that he put the car into the wall in turn four, destroying the car and giving himself a severely fractured skull and a number of minor lacerations.

During the running of the 1956 race, little known Keith Andrews, a Colorado Springs garage owner and a divisional winner in the 1954 Pike's Peak Hill Climb, drove Harry Dunn's 500B Kurtis roadster. While there was hardly anything unusual about the car in this, the heyday of roadsterdom at Indianapolis, there was something unexpected in the car's right front Firestone, which exploded in the northwest turn on Andrews's ninety-fourth lap. Andrews spun, made the car behave, and headed back into the pits for a right front replacement of rubber and a new issue of fuel. It could hardly be said that racing luck had smiled on him that day, inasmuch as the car finally stalled at the south end of the track. Nor was it riding with him in 1957, when he died at the age of thirty-six while testing a car for Italian driving champion Nino Farina. It was May 15 at 11:25 A.M. that Andrews again lost control of the northwest. He had just registered a lap in the 136-mile-an-hour bracket when the roadster spun, rear end first, into a concrete retaining wall on the inside of the turn, making Andrews the forty-first individual to lose his life at the track.

The passing of unobtrusive Keith Andrews prior to the 1957 race seemed to set a precedent that year for other difficulties to come in turn four. Rookie Mike Magill, a thirty-seven-year-old former stock car racer and air force veteran, spun the Dayton Steel Foundry car toward the end of the northwest corner. Enthusiastic Al Herman of Allentown, Pennsylvania, driving the same Dunn Engineering Special that Keith

Andrews had spun the previous year, was ten laps ahead of him when Magill spun, took both cars out of the race, and injured himself severely.

Magill and Herman appeared at the Speedway in subsequent years with somewhat better, if less than spectacular, results. Harry Dunn's white roadster, however, could not stay out of trouble long in the northwest turn. In 1958, the car crashed in turn four for the third year in a row. In the cockpit this time was Chuck Weyant, a midget car racer from Springfield, Illinois, who followed in the footsteps of Al Herman by stuffing the white car into the northwest wall. If ill luck indeed comes often conveniently packaged in sets of threes, then Harry Dunn's trilogy of misfortune had run its course for the nonce. When he returned in 1959 with Al Herman again at the controls; the car ran all 200 laps and finished an ominous thirteenth.

In preparation for the 1961 Indianapolis 500-mile race, Dr. Thomas A. Hanna examined seventy-six aspiring drivers. Their average age, Dr. Hanna reported, was 35.3 years, their average weight was 165 pounds, and their average height five feet ten-and-a-half inches. Three of them wore glasses while driving, and twenty had removable dentures. Fifty-nine of the men identified themselves as Protestants, seventeen as Catholics. All but three listed themselves as married.

"Steady Eddie" Johnson of Cuyahoga Falls, Ohio, seemed not to square too well with Dr. Hanna's 1961 driver profile. Johnson was contracted to drive for wealthy industrialist Jim Robbins, of Troy, Michigan, in whose car Johnson had finished sixth in 1960. At the age of forty-two, when most drivers have given at least minimal thought to retirement from automobile racing, Johnson had no such plans. His fabled steadiness on the track had served him well in every race at Indianapolis since 1952, and he would continue his extraordinary knack for avoiding trouble on the raceway until the 1966 race, his last. But in 1961 Johnson was not only the oldest man in the race, but also shorter (at five feet, five inches) and lighter (at one hundred fifty-five pounds) than Dr. Hanna's composite averages. Johnson qualified the Jim Robbins Kuzma (known as "Johnson's Jet") for the 1961 race with a four-lap run of

145.843 miles per hour; and while virtually no pre-race handi-capper would have laid money on Johnson as a potential winner, he seemed a prime candidate for a strong, first-ten finish.

Events turned out otherwise, however, and the 1961 race recorded Johnson's only race day mishap. At 2:20 P.M. Chief Starter Bill Vanderwater frantically waved the yellow bunting as yellow caution lights flashed around the course. The trouble was in the northwest, where, at 127 laps, Eddie Johnson had brushed wheels with Arizona's Wayne Weiler and began a protracted slide toward the inner edge of the track where he met the inner retaining wall. Parked on the middle of the track, Johnson waited momentarily while other cars swerved to miss his disabled racer and then hopped out of the car and over the wall to safer ground. By 2:25 P.M. a red rescue vehicle was at the scene, being motioned backwards by a United States Auto Club functionary stationed in turn four. But as the truck backed toward the stalled racer, a man fell from the rear of the truck. The driver continued in reverse, over the man's body and then about five feet past him. The victim, John Masariu of Danville, Indiana, was dead at the scene. Ironically, the entire incident went nearly unnoticed in this, the Golden Anniversary running of the 500-mile race at Indianapolis. The winner was A. J. Foyt, a Houston, Texas, driver half Johnson's age, who had connected with Victory Lane after four attempts at the Speedway.

Although the eyes of Texas were on Foyt in the oily 1963 race that went to Parnelli Jones, they were perhaps as much on the rest of the Texas contingent, which included Jim McElreath, Ebb Rose, Johnny Rutherford, and Lloyd Ruby. With consistently wretched luck that worked at cross purposes to his immense talent as a driver, Ruby would remain a sentimental favorite at Indianapolis for the remainder of his long career in the saddle of potentially winning machinery at Indianapolis. Having finished in the first ten in each of his first three tries at the Speedway, he retired from action in the Zink Trackburner at the 1963 race on the northwest curve at 126 laps, when he spun and caught the wall with his left rear wheel about twenty-five feet north of Grandstand H. The car then passed along the track and stopped on the infield grass. But in eighteen consecutive Indianapolis starts between 1960 and 1977, Ruby's third place finish in 1964 was as close as the Texan was to come to being first at the 500.

Like Lloyd Ruby, Jim Hurtubise seemed always to face immense crowd appeal with consistently poor luck in the race itself, as well as beforehand. It was on the fifteenth day of May in 1965 that Hurtubise was rounding the northwest during a practice run in his fluorescent red car, ominously christened the Tombstone Life Special (after an Arizona insurance company), when the throttle allegedly stuck. The result was a totally demolished car missing both right wheels, the result of a wall-banger that followed a 380-foot slide through the Speedway's fourth corner. Hurtubise himself was preserved from disaster both by divine providence and by Firestone's newly-developed fuel cell that prevented his right fuel tanks from rupturing. The spectre of the fire was a particular threat for the thirty-two-year-old sprint car hell-on-wheels, who had spent the better part of the previous year bedridden in the United States Army's burn center at San Antonio, Texas, recovering from devastating burns suffered during a 100-mile championship car race at Milwaukee. Undaunted by his pre-race spill in 1965, Hurtubise climbed resiliently into a latter-day Novi and went out of the contest after one lap with transmission problems.

Hustling a car that, at a distance, looked very much like Hurtubise's Tombstone Life Special, eventual three-time Indianapolis winner Al Unser of Albuquerque, New Mexico lost a wheel, struck a car driven by Joe Leonard, and lost all traction coming out of the northwest turn. Unser came to rest against the outside wall and unfastened himself from the bright red car, unhurt. He had been riding in third position. As the race wound to a close, the first two finishers in 1966 were British imports: Rookie Graham Hill finished first, while Scotland's Jim Clark trailed Hill's winning average of 144.317 miles per hour by half a mile per hour. The race, in retrospect, might well have gone to Clark, a drinker of Scotch and grape juice, if he had not spun on two occasions while leading the race in the northwest. On his sixty-fourth lap he had momentarily lost control of his STP Gas Treatment car, another screaming red creation, and narrowly missed the inside wall.

Somewhat the same thing happened on his eighty-seventh lap, when he spun around three times as he entered turn four. He had been leading on both occasions.

Southern stock car kingpin Lee Roy Yarbrough, unaccustomed to open-wheel racing cars, was a first-year man at Indianapolis in 1967, but he had only a modicum of beginner's luck. Having failed to qualify for the race the two previous years, he spun his Jim Robbins car in the northwest on the second lap of the race and then restarted, only to have the race stopped entirely at eighteen laps because of driving rains. When the race was restarted on the following day, May 31, Mario Andretti lost a wheel in the northwest. Once again, Yarbrough spun (this time to avoid Andretti), and was followed by Lloyd Ruby (replacing George Snider) in a Vel's Racing Team Mongoose. Both Yarbrough and Ruby slid off the track sideways, and each hit the dirt banking opposite the north chute. All drivers involved bailed out unhurt, while their cars remained in turn four for the remainder of the race, which went to Foyt, making him the fourth three-time winner in the Speedway's history.

It was the leader's 124th lap in the 1968 race when rookie Bill Vukovich, son of the 1953-1954 Indianapolis champion, made contact with Mel Kenyon. Vukovich spun and came to a stop at the head of the main straight, backwards. Kenyon continued around the track as Johnny Rutherford arrived on the scene, hit his brakes, and was shoved from behind by fellow Texan Jim McElreath. Although Rutherford spun around, both he and McElreath (nursing a badly crunched nose cone) regained control and limped into the pits for some heavy repairs. Smallish (145 pounds) Oklahoma-born Mike Mosley whirled low on the turn four apron, regained control, and followed the others pitward. The only visible evidence of foul play at this point was a considerable quantity of dirt and other debris on the track, and Vukovich, who had run to the outside wall for security, evidently changed his mind and returned to look his car over. Buckling himself into his Shrike once more, Vukovich was pushed to the pits, where he took on fresh rubber and charged back into the race, finishing seventh, a lap ahead of Mosley.

It was late in the steamy afternoon of May 21, 1969, and

Mario Andretti's prospects for winning the Indianapolis 500 were slim indeed. While registering laps at 172 miles an hour, a speed that would have handily captured the pole position that year, a right rear hub failed as Andretti wheeled his fluorescent red four-wheel-drive Lotus Ford through the northwest turn. Andretti's STP Oil Treatment car rammed the wall with considerable impact at the exit of the turn, transforming the machine into what accomplished chief mechanic Clint Brawner termed a "twisted wad of expensive junk." Considering the seriousness and force of the wall contact, Andretti was fortunate in receiving only facial burns and multiple body bruises. "As long as I can get out of something like this and be ready to go the next day," Brawner quoted Andretti as saying, "I have to feel lucky as hell."

Following the accident, Brawner uncrated Andretti's back-up car, a Brawner Hawk, which Andretti was openly unenthusiastic about driving. Qualifying at 169.851 miles an hour, Andretti started his fifth 500-mile race at Indianapolis in the middle of the front row and came home a winner. For Arizonian Brawner, it was the first win in nineteen years of questing at the Speedway. It was also the first win for the car's sponsor, controversial and rotund Andy Granatelli, who had once himself made an abortive bid as a driver at Indianapolis. "The instant Mario cleared the checkered," Brawner wrote, "Granatelli had taken off at a dead run, whooping at the top of his lungs toward the winner's circle." Brawner, who had thought that his driver had died during the horrendous pre-race crash in turn four, had put in an ironic month at Indianapolis. For Andretti, however, it was not the last run-in with the wall on the northwest turn. The following May 11, when he was on another high-speed chase around the track, the suspension folded in his 1970 McNamara, almost destroying the seemingly charmed Andretti.

Mike Mosley had not enjoyed the best of racing luck through the northwest turn at the Speedway since 1968, and was plagued there again in 1971 and 1972. At 159 laps into the 1971 race, Mosley's three-year-old made-over Gurney Eagle, powered by a turbocharged Ford engine, parted with a right front wheel, then spun and plowed into two parked racing cars that had been driven by Steve Krisiloff and Mark Donohue.

Bobby Unser, at the controls of Dan Gurney's Olsonite Eagle, spun to stay out of Mosley's way and rammed the wall in a burst of flame. The emerald grass stains on Mosley's helmet, meanwhile, were indisputable evidence of his having flipped over in the melee. Mosley was judged to be in serious condition with a broken arm and a broken leg. After Bill Vukovich looped his car and then continued through the turn, Gary Bettenhausen, still another second generation driver, voluntarily stopped his blue, wedge-shaped Thermo King Special to aid the injured Mosley. After a restart, Bettenhausen continued to a tenth place finish, his best effort in four Indianapolis starts.

Although he recuperated in time for the 1972 race, Mosley's fortunes were no better. Leading the race at fifty-six laps, his turbocharged Offenhauser lost a wheel and caught the wall toward the end of turn four. By the time he had leaped out of the car and rolled on the track to extinguish his flaming driving suit, his Vivitar Special had parted with two wheels. Condemned once again to spend a dismal summer recovering from burns, Mosley's 1973 reappearance netted him a tenth place finish.

The 1973 race proved to be the final one for highly touted Peter Revson, who in his five Indianapolis starts either finished well or did not finish at all. With three laps down, Revson smacked the wall in the fourth turn without injury to himself. Over-eager to remove Revson's Gulf McLaren from the track, the rescue team that brought the yellow car off the track "on the hook" (suspended by a cable) managed to drop it, damaging it even more severely. Revson, in the meantime, assembled his gear and departed the Speedway en route to Monte Carlo, where he hoped to break the bank at the annual grand prix. On March 22 of the following year, he was to lose his life while testing a car for the Kyalami circuit in South Africa.

*   *   *

And where are they now? The tree is gone, Mickey Rooney (for all practical purposes) is gone, *The Big Wheel* is as good as gone, unless one is willing to wait for its occasional 3:00 A.M. television viewing time. The northwest turn, obviously, is still there; and so, God willing, am I. On race day U.S.A. (if the past is any indication) there will be daring men, young and not so young, who will slim their racing cars through the Speedway's fourth corner, destined to win the world's richest motor derby that will net them over a thousand dollars a minute: high pay for high risks.

Chapter 7

THE MYTH OF THE
MONTH AT INDY

Of course, nothing is universally admired. If the staging of the Indianapolis 500 reaches a great many lives, it also misses touching a great many other lives. Despite its immense popularity (for at least one month of the year), the race somehow fails to arouse the attention of most mature, adult Americans who accord the Indianapolis race about as much recognition as the Calgary stampede. And while there are relatively few individuals of certifiably sound mind and clear judgment who have any negative feeling toward the Calgary stampede, the same cannot be said for their attitudes toward motor racing, especially that particular form of racing practiced at Indianapolis. It is known, for example, that ABC's same day coverage of the 1979 race was viewed by a disappointingly low percentage of metropolitan New York television viewers. This is a regrettable fact of life for racing people to face. They know full well, for instance, that the public at large sees automobile racing as having no significance, and that it is furthermore a thoroughgoing excerise in the most abject futility: 500 hazardous miles to nowhere except perhaps death and destruction — a frivolous, counterproductive misappropriation of time, energy, materials, and other cherished resources that ought to be dedicated to more constructive, perhaps even utilitarian ends.

The Speedway has weathered numerous bleak times, but none perhaps quite so threatening as the summer of 1955. While the race has always had its militant detractors, it was the gory demise of Bill Vukovich on the Speedway's backstretch (while he was apparently en route to an unprecedented third consecutive victory) that came uncomfortably close to putting the future of the Memorial Day race on its ear. Vuky's passing had somehow called the whole (seemingly dubious) rationale for motor racing into immediate question. Less than a month later, tragic circumstances in France (of all places) dealt the Indianapolis cause another sucker punch: During the twenty-four hour race at Le Mans, eighty-two people were reported dead and another seventy-six were accounted injured when Mercedes driver Pierre Levegh hurtled his airborne racer into a portion of the 250,000 spectators assembled for the race. *Life* magazine, which had been highly critical of the Vukovich accident earlier, also gave the Le Mans tragedy flamboyant photographic and editorial coverage. The Mercedes's hood, it was reported, "decapitated tightly jammed spectators like a guillotine. The engine and front axle cut a swath like an artillery barrage. And the car's magnesium body burst into flames like a torch. . . burning others to death."

Before the first session of the 84th Congress that July, Oregon Senator Richard L. Neuberger made an impassioned appeal for the discontinuance of motor racing in America. "I doubt if there is as much bloodshed in Spanish bull rings as today occurring on automobile racetracks in the country," he said. "If automobile racing is necessary to perfect motor vehicles, as proponents of racing ridiculously claim, then I suppose we next will hear that we must run stallions off cliffs to improve horseflesh." He continued, "The deaths on our highways are sad and tragic, but at least they are not purposely staged for profit and for the delight of thousands of screeching spectators." Although Neuberger failed to propose any legislation to prohibit motor racing, his senatorial diatribe fell on a good many ears that were anything but unsympathetic. Impassioned controversy over the future of America's premier motor race continued to escalate.

Back in Indianapolis, columnist Bill Eggert hastened to the defense of the Speedway. "Because it was Bill Vukovich and not some nameless Joe, there is talk of halting 500-mile races," he wrote. "The truth is that the Indianapolis Motor Speedway is safer than a highway. In thirty-nine races since 1911, 350,000 miles have been driven there in races. Seventeen drivers have lost their lives. Others have been killed — mechanics and spectators in earlier days, but since World War II only two drivers — Shorty Cantlon and Vukovich — have been cut down in race day traffic." But in spite of what evidence Eggert and other Speedway defenders were able to marshall, the safety-minded American Automobile Association, under whose supervision races at Indianapolis reached back to the track's inception in 1909, abruptly withdrew its heavy-handed sanctioning of the 500-mile race. The announcement of the AAA withdrawal came in August 1955, leaving a vacuum that was filled by the hastily organized United States Auto Club, which relied upon many former AAA personnel to staff its ranks.

While no one — in or out of racing — cavalierly dismisses the loss of life and limb at Indianapolis or anywhere else, there is a grumbling consensus that as long as there are cars, there will be races. Indianapolis critics have not been inclined to extend their grievances to embrace such other ritualized and widely condoned manifestations of anxiety, energy, and aggressiveness as soccer matches, football games, prize fights, bull fights, and ice hockey encounters, all of which enjoy somewhat more the mantle of respectability. Automobile racing in its numerous forms has traditionally been less culturally accepted as a sufficiently civilized form of healthy competition, notwithstanding its various other sporting analogies that have no less potential for institutionalized havoc. Janet Guthrie, three times a participant in the Indianapolis race is one of the few who own up to the problem. "I think that racing's image needs all the help it can get," she told interviewer Bill Lyon. "It traditionally has been a low-brow image; people tend to think drivers are a bunch of cretins running around with their foot stuck on it."

The sports review on anyone's eleven o'clock news report tells us much about the recognition of automobile racing by telling us nothing at all. Baseball scores are of primary importance, followed by anything remotely newsworthy in the worlds of tennis and golf. Following that, the emphasis turns to table tennis and pocket billiards.

Indianapolis's relatively dim recognition is all the more ironic in light of America's obsessiveness about the motor car and its pervasive influence over the shape of modern American culture. Where but stateside does an automobile serve so conveniently as a kind of oblique index to an individual's personality, his self-esteem, and even his intrinsic personal worth? This preoccupation with the motor car easily transcends its purely practical mission as a means of solitary transportation and has unquestionably acquired significances that reach in widely different directions. One of these is on the speedway — any speedway — where the automobile is introduced as a glamorously contrived projectile that aims to terrify as it entertains. At Indianapolis, where automobile racing has been staged with more regularity, ingenuity, and stability than anywhere else, the motoring mystique finds its highest expression today.

Still another irony: Whereas the horse has largely been detached from its plow and dispatched to the parade ground and the pari-mutual racetrack, the automobile's partial removal from street to speedway has somehow not been greeted with ready approbation and overwhelming public approval. Horse racing out-draws motor racing (and all other sports, for that matter) at the turnstiles because of its greater frequency and because of its lure of legalized wagering. But aside from these circumstances, automotive competition has still not yet been granted its full measure of legitimacy, even in the minds of a substantial number of Americans who worship their wheels above all else. True, there are copious numbers of automobile idolaters who cannot identify with the Indianapolis racing car because of its wildly exotic characteristics that seem light years removed from anything observed rolling down an American street. Then too, the Speedway at Indianapolis is a rather parochial and self-limiting interest, regardless of the immense following it sustains for one frantic month of the year. Every true Indian-apolis buff knows this. When confronted with a person uninitiated into the ways of Indianapolis, the 500-mile race addict must field three inane questions the best he can: Do you drive those cars yourself? Did you place any bets? Was anyone killed?

In its early days, auto racing in America was far more a carnival-like, county fair attraction. Like any number of other ephemeral Sunday summer afternoon monkeyshines, the participants and their paraphernalia were packed and well down the road by the time the sun set. But this carnival ingredient survives in auto racing today, even at Indianapolis. The proof is there for the taking: One need only try the vicinity of West Sixteenth and Crawfordsville Road on the evening prior to the race. But if that carnival ingredient is at all captivating in the short run, it is regarded with at least a modicum of suspicion in the long run; and if the great Indianapolis extravaganza owes a large proportion of its appeal to its brassy show biz characteristics, then that fact also has its consequences. Like other theatrical performers, racing car pilots are likely to be regarded as travelling players, rootless drifters, and nomadic gypsies perpetually in transport to another race in another town before still another audience. However fluid and mobile the tempo of American life has become, there remains a certain staid respectability that comes from putting roots down. The Speedway at Indianapolis provided the family of American auto racing an at least titular home when it became unofficial headquarters for this otherwise wandering enclave of speedsters.

Judged by their working and playing habits, racing pilots of the sort who compete successfully at Indianapolis run the danger of resembling actors more than athletes. Resemblances such as this keep automobile racing relegated toward the bottom of the sportsdom's Great Chain of Being and toward the bottom of the sports recognition order for the broadcast of Everyman's eleven o'clock news report. Viewed from the outside, at least, motor competition (including that rarefied brand executed with adroitness and grace at Indian-apolis) appears to be less physical and less predicated upon gifted coordination and methodically programmed athletic conditioning than many other sports. An old and still current joke that finds its way into racing circles is that participants require only as much physical fitness as that provided by lifting skirts and raising beer bottles. Although there have always been those inside the racing scene who advocated strict, systematic regimens of strength improvement as preparation for a dead run toward Indy's checkered flag, vigorous exercise is an idea whose time at Indianapolis has not yet come. Beginning, it seemed, in the 1950s, there was minimal lip service given to the desirability of body conditioning and preparedness, although the only apparent manifestation of it was a temporary vogue of squeezing rubber balls as an aid to improving a driver's grip on the steering wheel. When the Speedway's chief starter Pat Vidan arrived at Indianapolis with his rainbow assortment of custom-made flags in 1962, he also brought with him an advocacy of physical fitness which assumed the form of an exercise study located about two blocks away from the Speedway's southwest turn. Although Vidan succeeded in securing several drivers as clients, the business ultimately evaporated in a cloud of perspiration.

So if there is a problem with the Indianapolis driver being recognized as an athlete, there is also a problem in distinguishing the performance of that same driver from the performance of his car. Whether or not one can distinguish the dancer from the dance, one cannot always separate the driver from the car when the two are performing as one. Part of the problem with motor racing's sports visibility centers around the bromidic but still vital question of whether the spectator is witnessing the virtuoso performance of a man or a machine at Indianapolis. From a scorer's point of view, the credit goes to the car. It is universally agreed that a driver at Indianapolis or anywhere else can scarcely hope to get very far with a comparatively inferior racing car. Bad racing cars are quaintly referred to as "pigs" or "boxes," if not in still more deprecating terms. But the consensus seems to be that making it big at Indianapolis rests a little more with the quality of the machine, rather than the quality of the person stuffed inside it, although there are informed opinions to the contrary.

But the driver's particular role and function and overall

importance as athlete has sometimes been held up to question. His role is aggravated all the more by the recognition that at Indianapolis, little more than the bulb of his helmet is visible. Die-hard advocates of short-track, open-wheel racing argue that they are at least able to see the driver at work from his waist up, and that they are more reassured that the figure behind the wheel is a man rather than a robot. Nevertheless, committed Indianapolis enthusiasts are far more interested in the progress of the driver than the car, and they conceptualize a triumph at Indianapolis as a human victory instead of some technocratic tour-de-force. Should the race ever cease to be read in other than human terms, its potential for creating and maintaining public interest would diminish substantially.

Stronghold of American oval track automobile racing that it assuredly is, Indianapolis gives tacit, ironic acknowledgment that the spectacle it strives so diligently to promote is not altogether legitimized to the degree that it might like to be. As a sporting activity, the annual 500-mile race finds itself in a paradoxically defensive stance. From the perspective of one well outside the racing establishment, that defensiveness speaks as loudly as the belch of racing engines in May. But why the defensiveness? Lack of sporting recognition is one reason. A shortage of broad-based public approval of automobile racing is another. Organized with the most august of intentions, the cabalistic United States Auto Club, whose offices are located within earshot of the Indianapolis Motor Speedway, has in the twenty-five years of its existence succumbed to an advanced stage of cronyism and parochialism — the same attitudinal combination that once beset the American Automobile Association before it. The United States Auto Club shows every indication of having been driven into a corner by a generally suspicious public, skeptical of the basic efficacy of automobile racing. The result is that USAC and its followers have clannishly withdrawn into their own endemic world replete with its unique language and its jealously defended sense of separateness. The penalty for this isolationism is the regrettable lack of sophistication that characterizes USAC and, for that matter, the front office of the Indianapolis Motor Speedway. Their innate sense of defensiveness has also resulted in a disinclination toward public communication of part of their mission: to advocate and recommend the somewhat esoteric delights of automobile racing to a largely uninitiated and therefore mainly indifferent America.

This shortcoming has not gone unnoticed. When the United States Auto Club began touting automobile racing as the Sport of the Seventies, it fell conspicuously short of promoting its Indianapolis car circuit to full media potential. It was over the enervating winter of 1978-1979 that a substantial number of championship car owners became disgruntled enough over what they considered the antiquated means and ends of the United States Auto Club to form a defiant splinter-group sanctioning body of their own, calling it Championship Auto Racing Teams (CART). The recidivism of the United States Auto Club was not the only thing at issue. Limited prize money at all championship races (not excluding Indianapolis) became still another grievance. The two most imposing figures behind the CART banner were Michigan's Pat Patrick and controversial entrepreneur Roger Penske, each of them wealthy (and therefore powerful) bankrollers of top-line Indianapolis racing machinery. "Unlike baseball, football, and basketball," said Dick Stahler of *Car and Driver*, "auto racing cannot count on automatic media coverage — it has to work hard for what it gets. So maybe we're seeing the first step toward the inmates taking over the promotional department of the asylum."

Perhaps so. But the emergence of CART threatened not only to divide the future of Indianapolis car racing, but also threatened to shatter the existence of USAC as a credible sanctioning body. Although the United States Auto Club has failed over the years to transcend the limitations of its own very circumscribed perspectives, it has at the same time provided (along with the Indianapolis Motor Speedway) a gathering ground and forum for the most vital and influential contingent of motor racing personalities on the planet Earth. Ostensibly both nonprofit and laudably democratic, the United States Auto Club's brief history has been punctuated by continuous and sometimes acrimonious dissention, as well as largely unexplained adjustments in administrative personnel. It might also be noted that while USAC's function as administrator and supervisor of the annual 500-mile auto race at Indianapolis has yet to be improved upon, it has nonetheless inherited the American Automobile Association's legacy of bureaucratic pettiness and perversity toward its membership.

Today the United States Auto Club seems to conceive of itself as the guardian, benefactor, and protector of its sizable membership, whose whims and desires it purports to follow. It is the umbrella under which traditionalist (primarily open-wheel) competition strives to perpetuate itself. What limited security it may have to offer comes through the apparently common recognition within the membership that what is good for auto racing is therefore good for them. While the USAC constituency has been beleagured over the years by factionalism and schisms, there appears to be a vague consensus that the plight of open-wheel automobile racing is served best if it remains largely white, middle-class, and male-oriented, and as long as it nurtures its traditional domestic American flavor. Indeed, the official red, white, and blue crest of the United States Auto Club is superimposed over crossed checkered flags. It is behind this ostensibly proud symbol of convergence of car and country that the drama of the 500-mile race is reenacted annually. In other words, the logo is the message.

The myths established, nurtured, and perpetuated by the Speedway's sometime bizarre history are perhaps too varied to categorize conveniently, although they are not difficult to identify. One such myth, and a fundamental one at that, finds its expression in the almost mystical yoking of man and machine, to the end that both function as a magnificently integrated organism that embraces both human judgment and intuition with feats of mechanical ingenuity. This wholeness is not only desirable, but necessary to the optimum performance of the car and its intrepid passenger. "And that's what it's all about," comments regular Indianapolis driver Johnny Parsons, son of the 1950 winner. "Trying to get the car to feel like part of your body." To Parsons and other drivers who have transformed driving into a mystical experience of sorts, the car is, or should rightfully be, an extension of one's consciousness. To help that relationship flourish, Indianapolis cars are fitted to the driver's body like a pair of tailor-made leotards, and when he takes to the wheel, it is like easing into some great mechanical cocoon. Racing car builders go to some pains to ensure that their drivers are accorded as much comfort as their uncomfortable cars will admit. It is imperative, therefore, that the contour and the padding of the driver's reclined seat are to his satisfaction, and that his legs do not chafe abrasively against any of the car's cockpit components. No less important for comfort and for safety's sake is the positioning of the windshield in such a way that it prevents wind turbulence from gusting down upon the driver's chest and then up under his helmet. After these and other amenities are attended to, it is the business of the driver to know intimately the personality of his car as it reveals itself at speeds well over two hundred miles an hour, and in an endless sequence of left hand turns.

It has been pointed out with some frequency that the contemporary Indianapolis car (although its form follows its function) resembles a scarcely sublimated phallus. Whatever overt similarities that exist may be purely coincidental, but then again perhaps not. Racing is very much the machismo preoccupation, and its participants are not untypically assertive in their real or supposed virility. "Drivers, especially the well-known ones, have all sorts of good-looking women chasing after them," Indianapolis veteran Mel Kenyon wrote disapprovingly. "If a driver wants to go that route — and most do — they have plenty of opportunities to play around."

Popular Jan Opperman concurs. "Before I discovered Jesus," he told writers Phil Berger and Larry Bortstein, "I was a typical race driver, you know, on an ego trip. And I used to party. There wasn't one race when I didn't have some woman or another with me. I mean, I dig chicks. I still like to look at 'em, but I'm straight now with my old lady. Mary, my wife, that is."

Albeit there is not a great deal of latitude or choice in the particular shape of racers at Indianapolis today (because they are reflective of both the immutable laws of physics and the sometimes peevish regulations sent down by the United States Auto Club), the cars themselves remain sexually suggestive. Vividly painted, handsomely lettered, low slung, and fearsomely aggressive, they have a way of letting even the most sexually moribund observer know that they mean erotic business. Automotive historian Griffith Borgeson was neither the first nor the last to remark on the relationship between the racing car, its driver, and the combined performance of both on the track when he wrote, "A very real part of the thrill is sexual, a statement which will not come as news to most psychologists nor to most members of the racing fraternity." He continued, "There are those of us who very consciously can experience degrees of orgiastic transport with a suitably inspiring mechanical companion." Referring specifically to the oval track driver who finds himself magnetically drawn to Indianapolis, he continued, "The balls-out stand-on-it-and-turn-left charger is typically a person of very strong, virile libido. It seems to be and probably is an occupational prerequisite."

Inside the racing fraternity, the social forms and gestures that accompany the process of racing cars at Indianapolis are themselves a direct outgrowth of the sport itself. We know, for example, that the pressures and requirements of the racing fraternity as a whole have a great deal to do with the way the members of the fraternity behave toward one another. If its members are unalterably clannish and exclusive, those tendencies are an expression not only of occupational defensiveness, but also of shared goals and mutually held values. The reward system in open-wheel racing that says all roads must inevitably lead to Indianapolis is largely borne out in fact. Those whose lives are dedicated to deriving a living from following the racing circuits across America are those whose ultimate shrine is to be found in Speedway, Indiana. They make their way to that shrine in successive stages of perceived fitness and eligibility as determined by the well-entrenched values evolved by the peer group itself. Because Indianapolis is almost universally recognized as the penultimate achievement in American (at least) motor racing circles, its doors are open to relatively few eligible contestants. Of the few who are called, even fewer are chosen.

The sometimes arduous process of credential gathering that permits a driver to be at Indianapolis at all may well reflect up to twenty years in accumulated experience and reputation. In Gasoline Alley there is more respect accorded an aspirant who in the view of the clan has properly served this apprenticeship than is accorded a contestant who has somehow found a way to short-circuit the novitiate phase of his career behind the wheel. Properly accumulated racing experience on the part of the Speedway neophyte driver reassures the old-line Indianapolis establishment that the candidate knows well the ritualized rules of the game and is constitutionally able and willing to abide by them. Not everyone is.

There have always been drivers (talented and accomplished drivers, at that) who did not seem to fit the Indianapolis mold, but who ultimately did themselves credit on the two-and-a-half-mile course anyway. Their successses were at times a source of disquietude to traditionalist Speedway pundits, because those successes tended to cast some doubt on certain long-held (and probably erroneous) convictions about what it takes to be an Indianapolis driver. Some of the more successful personalities on the track at Indy were generally considered to have come up from corners of the racing world that were considered suspicious. Jim Clark, Graham Hill, Mark Donohue, Peter Revson, Sam Posey, Mike Hiss, Tom Bagley, and Janet Guthrie each seemed at one time or another to be a subversive departure from the comfortably stereotyped Indianapolis candidate. Most of them had raced the European road course. Most of them had been to college. Some of them knew a few principles of basic engineering and physics. Worst of all, one of them was a woman, and her marked determination to motor through the macho barrier at Indianapolis was at the outset, at least, the ultimate insult to male-dominated Indianapolis. To make matters worse, each was a product of having raced a bewildering array of sports cars, grand prix cars, and formula cars of different descriptions. Clark, Hill, and Donohue were difficult men to ignore at Indianapolis, for the simple reason that each of them registered a win there.

Connecticut artist and writer Sam Posey, the stepson of a New York physician, raced at Indianapolis one time (1972) and completed 198 of the full 200 laps, finishing in fifth position. Hardly the prototypical Indianapolis driver, Posey had experienced more than his share of frustration in convincing the sages at the United States Auto Club that he should, because of his distinguished career as a road racer, be given the go-ahead to try Indianapolis. He had correctly recognized that by the late sixties road racers like himself were converging on the Speedway in increasing numbers and that they were enjoying considerable success there, partly because of their familiarity with rear-engine racing cars, a relatively new phenomenon at that time. "The USAC committee which ruled on the eligibility of rookie drivers was the first line of defense against this invasion," he wrote in his autobiographic *The Mudge Pond Express.* "In this context, 'eligibility' is a code word for 'acceptability to the Indy establishment.' At the time my application arrived at the USAC office the committee was doing all it could to make things difficult for road-racing drivers."

This is not to suggest that the USAC opinions about who should be eligible for a try at Indianapolis have always been misguided. Speedway traditionalists have never quite recovered from an "I told you so" situation that occurred in 1976, for example. Thirty-one-year-old Eddie Miller, of Lakewood, Colorado, had not only paid for the privilege of driving ("renting" might be a more appropriate term) a competitive car owned by Gearhardt Racers of Fresno, California, but had also agreed to provide a life insurance policy on himself as part of the arrangement. By candidly held Speedway standards, the apprenticeship that Miller had served (consisting of experience in sprint cars, Formula Fords, and Super Vees) was considered unorthodox enough to be at least somewhat suspect in the minds of the Indianapolis old guard. They may have been right. In phase two of his high-speed driver's test, Miller misnegotiated the Speedway's southwest turn, spun into a ditch, hurtled over two fences, and landed on his head next to the tunnel in the south chute. Having come within a flick of destroying himself in the decisive way that he had destroyed Don Gearhardt's blue Thermo King racer, he was perhaps blessed in receiving only a broken back in what had been an unusually violent, rampaging spill. And although crack-ups are, one might safely say, nothing especially unusual at Indianapolis, old-line racing gurus shook their heads knowingly in the positive recognition that Miller, because of the paucity of his professional experience, should not have been out there in the first place.

* * *

Inside the track gates, the springtime motif of an Indiana May is itself emblematic of renewal. Early in the month the intermittent activity of men and cars at the Speedway (punctually broadcast by local radio stations at thirty-minute intervals) has the unmistakable suggestion of a fertility rite that increases its force and momentum with the passing of each day. The spring opening of the Speedway is a time for the gathering up of psychological strength for what is by all odds the most momentous and raucous racing roundup of the entire year. May in Indiana means among other things that the weather can, and usually does, vacillate unpredictably between the two extremes of frigid rain and scorching aridity. The trees and shrubbery in and around the Speedway have not long been foliated, and the grounds have only recently been restored to the green of summer. The dead gods of a dormant Speedway have not long been awakened, and a quickened spirit of rejuvenation is written across the entire scene. The fertility expressed in that landscape finds expression in other ways as well. The racing clan well understands that it is a fertile time to amass a great deal of money in a short time, and that a few of the competitors will accomplish precisely that before the pageant is over. There is also an understanding that it is a fertile time to metamorphose oneself into an instant celebrity, and there will be persons who manage to do that as well. It may also be an excellent time and place for a driver to ingratiate himself with monied individuals who are prepared (if they are also persuaded) to underwrite him with the wherewithal that could well finance a sweet season spent on racetracks from Ontario to Trenton.

The drivers who haunt Gasoline Alley and who are in perpetual quest of dollars and celebrityhood form a variety of racing types. Populating the center stage are certain determined types who are, or would like to be, race day protagonists: the top dogs, the underdogs, and the hot dogs. The first group has established itself well enough in past races so that it is almost certain of obtaining a good car to drive. The second group would like the opportunity to prove itself, and the third group evinces a chancy do-or-die attitude not necessarily admired inside the racing fraternity. If these categories seem excessively simplistic, they are further com-

The great Anthony Foyt after his unprecedented
fourth Indianapolis victory, 1977.

David Knox

plicated by the introduction of certain other regional driver
types who have long been in vogue at Indianapolis. Among
them is the collegiate and well-urbanized easterner, the neo-
cowpoke, and the middle-class mid-American. Superimposed
over these are the second generation drivers with excellent
dynastic name recognition like Duane Carter, Johnny Parsons,
Bill Vukovich, Al and Bobby Unser, and an occasional driver
from beyond the Atlantic.

It is the westerners and middlewesterners who, because of
their pervailing oval track orthodoxy and their historic affin-

A. J. Foyt pulls out of pit in car #14 on his practice run, 1979.
David Knox

ity for left-turn-only motorsports, have influenced the Indianapolis scene most. Even so, scarcely anyone would quarrel with the nomination of Houston's balding Anthony Joseph Foyt as the all-time, classic, made-to-order Indianapolis competitor: twenty-two times a Speedway starter, four times a winner. Two-fisted, devotedly pragmatic, gamey, unlettered, and unequivocally blunt, A. J. Foyt (himself a second generation racer) embraces the compulsive tunnel vision requisite to the ultimate performing genius in all avenues of questing. But like virtually all old-line Indianapolis regulars, Foyt had not only fulfilled the ritual apprenticeship before coming to the Speedway, but has also managed to evolve into a shrewd racing tactitian, a self-made engineer (who never advanced through the eleventh grade), and above all a remarkably intuitive and subtle orchestrator of the potentially lethal racing cars that he barrels around a multiplicity of race courses in and out of the continental United States. Like him or not (and there are a substantial number of racing insiders who do not), Foyt comes closest to fulfilling completely the attributes of genius and excellence as they are construed at Indianapolis. His biographer, Bill Libby, reported in 1974 that Foyt's "personal worth had been estimated at $10 million," and that, besides lending his name and counsel to the largest Chevrolet dealership in Texas, he had financial interests in "oil wells, race tracks, real estate, shopping centers, and motels."

All such on-track and off-track accomplishments have made Foyt the reigning role model for the Indianapolis racer. There is much more to the Foyt mystique than the image of a man who has collected laurels from Indy to Daytona to Le Mans, for he also is representative of down-home Texas, and a sterling example of the limitless heights the inspired bourgeois can still aspire to and attain in contemporary America. The genuineness of his Speedway percipience, combined with his surprisingly gifted head for business, may well (as is persistently rumored) make him the next president of the Indianapolis Motor Speedway.

It may come as news to some that there are other luminaries at Indianapolis besides Foyt. Many have served racing apprenticeships every bit as rigorous as his, but have not been quite so skilled at remaining alive and relatively well. This is not to suggest that Foyt has escaped serious injury. During the 1972 100-mile dirt-track race at Du Quoin, Illinois, fuel that had carelessly been splashed over his hot exhaust pipe during a pit stop ignited as he rejoined the race. When flames licked their way into the cockpit, he was left with little choice other than to bail out of the moving racer with his driving suit ablaze. In doing so, the racer's left rear wheel steamrolled over Foyt's left foot, mauling it substantially. To increase the seriousness of the accident, it was that same left foot which had been mauled once before at Riverside, California, in 1965, during the running of a stock car race, when Foyt sailed end-for-end through the atmosphere and came to rest amid smoke and debris well outside the racecourse. On that occasion

Inside the cockpit of one of A. J. Foyt's many Sheraton-Thompson Specials. Note the gauges rotated so that all critical "redline" points will read exactly at noon. Gauges can therefore be read with with peripheral vision.

Patrick O'Daniels

Foyt's injuries were numerous enough to defy categorical description. In 1966 he crashed again, this time at Milwaukee's one-mile paved State Fair Park, where he suffered burns about the head, neck, and hands. A listing of Foyt's injuries incurred in the line of duty would indeed be ambitious, although by dint of intuition, determination, luck, and extraordinary singlemindedness, he has managed somehow to prevail in circumstances that have killed outright a good number of his friends and companions in racing or else have injured them to the extent that they never drove competitively again. His survival alone since his initial race in 1953 at the age of eighteen is a singular accomplishment in itself. His first crack at the Indianapolis 500 was in 1958, and among the thirty-three drivers who started that race, twelve eventually died in racing accidents; the rest of them, excluding Foyt, have long since retired from active competition.

Seeing friends perish on the race track is a problem that Foyt and others in the racing fraternity have had to come to terms with. It can hardly be said that the racing clan at Indianapolis gives up its dead easily. For years, those members of the fraternity who had been lost over the previous twelve months, whether from accidental or natural causes, have been accorded recognition. Twelve minutes prior to the flagging-off of every Speedway race comes the ritualized playing of "Taps" by the combined United States Armed Forces Color Guard. Their somber notes (themselves in contrast with the elevated excitement of the occasion) are in memory of service men and women who unselfishly defended their country with their lives, but also in memory of racing's fallen. Beyond this solemn obeisance, different kinds of gestures are made by the racing subculture to preserve the memory of those comrades-in-arms who have allegedly defended the cause of automobile racing by coughing up the ultimate price. Indianapolis race winners are accorded a kind of symbolic immortality by having their stern facial likenesses embossed on the checkerboard side of the huge Borg-Warner trophy, itself the most revered totemic object in all of car racing.

There is a very strong impulse among racing people, particularly the Indianapolis-oriented among them, to sustain old memories at nearly any cost. The Indianapolis 500 Old Timers Club, which maintains an aging membership roll of over four hundred, has been in existence for more than twenty years, and stations a mobile lounge in the Speedway's infield for the pleasure of its constituency. Organizations like it have come into being in the East, the Middle West, and the far West. When the Williams Grove Speedway Old Timers Club was organized at the famous half-mile dirt track in Mechanicsburg, Pennsylvania in 1975, the membership responded by convening a gathering of vintage racing cars and (where possible) their vintage drivers. The group even managed to resuscitate two beloved, deceased Indianapolis veterans for the occasion: Someone appeared holding two life-sized beaverboard mannequins. The first was the likeness of Ted Horn, who died at the age of thirty-eight after a dirt-track spill on the Du Quoin mile oval. The other likeness was that of "Bronco Bill" Schindler, the one-legged (because of a 1936 racing mishap) driver whose life ended at the age of forty-four on the half-mile dirt track at Allentown, Pennsylvania, in 1952. Said an accompanying bulletin, "This is an era of non-hero worship. Where would auto racing be without it? . . . these two HEROES will always be on our minds at every convention. We must honor all our dead heroes of the speedway as well as our fortunate live ones. This is what racing is all about." Said one onlooker, "It was eerie the way those two figures were made to stand there. Spooky."

People on the inside of American motor racing circles have extensive and usually accurate memories that spur on their devotion to those cohorts who have been cut down in action and to those who have been severely injured at Indianapolis and elsewhere. One particularly fertile expression of that devotion is evidenced in the fairly recent tendency to recover, restore, and preserve racing momentos. The Indianapolis Motor Speedway's laudable successes at procuring and rebuilding vintage racing cars is a gesture of tribute to the personalities who were historically identified with them. The racing fraternity's all but religious veneration for their quasi-holy artifacts has extended itself also to the accumulation and display of other relics that form a seemingly endless inventory of helmets, goggles, driving gloves, soiled bandanas, and oily racing uniforms. Displayed beside them are antiquated spark plugs, carburetors, pistons, and connecting rods—each reflective of the Speedway's keen reverence for its seventy-year heritage. The metallic blue helmet with the felicitous cartoon figure painted across its frontal edge once belonged to the late Sammy Sessions (who, after a life on the speedways of America, killed himself in a snowmobiling accident) during his innumerable racing forays. Donated to the Speedway by Session's widow, the helmet finds its *raison d'être* as a poignant reminder of a man beloved in an extensive historical procession of real racers.

Beyond the walls of the Motor Speedway's museum, the most curious single assemblage of racing artifacts is without much question barely outside the benign village of Urbana, Ohio, about forty miles west of the state capital in Columbus. It is here that one Robert McConnell, a vice-president of the Desman-Stephens Manufacturing Company and president of a concern called Gaslite Auto Parts, maintains a comprehensive collection of replacement pieces (most of them reproductions) for vintage Fords, specifically Model T's, Model A's, and early V-8's. To the antique Ford fancier, McConnell's inventory is a veritable automotive horn of plenty.

McConnell, who in appearance and by inclination resembles a mustachioed Sherlock Holmes, is willing for a price to furnish anything from a set of four emergency brake band retracting springs for a Model A to the left-hand water pump on a 1937 Ford V-8. But despite the efficiency with which his esoteric inventory is lovingly collected, organized, and dispatched to any point, vintage Fords are not McConnell's primary passion. His métier is racing cars — the older and more renowned the better. "Model T's are like two peas in a pod," says McConnell, who declines to reveal either the number of racing cars in his possession, or the dollar figures that have paid for more midgets, sprint cars, and Indianapolis racers than could be contained at one time on the Urbana High School basketball floor. "I've never been a racing driver," he continues, "but I have admired racing, and I am a fan who got himself involved. Back in the fifties, I couldn't see why anyone would want to fight the traffic at Indianapolis, and that's the last place I wanted to be on Memorial Day weekend." His attitude has changed completely now, and McConnell has become the unchallenged king of the private racing collectors. He reasons that if Model T's really are like two peas in a pod, then racing cars are nothing if not unique and individual creations, each one unlike the other. "Each race car is unique," he says, "not only because of the history behind it, but because of how it performed for the driver, and because of its engineering. Some cars did well, and others — well, others were merely trying." But what prompts a man to acquire racing cars? "It's like a lot of things you can get carried away with," he theorizes. "It's the same as saving spinning wheels or different types of barbed wire. Racing until recently has been overlooked. Maybe this is why I was able to get in on the ground floor."

McConnell's primary cache of cars is in one of two large, temporarily unheated garages. The one closest to the door is a battered old Packard racer once driven by Ralph DePalma; McConnell found it stashed under a porch in "a bad Detroit neighborhood." Next to the abused Packard is what remains of the Sampson Special the eastern driver Walt Ader trailed to twenty-second place in the 1950 Indianapolis 500. The car's paint is missing. Also missing its paint (as well as its engine and its wheels) is the Pat Clancy 500-B Kurtis roadster whose best finish at Indianapolis was a third in 1955 with California's Jim Davies driving. "I've got the other bits and pieces to finish it out," McConnell explains. "It hasn't been cut or changed any. It's pretty straight." Toward the back of the garage, illuminated by fluorescent lamps, is a machine of more recent vintage: the 1971 Utah Stars Special that Lloyd Ruby experienced gear trouble with and finished eleventh in. It is a red, white, and blue 1970 Laycock Mongoose that was once owned and entered by Gene White Firestone. "I am told that it cost White and Firestone roughly a million and a half. It holds the fastest straightaway speed currently on the Speedway because it did not have any wings to slow it down and because the blower once stuck open on the frontstretch."

Wearing what remains of its 1950 paint is the car once sponsored by George Hoster. It was a nonqualifier that year, but its history reaches far back. "I believe it is the old Louis Meyer Tydol car," McConnell speculates. "There were three cars built of this type, but this one's been changed. It was rebodied by Art Hoyt in 1949. I'd like to trace it back still further, but I'm having problems with that." Next to it rests the tattered remains of the Troy Oil car, driven to tenth place in 1949 by Norm Houser, and to sixteenth the following year by Gene Hartley in his rookie year at Indianapolis. "It was lengthened and shortened as the cars were back then," he recalls. "It was run as a sprint car, for instance. Bill Mackey was killed in it over at Winchester. At that time the tail was so bashed in that it was replaced without the original headrest on it. I found the car in Kokomo." His attention rages over the room filled with sadly defunct cars. "This over here is the car that Al Gordon drove to the west coast national championship in 1933, and that yellow one over there still intrigues the heck out of us. It looks somewhat like the Miller Fords in design, but notice that the riding mechanic sits ahead rather than behind the driver. Somewhere, sometime, someone will be able to tell us what the car was. It has a nice aluminum body, but everything else is pure junk. This car back here is a sprinter. Auto Shippers Special. Ran in the forties. Bill Nagy drove it. Other than that I don't know a lot about it. That number 3 over there was one of Mauri Rose's first rides. I have a picture of it taken at Winchester in 1928."

Pushed unobtrusively against a back wall is the 1931 Indianapolis winner, the Bowes Seal Fast Special driven by Louis Schneider, who had started the car thirteenth. In its eight Indianapolis starts between 1930 and 1939 it finished all of the way from first to thirty-second and last. "It was sitting in Indianapolis until a couple years ago," McConnell reports. "If you look at the front end of the car, you will see virtually no changes from the way it was originally. And if you count the rivets down on the hood, you'll find the third rivet missing. Then look at Emil Andres's qualifying picture in 1939, and you'll find that third rivet still missing. This is one of the Millers that was built with the steering support outboard. It has a Duesenberg, which was installed in 1948."

But the jewel of Bob McConnell's collection is fragmented and resting in more than three garages awaiting its full restoration. It is the original Ted Horn sprint car, built in 1939. It campaigned until 1961, when it appeared briefly with a Cadillac engine under the hood and Mario Andretti in the driver's seat. "This is Horn's really famous car," McConnell says of the man who in ten Indianapolis starts between 1935 and 1948 never finished worse than fourth nor better than second after his rookie year. "Cars like this one are very definitely objects of veneration. They are not only historical; they are an extension of the driver's personality. In the case of Ted Horn, I don't know of anybody who disliked him. He was strictly a hero, and the car is part of the man who drives it. I have a couple of cars that were never raced, and they don't hold as much interest. But the ones that have a history and a tie-in with various personalities are the ones we like: the more famous, the better. If you had Babe Ruth's bat, it would be the same kind of thing."

McConnell purchased the car from New Jersey 500 photographer-historian Bruce Craig. Prior to that time, Craig had systematically gathered pieces and parts of the original car from its numerous intervening owners. Those earlier owners, in turn, had saved the original components as if they were indeed sacrosanct. For McConnell, the acquisition of the car meant painstaking, retrospective inquiry that involved notifying each of the car's previous owners that the original parts were being actively solicited. Horn's machinist-mechanic Dick Simoneck provided the car's original patterns, and good-luck emblems for the dashboard. McConnell, in the meantime, found the car's (presumably) original engine some years ago in Pennsylvania. "I try to have the car exactly as it was," he reflects philosophically. "Some cars I'm fussier about than others." The Horn car, with its reverential respect in the minds of hundreds, became for Bob McConnell something to fuss over endlessly. Having heard about the restoration of the Horn car, George Moore of the *Indianapolis Star* commented that although Horn had never won at Indianapolis, "he was regarded by drivers, mechanics, and owners alike as a race driver's driver. It is fitting that a portion of his life can be preserved in memoriam."

But if the car is an extension of the driver, then McConnell and others have gone to some pains to find a driver whose vintage matches that of the car. "When we take a car out to run it," says McConnell, "we normally try to find a driver who drove on that particular track. Most former drivers are greatly pleased to meet their old cars again. They like reliving those memories. There are a few men in racing with bad experiences behind them, and they have tried to put these experiences out of their minds. They don't want anything to do with it. But I find this in the minority. We give some the opportunity to ride in different cars, and most of them are eager to do so."

If accumulating and interpreting memorabilia is one avenue toward the ritualization that has found support inside the world of Indianapolis racing, still another is the conduct of the "thirty days in May" that lead first toward the actual running

Prerace scene at turn 1 (southwest).

of the race, and then away from it. To be on the Indianapolis scene during the race month is to subject oneself to a gradually elevated scenario of heightened anxiety and outrageous social humbuggery. On the day that the Speedway throws open its gates to the public for the witnessing of initial practice runs, the appearance of racing cars on the track is musically anticipated by the uniformed appearance of the Speedway High School marching band, and then by ceremonies of renewal that call for a brief round of cordial addresses from the balcony of the Terrace Tower by the president of the Speedway and by other locally esteemed personalities. Among the latter are copious representatives from the socially ambitious, upper-middle-class retinue of the 500 Festival Committee, composed of ubiquitous civic-minded individuals, all of whom are attired symbolically (and conspicuously) in Speedway black and white. The organization's thirty-three directors (lately increased to thirty-six) are, according to one press release, "key people in the community" behind whom are "nearly 5,000 volunteer workers," consisting presumably of something less than key people in the community.

Present also on this first of the May Speedway days is the 500 Festival Queen, who is given a customary bouquet of roses, a scholarship, a jewelled tiara, and a pace car replica furnished by whatever Detroit automaker is favored by the Speedway that year. "Not to be outdone by Atlantic City," a bulletin issued from the 500 Festival Associates explains, "a queen contest was added in 1959," two years after the original race celebration was instituted. Originally, the celebration had consisted of a parade, a select Governor's Ball, and a non-select community dance. Today, however, the Festival Committee has enlarged its mission from a single day celebration to a flurry of social paradigms that require almost the whole month to act out. Besides the televised parade (known officially as the 500 Festival Memorial Parade) and the Governor's Ball (now known as the "Queen's Ball"), certain local residents are smitten by such neighborly occasions as the Queen's Coronation Pageant, the Mayor's Breakfast, the Festival of Arts Exhibit, the Children's Activities, the Radio-Controlled Car Race, the Gin Rummy Tournament, and the Mechanic's Recognition Party. It is clearly the most socially active phase of the year for Indianapolis. "A hundred thousand details are worked out in hundreds of committee meetings," says the communique from the Festival Associates. "Meanwhile, sponsors are found to pay the price of floats. Artists are found to design them and builders to build them. Bands are selected. Celebrities are invited. Tickets are sold, as is the Festival souvenir program advertising. All of the other events are planned and organized, and suddenly, the merry month of May has begun."

After the merry month has commenced out at the track with a round of addresses and musical interludes, the track is inspected (as is the usual custom) before the cars take to the course for their annual "shakedown" runs. In times past, the opening of the Speedway for practice laps was accompanied by a furious quest on the part of several drivers to be first on the course. Their desire was evidently founded on the assumption that being first on the track on this first day of practice runs was a gesture that would bode well for the remainder of the month. In 1974 the Speedway's opening day fell on May 6, when the first two cars anticipated the green signal light and rushed prematurely down pit lane, sending crusty seventy-one-year-old USAC supervisor Walt Myers to Methodist Hospital with fractures in both his hip and wrist after he had stumbled in an attempt to keep from being run down.

While there is admittedly a great deal of pretense and ill-disguised stupidity on and off the Speedway, the electrical days of May are unlike the days of May anywhere else. For those caught up in the Speedway scene who have a knack for ignoring the ludicrous, these are the most cherished days of the year. Once they have passed, there is an awareness of another eleven months and a dreadful winter to contend with before the scene will be restored again. As the days pass, there comes the gradual but ever more determined influx of participants and spectators. Among the witnesses are numerous busloads of elementary school children escorted by their mentors on what passes for educational field trips happily removed from the pressures of geography and arithmetic. Unlike the children, whose every move is supervised and monitored, other spectators have a propensity for strolling at random from one region of the ground to another. Some assume their personal outposts around the two-and-a-half mile track, where they assert something akin to squatter's rights. Equipped with stopwatches and wirebound notebooks, they hail the reappearance of their cherished whizkids by logging lap times and by soliciting enough autograph signatures to nominate Dolly Parton for president. Their demeanor confirms that the preparations they witness are an experience shared among thousands of diverse individuals. It also confirms that the Indianapolis experience is, among other things, an organized reunion of the Indy car set for the purpose of rekindling friendships while witnessing the evolution of another race month at the old ritual ground. Wage slaves with nine-to-five regimens absent themselves surreptitiously from their shops and offices, preferring instead to loll away the hours nourishing their fantasy lives to the tune of wailing Cosworth engines.

On the track, drivers pursue their usual occupational duties of finding speed, while also attempting to find which parts of their cars are weak enough to pose problems in the race itself. In the pits, crewmen maintain a detailed record of changes to the car's chassis and engine settings. A rookie driver who has been given the provisional clearance by USAC to learn both his car and the track it navigates is obliged to wear three taped-on stripes at the rear of his car. The symbol tells others on the course that his apprenticeship is still not concluded because he has not yet passed the required driver's test before a board of peer-judges, and is therefore to be regarded with an extra measure of caution. Once the driver's test (a solo performance) has been disposed of, a qualification run later on will constitute still another solitary run on the track, under the most exacting surveillance by multitudes of witnesses, among them the most celebrated figures in the realm of automobile racing. At Indianapolis, every performer auditions, regardless of his reputation, and in that audition presumes to display his prowess at the controls without sharing the track with his fellows. The great spectacle of qualification runs (which many experienced race-watchers esteem more highly than the race itself) establishes the separate identity of each would-be competitor on race day.

When the public gates break open at five in the morning, race day is finally and irrevocably on. And when the motorcycles, passenger cars, and pedestrians stream through the gates, the great influx is the final and most significant tribute to the nearly religious fervor over the race that has been gathering momentum during the month. The management has, over the past several years, been fairly consistent in its programmed sequence of events. Those who have been inside the Speedway on race mornings in the past come to expect an essentially identical and ritualized bill of fare. At 7:30 A.M. a caravan of pace cars is lined up in downtown Indianapolis at the Indiana National Bank on Ohio Street. On the bank's fifth floor, a continental breakfast is in progress for participants who, minutes earlier, have received their race day credentials and who will ride the caravan into the track with all the seriousness of purpose with which Hannibal crossed the Alps. Five miles away, out at the Speedway, all competing racers have been pushed along the pit wall in race readiness. Some of the cars are covered by blue and yellow tarpaulins that say "Goodyear." It is 8:00 A.M. By 8:30 A.M., those who were last seen eating breakfast in the Indiana National Bank are now reported to their pace cars. Led by police escort, the caravan leaves the bank at exactly 9:00 A.M., and makes its way to the track by way of West Sixteenth Street. The caravan enters the track through Gate 2, and then dips into tunnel 2, finally coming to park in the Speedway's museum lot. Twenty minutes is allocated for the participants to exit their pace cars, following which the assemblage is ushered through the automotive museum in half an hour. As the cars are pushed into position at 9:45 A.M., the Purdue band intones the sentimental Indiana favorite, "On the Banks of the Wabash," written by Theodore Dreiser and his gladhanding brother Paul. At exactly 9:50 A.M., the various queens, princesses, VIP's, television heroes, politicians, captains of industry, and professional warriors are installed in their pace cars once more. It is now 10:00 A.M. This so-called celebrity caravan makes its way through the garage area and then onto the track for a single lap. Returned to the starting line, they disembark (at the rate of four passenger cars at a time) in front of the Master Control Tower, where the late Sid Collins once held forth. By 10:34 A.M., it is time for the usual track inspection by the chief steward of the race, who eventually returns from having circled the track slowly, but in time to hear the thunderous chords of "The Star Spangled Banner" as rendered by the Purdue Band.

The national anthem is played with sixteen minutes remaining until race time, and it is sounded partly in affirmation of Memorial Day (which is still more than thirteen hours away) and partly in keeping with the nationalistic occasion that the 500-mile race has maneuvered itself into being. At 10:47 A.M. comes the Invocation, which is partly out of deference to the race's being run (in recent years) on Sunday in a region where most natives would be inclined to agree that the proper place for a God-fearing Christian on Sunday morning is not at the Speedway, but in church. By this time, at any rate, the duty to both country and God has been perfunctorily disposed of, and it remains (with twelve minutes left before the start of the race) to pay tribute to deceased service men and women as well as to those who have (by some oddly conceived analogy) died motor racing. At 10:50 A.M. the Purdue University All-American Band strikes up "Back Home Again in Indiana," both lilting and sentimental. As the sounds waft over the Speedway's ample acreage, thousands of parti-colored helium-filled balloons waft skyward and eventually drift out of sight. There are now seven minutes remaining before the start of the race, and almost everyone's attention is directed toward the front of the starting field, where, according to the precedent established by the late three-time winner and Speedway president Wilbur Shaw, comes the familiar stern command: "Gentlemen, start your engines." Well in excess of three hundred thousand spectators hoot their approval, and their sound is superseded by the engines of thirty-three racing cars which are, at this precise moment, supposed to sputter into life. Invariably, there is at least one that refuses to fire, and the attention that has been directed to the front of the pack moves to wherever the unobliging car may be.

At Indianapolis, the climax comes not at the end, but at the beginning. The command for engines to be started is perhaps as much a treasured moment as the start of the race itself. Owing to the necessity of warming racing engines gradually, all thirty-three cars creep stealthily away from the starting line, falling into what is intended to be racing formation on the backstretch of the Speedway. Once on the track, the first obligation of drivers is to provide a ceremonial parade for a single lap behind the pace car. This gesture may be the only opportunity that amassed throng has to view all contestants at the same time, for generally there is at least one who, for one reason or another, falls away from the back at the start of the race or indeed even prior to that. It is doubtful that, at the end of the day, a random spectator can remember having seen specific cars in the race, inasmuch as some contestants remain in competition so brief a time as to be virtually unnoticed.

At the conclusion of the pace lap, the pace car begins to

The pace lap through the south chute, 1965.

Indianapolis Star

accelerate its speed until the cars are led to the starting line and to the waving of the green flag. At the time of the theatrical unleashing of the green, the southbound speed is roughly 100 miles an hour, and by the time the cars are on the northbound back straightaway the speed will have increased to more like 200 miles an hour. The convention of using a pace car to escort the pack of thirty-three for the start of the race is, at best, anachronistic. While it is true that the USAC high command who occupy the pace car are able, to some extent, to size up the formation of cars behind them, another point of view has it that their presence on the track is perhaps more of

Indy Myth   209

The start, 1974.

Indianapolis Star

a hindrance than a help. After the disastrous incident when the pace car failed to slow down on the pit driveway and plowed, headlong, into a special portable grandstand for the use of photographers, the pace car has been driven by professional drivers such as former winners Jim Rathmann and Sam Hanks. During the bungled start of the race in 1972, however, the pole car driven by savvy Bobby Unser threatened to cold-nose the behind of the Oldsmobile pace car after its occupants signaled that there would be no start. As several drivers raised their arms to warn those behind them not to anticipate the green flag, the green flag flew anyway. For several seconds, contestants did not know whether the race was underway or not. Some surged forward, and others momentarily held back.

Those who value the pace car most are those who produced it, and the value they find is in advertising. In view of the long-standing liaison between the Speedway and American industrialism, it is small wonder that the cars that first appear off turn four at the start of the race are polished Detroit productions, rather than fire-eating, low-flying racers of the Indianapolis ilk. Because commercial interests, above all else, lead the ceremonies at the Speedway, ("Where Business Locates in the Winner's Circle"), the occasion itself becomes in part a commercial festival in praise of free enterprise. In proper tribute, the Speedway sees to the placement of business executives around the track perched on the backs of convertibles, and finds a way to interview them over the hugest of all known public address systems. This is a publicity payback for industrial sponsorship of racing cars and for contributions to the overall purse to be divided among the thirty-three contestants. But in certain instances, business involvement in the race is still more pervasive. Some feeling in Gasoline Alley has it that the Goodyear Tire and Rubber Company dictates (but well behind the scenes) much of what happens and fails to happen each May at the Brickyard. Goodyear is at present the only supplier of tires at Indianapolis, and is therefore in a unique position to exert substantial leverage over the conduct of the month. When the pace lap is run on race day, there are 136 Goodyear tires rolling on the Speedway, counting those mounted on the specially prepared pace car. Through one means or another, the Indy crowd knows this, and any identification with Goodyear, such as the donning of a Goodyear cap (along with a blue Goodyear jacket) is a way of communicating that the wearer is (or would like to appear) close to racing's inner circle, and is proud to be so. Notwithstanding, a Goodyear outfit is a vestment of a lower order. At Indianapolis, as everywhere else, what you wear may tell us who you are. The ultimate thing to be seen in at Indianapolis is the fireproof Nomex driving suit worn by the drivers themselves. The crowd seems also to be aware (because it is difficult *not* to be aware) that Ashland Oil products are used by most of the crews; and it is Ashland Oil, like Goodyear and Monroe (the shock absorber manufacturer) that has elevated its products to the level of venerated cult objects worthy of uncommon respect and reverence.

Among the people who find it difficult to become aroused over the prospect of a tire or a quart of motor oil, the lament is often heard that after the race has been started, all that remains in store for the spectator is the monotonous prospect of bullet-like missiles hurling around the track 200 times, provided they can withstand running that long. It behooves one, they think, to gather one's belongings and meander toward the exits in the ominous anticipation of the inconceivable crush of bodies that will develop inevitably in about three-and-a-half hours. This is not the attitude of an Indy devotee, who views the race as a ritual journey of 500 miles run over a pathway consecrated by the memory of mythic daredevils like Shaw, Horn, Nalon, Mays, and Foyt. The prospect of these cars going around the track producing an almost uninterrupted and curiously harmonic, mournful howl is a highly significant benchmark in the year of an Indianapolis addict. This strange interlude is made all the more poignant because the usual running time of the race is but three-and-a-half hours in approximate duration, and when the commotion finally comes to an end, it is with some regret.

During the course of the race, therefore, it is incumbent upon the spectator to be as attentive as possible. He may well regret pausing for lunch, because to do that is an irritating distraction. He definitely resents the gnawing prospect that he may be obligated to visit a rest room. If the latter becomes absolutely imperative, he may scramble out for his pit stop (so the old joke goes) during a yellow light period in the race, when the drivers themselves are pit stopping also. The expert spectator hopes, therefore, that he will be emptying his bladder at the same moment when they are filling their tanks. This kind of quid pro quo is a trade-off that each Indianapolis fan must confront in his own way. Unlike the dilettante, the genuine Speedway afficionado is virtually never bored during his hours at the Speedway, even at a time when it is raining and when ostensibly there is nothing happening. When the track is open to spectators and the rain falls, racing fans still ironically persist in paying admission to come inside the Speedway. All of racing's people have an almost limitless capacity to wait, just as they did in 1973 when many thousands lingered for three days to see the race run. After the race is over, there are also many thousands who show reluctance to evacuate the grounds; they still persist in waiting for something more to take place, even though the show is officially over.

Under the heading "Order of the Day," the Speedway's race day program tells us that "at the end of the race the presentation will be made to the winner and he will be driven around the track in the pace car for the acclamation of all present." There are many beery spirits who wait for this to happen. The winner of the race brings his car to a stop in front of the Terrace Tower, where both he and the car are elevated on a huge ramp decorated in black and white checkerboard. Celebrities, beauty queens, crew members, and media people all converge on the new Indianapolis champion, who is encouraged to swallow the ritual goblet of milk provided by the American Dairy Association and subjected to a preliminary interview on radio and television after he has removed his helmet and replaced it with a jaunty Goodyear cap. Following his drive around the track in the back seat of a convertible pace car, he is dispatched to the Speedway Press Room for a second interview with ladies and gentlemen representing dozens of newspapers and other periodicals at home and overseas. It is here that he responds to the hackneyed but annual inquiry: "How was it out there?"

A winner at Indianapolis is much more than king for a day. With his likeness frozen eternally on the side of the Borg-Warner trophy, he achieves a form of immortality, regardless of what may befall him after that. Most Indianapolis winners, because of their sudden affluence, begin to shun all but the richest-paying races on the United States Auto Club schedule, or wherever else their professional licensing may permit them to compete. Although the schedule of racing after Indianapolis inevitably varies from year to year, racers have generally gravitated toward certain ports of call. Milwaukee, as every racer knows, follows Indianapolis on the established traditional circuit. Salem runs on the Fourth of July, DuQuoin on Labor Day. Schedules inevitably change every year, and yet the season that runs from spring to fall and beyond does have a pattern to it. The racing season leads away from, and then toward, Indianapolis, which is always the crowning mark of the year. Like placing one more silver dollar in a one-armed bandit, the defending Indianapolis champion typically longs for another try at the greatest of all racing jackpots; and a one-time winner at Indy may be likened to a first term president: He did it once, but can he do it again? Once a man registers a win at the Brickyard, he plays a curious game of king of the mountain as he makes a quest for a repeat win the following year. Al Unser, who triumphed in 1970 and 1971, waited for his third Indianapolis win in 1978 before making the somewhat inscrutable remark that in retrospect, he should have come home a winner in *all* of his thirteen Speedway outings. His comment, while largely passed over in the press, seemed to hint at more than an offhand remark by a man in the delirious excitement of an Indianapolis triumph. Had he, in the dotage of his days at Indianapolis (having now reached the venerable age of 39), at least partially unlocked some ineffable riddle of the old track with its tunneled straights and problematic turns?

One would rather hope not, for the Speedway, with its intriguing heritage, frustration, calamity, spectacle, and surprise, might well be the less for it. The demythologizing of Indianapolis, like the demythologizing of the Church, would be as pointless as it is hopeless. Perhaps more than anything else, a month at the Motor Speedway is an experience to be regarded as a theatrical one, where the spectators enter through one avenue and the players through another. It is not until the curtain of nightfall descends that identities are restored, when the participants have removed their masks and the immense audience has ceased its role as a vast supporting chorus in a mythic pageant of quest, failure, and fulfillment that has lasted from sunrise to the close of the day.

MOVIETONE

In a darkened room, I sit alone with a whirring motion picture projector, while silent black and white images, moving faster than real life, flicker across the screen. Momentary sequences of awkward-looking, bullish racing cars with huge hoods and narrow tires sail round the corners and on the straightaways at Indianapolis. Thousands of spectators seem to rise from their seats, as if on command. One car slides sideways, out of control, while another moves wide on the track, colliding with the first. Both cars ignite while the second car veers through the railing and out of view. The first car rolls over, leaving a human form on the track. A third car enters the picture, pinches abruptly to the left, explodes through the inner guardrailing, and turns over. A succession of other cars squiggle through the fire that has erupted on the track. Drivers gesticulate as they pass the scene of the wreck, moving low on the track.

To be involved with automobile racing in any way requires that one accept the bad with the good. Metaphoric of life experience itself, the history and progress of racing at Indianapolis is weighted heavily on the side of pleasurable and memorable interludes that, even if they cause one's blood pressure to rise, are not to be forgotten. Participants have indeed paid a high price to compete there, but it has somehow always seemed worth the cost, even when it ostensibly seems difficult to justify. Those who sustained injuries and lost their lives were involved in a continuing struggle for acclaim and other rewards not easily come by. At Indianapolis, the game is much more than a question of win or lose. It is a question of survival itself. The quest, in the long run, seems neither more nor less absurd than any other burning aspiration that one might entertain. Triumph and tragedy at Indianapolis have impressed me as being more purely defined and expressed on the two-and-a-half-mile track than they have in any other theatrical arena that I have found. I am reminded often of the Puritan notion that to apply fully such talents as one has and to pursue some calling in life is to fulfill one's divine purpose in living, even if it results in one's dying.

INDEX

217